Land, Wind, and Hard Words

A STORY OF NAVAJO ACTIVISM

JOHN W. SHERRY

UNIVERSITY OF NEW MEXICO PRESS

ALBUQUERQUE

Library of Congress Cataloging-in-Publication Data

Sherry, John W. (John William), 1961–

    Land, wind, and hard words : a story of Navajo activism /

John W. Sherry.— 1st ed.

      p. cm.

Includes index.

   ISBN 0-8263-2281-6 (cloth : alk. paper)

   1. Diné Citizens against Ruining Our Environment

(Organization) 2. Environmental protection—Navajo Indian Reservation.

3. Navajo Indians—Land tenure. 4. Navajo Indians—Government relations.

I. Title.

   E99.N3 S47 2002

   333.73'16'089972—dc21

                                       2001008065

contents

In the spring of 1996, a couple years after most of the events described in this book had transpired, I was with Lori Goodman, one of Diné CARE's founding members, and currently the organization's secretary, treasurer, and de facto executive director. We were attending the annual Navajo Studies Conference, an event that brings together presenters from a wide variety of disciplines: resource planners, environmentalists, educators, policy analysts, economists, social workers, and, of course, more than a few anthropologists. The Diné may be, according to one anthropologist, "the most studied people in the world."[1]

Lori noted that there seemed to be a lot of talk being promulgated with a great sense of authority by a great number of people who were clearly not Diné, for an audience consisting likewise of many non-Diné. While trends indicate this seems to be changing, she still found it somewhat disconcerting.

If there is one message that the members of Diné Citizens Against Ruining our Environment would wish for the world to hear, it would be that their people, the Diné (Navajo) elders, the people who still live off the land, need to be given the opportunity to speak for themselves.

As we walked back to her car in the cold wind, she asked me simply enough: "How come you haven't written a book about us?"

I didn't know if she was joking or not.

By this time, it had been about four years since the first time I came stumbling rather blindly onto the reservation. She and the other members of Diné CARE were, I am now embarrassed to say, the "subjects" of my dissertation research. In the course of this, as a way of "fitting in," I had developed a working relationship with them, helping with some of the writing that inevitably formed a part of their work as environmental-justice activists on the Navajo Nation.

Each of the local efforts in which they were engaged—some were conservation efforts, some were outright conflicts with governmental or corporate entities—required a surprising amount of writing and bureaucracy. Examples included letters, memos, and other correspondence; a quarterly newsletter; press releases; written resolutions; and, perhaps most important of all, a lot of bureaucratic requirements placed on their organization by the government, grant makers, and other powerful outsiders to whom the members of Diné CARE found themselves accountable in a variety of ways.

These people are activists, not bureaucrats. While most had been raised speaking Navajo in the home, they are without exception well educated and intelligent, perfectly capable of reading and writing in English. Still, they recognized that their time was often better spent doing the many other things that made up the life of activism—much of which involved intensive "face to face" communication with all kinds of people around and beyond the reservation (this book discusses some of that "face work"). So, they graciously offered me the opportunity to get to know and understand their work through the process of helping them produce some of the documents mentioned above. It actually provided me with a nice chance to discuss with them, often at great length, their perspective on both the current condition of the Navajo people and the motivations underlying their own work.

Of course, by this time, the relationship had become more than a "working arrangement." The people of Diné CARE had been amazingly generous, providing me with a place to live, food to eat, and they even paid me for my work out of their meager budget whenever they could.

Adella Begaye, who features most prominently in this book, calls me her adopted son. Once, at a meeting, the members of Diné CARE framed their predicament in terms of the long historical problem of "white people going after our land." After the use of the term "white people" a couple members looked my way, half apologetically. "Don't worry about him," Adella said dismissively, "he's my son, he's Diné."

That, in a nutshell, captures both how generous they have been with me, and how difficult it has been to write this book. When Lori suggested I should tell their story, it seemed like a good idea. I had seen how they had been handled by some members of the media—particularly during the sad days at the end of 1993. I thought I knew them well enough to tell the story from their perspective.

Of course, I was wrong. I can't tell the story from their perspective. I can try and include what I think are some of the most important things they've told me, to indicate what I think their perspective may be, but ultimately, I can only tell this story from my own perspective.[2]

This has been a humbling and learning experience. After having seen what looked like caricatures of these people—my friends, my heroes—in print, I have turned around and produced, unfortunately, little more than an analogous objectification of those same friends. Limited writing skills may be part of the problem, but only part: all writing, all representations we create, are inevitably doomed to particular limitations and distortions.

There is some consolation in a couple facts: First, this is nothing new for anthropologists. The discipline has struggled over the past two decades to get beyond the authoritative descriptions of "this or that culture." Such descriptions have dominated ethnographic writing throughout most of its history, but since the 1980s there has been a distinct effort to be more open and honest about the fact that all our representations are constructions, from the author's perspective, of particular experiences with other human beings who also actively construct the world around them.[3] This is equally true, of course, for the "hard sciences," though less often admitted: we can no longer claim that "things" (from subatomic particles, to trees, to other people) naturally speak for themselves through our writing and our representations of them.[4]

Second, and more importantly, despite all my misgivings, the people of Diné CARE themselves have never stopped encouraging me to continue. They have read and commented on drafts, giving me corrections and feedback, and told me a number of times, "it's OK, keep going."

For all their generosity, I gladly offer the author's royalties from this book to the people of Diné CARE.

one

Leroy Jackson stood in the middle of a corral beneath a scorching August sun and looked to the east. There in front of him, miles of junipers and pinions melded together over a vast, gently rising slope, creating the illusion of a landscape more lush than it really was. Above the trees, far in the distance, loomed the gigantic red cliffs of the Lukachukai Mountains, gleaming like magnificent copper walls in the brightness of mid morning.

A summer storm appeared to be gathering over the mountains, distant white billows climbing tens of thousands of feet into an otherwise deep blue sky. With any luck they would soon discharge what the *Diné*—the Navajo people—call the "male rain."

For the Diné, maleness is associated with aggression, with fierceness. It aptly describes the kind of rain that the summer storms bring. It is usually accompanied by vicious displays of thunder and lightning. The rain itself comes down with an aggression all its own, not wetting the ground so much as pelting it, attacking it. Anyone who has been caught in such a storm does not soon forget it.

But for all their violence, those rains are precious. Breathe deeply and smell the air after a storm in the middle of a hot summer afternoon, or feel it on your skin, and it becomes obvious why the Diné consider the rains a gift. They cool the air, and clean it. They contribute to a rich forest ecology in the Chuska mountain range (of which the Lukachukai Mountains are a part). Large ponderosa pines and gambel oak fill their slopes. Higher up, Douglas fir, white spruce, and aspen can be found. Deer, wild turkey, beaver, cougar, and black bear still inhabit those mountains, though their numbers are dwindling. It is a completely different world from that of the deserts only a few thousand feet below.

Leroy gazed at the distant possibility of a storm only briefly. All of that was miles away. Rain was neither a concern nor a hope where he stood, and there was work to be done.

Specifically, there were sheep to treat. Leroy had acquired, through a recent trade, a small flock of *churro* sheep. He and a rather ragtag crew now stood before the sheep with a few bottles of worm medicine, strips of cloth, some rope, and a couple of cheap plastic syringes that Adella (Leroy's wife) had managed to pilfer from the Indian Health Service clinic where she worked.

Many changes have swept the Navajo Reservation, but this is still sheep country. Their wool is spun into rugs and tapestries, a tradition for which the Diné are famous among collectors. Their meat is roasted or cooked up into mutton stew. No major ceremony or gathering occurs without the slaughtering of at least one sheep to feed the attendees. Everyone takes part in some aspect of raising and caring for sheep, even though these days most local residents are wage earners and not shepherds. Rodeo—an outgrowth of the sheeping economy—is a passion for many Diné men.

Then there was Leroy. He couldn't rope. He couldn't ride. He was definitely not into rodeo, although on one occasion in his wilder, younger days he did manage to last five seconds on the back of a bucking bull. "I could do that," he told his buddies as they watched a bull rider from the safety of their seats. "We bet you can't," they replied. "It was so stupid,"

Adella recalled about that ride many years after the fact. "I couldn't even stand to watch."

For a guy who on more than one occasion denounced "all that Horatio Alger, power-of-positive-thinking stuff," as "a bunch of gobbledygook," Leroy sure seemed to have the energy and confidence to take on all kinds of challenges—or get himself into all kinds of trouble. Some of his family and friends found it mildly amusing that his first foray into sheep was with churros, of all breeds.

Churros arrived on the Navajo homeland hundreds of years ago with the first Spanish, possibly even with Coronado and his retinue, as they blundered and plundered their way north in search of the fabled golden cities of Cibola.[1] One rarely sees churros on the Rez anymore. They are wild and unruly, too much trouble for most people. Crossbreeding efforts by traders, the government, and the Navajo people themselves to create more marketable wool from more docile flocks have given rise to other breeds.[2]

Leroy didn't seem to care about the trouble involved. He wanted churros precisely because of their historical legacy. He wanted the original Diné breed.

Standing in the corral with an expression of intense enjoyment on his face, he swung a lasso above his head, then sent it crashing awkwardly into the dust with a clap that only startled the sheep and sent them scurrying from one corner of the corral to another. He laughed and muttered a thinly veiled profanity (it sounded something like "sheeuh"), then ditched the rope and took off running to try to grab one of the churros by its long, curling rack.

They scattered in confusion. One savagely rammed what it took to be a weak point in the corral, a stretch of chicken wire attached to a post made out of a twisted juniper limb. The fence shivered and held. The ram, dazed and now tangled by one horn, hung limply for a moment then began to buck wildly to free itself. These were definitely not your ordinary docile breed of sheep.

Assisting Leroy that day was a *bilagáana*[3] anthropologist, to whom he had been introduced a year or so earlier, at the Denny's Restaurant along Interstate 10 in Tucson. The young man had been interested in coming to the Rez and "helping out."

"So, you're in school down here," Leroy said by way of small talk. "What are you taking?"

"Anthropology."

Leroy threw his head back and erupted in a crackling burst of laughter. Years later, the anthropologist still couldn't decide what that had signified. Was it genuine amusement, or was it the type of laugh that overcomes some people when they realize they've been thoroughly and perversely mistreated by fate? "Into each life some rain must fall, . . ." writes Vine Deloria, "But Indians are cursed above all other people in history. Indians have anthropologists."[4]

One of the basic tools of anthropology is "participant observation." After more or less arbitrarily descending on some particular community and calling it home, the researcher attempts to establish a legitimate presence by participating in the local daily routine. This practice is intended to provide a way of fitting in while at the same time permitting more or less surreptitious scrutiny of the locals. Some anthropologists have managed to pull this off. Gladys Reichard, who spent much of her adult life among the Diné, became a proficient weaver, a highly valued skill in the *Diné Bikéyah*.[5] Others wind up sticking out like sore thumbs, and more often than not lack any semblance of the most rudimentary proficiency in any of the activities that make up local daily practice—as was painfully clear that day in the corral.

Leroy and the anthropologist were joined by Leroy's son Eli. Eli was his father's son, in a number of ways. The first time he met the anthropologist his reaction was about as ambiguous as his dad's had been. "Come over here," Leroy said to him the day the anthropologist arrived on their doorstep, "I want you to meet someone."

Eli stopped dead in his tracks in the middle of the room, some fifteen feet from the door, at which point he simply stared, motionless and inscrutable. After a few seconds he slapped a tiny open palm to his forehead and fell backward to the floor, landing flat on his back, as if he had knocked himself out. Leroy turned back to the anthropologist, laughing and shaking his head, slightly embarrassed. "My son, he's a little strange sometimes."

Eli was about four years old at the time, and all but the smallest of these churros easily outweighed him. Besides being faster and more agile than most other breeds, the rams had two sets of racks, one that curled back around like wild bighorn sheep, another that corkscrewed straight up into sharp spikes. They were still edgy and skittish from their long trip to the Rez (they came from somewhere up in Oregon). They looked as though they could have run Eli down at will.

The final member of the deworming party was the only one actually suited for the job. Ervin, Leroy's brother-in-law (married to Adella's sister), was older than Leroy and had spent his life with sheep. He had a long, lean frame, and a very good-natured, avuncular appearance. He kept his salt-and-pepper hair cut short and neatly combed. He only spoke a few words of English; he mostly spoke only the Navajo language, *Diné bizaad*.

Ervin worked the rope with deceptive ease. Just a quick sidearm flip, that's all he used–no Wild West show loops above his head, no contortions when he let it fly, no wasted motions at all. With a flick of his arm he sent the rope hovering inches above the ground under the belly of a sheep just long enough to snare it by the back legs. He rarely missed. Then it was up to Leroy and the anthropologist to grab the animal, shove the syringe down its throat and mark its horn with a piece of rag.

Besides the four of them, no one else was around. The rest of the extended family had long since gone to the summer homesite up in the mountains, where their collective flocks were getting fat on greener pastures in the shade of the pines.

It was hot. The sheep kicked up clouds of dust. There were no shady pine trees within miles. But it was a good day, primarily by virtue of the fact that they were engaged in a very rewarding activity. The Diné elders say that the sheep are a gift of the Holy People. When properly cared for, the flocks multiply; when the people use them wisely, the Holy People bring rain, and everyone—all living things—prosper. Most people here know all their sheep as individuals. (One sickly churro lamb, in fact, would come to think of itself as Ervin's house pet.)

There's a different sense of time involved in caring for the sheep. It's not governed by clock time. It feels wholly separate from "linear time," with its burden of history. It is more a matter of rhythmic time, cyclic time. It involves annual migrations up the slopes in the spring and back down in the fall—at least for the families lucky enough to have home and grazing permits in the mountains. It involves the daily search for pastures. Twice a day, in the mornings and again in the late afternoon, almost everywhere throughout the Navajo Nation, you can see Diné shepherds, mostly elders, or in the summertime young children, walking in the fields or along the roadside with their sheep, occasionally on horseback, or keeping watch from the cab of a pickup truck parked at a short distance. Such work doesn't lend itself to a life of participation in the wage economy, which is why few people of working age on the Rez are able to pursue it anymore.

As they worked their way through the flock, Ervin changed his approach and gave his rope an overhand toss right into the middle of them, catching a big ram by one of the horns. Ervin anchored himself and reeled in the sheep while Leroy and the anthropologist advanced on him quickly but cautiously, trying to keep him cornered while he kicked and dodged and tried to run around them.

Eli stood a short distance away, his back to a large, heavy, stainless-steel trough that rested on the ground in the middle of the corral. He made a move to help, but with all the flailing he couldn't find an opportunity. Leroy grabbed the sheep's horns and yanked his head back, while the anthropologist stuffed the syringe deep down his mouth into the back of his throat. The poor sheep's eyeballs rolled back into his head, and his thick tongue bobbed in and out of his mouth as he began to gag. Phlegm shot from his nostrils onto the sleeves of their shirts, which were already soaked with sweat and caked with dust. Leroy tied a strip of red cloth to one horn to mark him as "treated."

Before they could get the rope off the ram bolted from their grasp. He sprinted across the corral, pulling taut the rope, which was still wrapped around Ervin's wrist. It all happened so fast. The ram passed directly in front of Eli, trapping him between the rope and the trough at the center of the corral. Ervin did not even have time to let go.

The rope pulled across Eli's stomach and, in a freakish, eternal instant yanked him backward, flipped him up over the rim, and slammed him into the bottom of the empty trough with a hollow thud.

They all held their breath. Eli lay there without moving. Leroy scrambled toward the trough.

But then two tiny hands emerged from the recesses of the basin and grabbed the rim on either side. Eli looked up with a thoroughly alarmed expression. He wasn't crying—maybe he was too stunned to cry. He slowly removed himself, gingerly but calmly placed both feet back on the ground, and proceeded to brush off his tiny little black jeans unselfconsciously, like a miniature rodeo star. As the rush of relief hit, they began to laugh uncontrollably.

"I'm sure glad his mother didn't see that," Leroy finally sputtered.

■|

A couple hours later, they walked down to the corn fields, tired, dusty, and stinking. Eli's tumble into the trough didn't seem to have any lasting effects. He continued to practice with his own rope, whipping it viciously through the air, producing a high-pitched whistle.

The corn was tall and green. A gentle breeze blew through the stalks, ruffling the leaves and cooling them down. Like the sheep, corn plays a central role in the Diné way of life. No morning prayer is complete without the sprinkling of corn pollen, and an offering, on the tongue, to one's inner spirit.

Here is how First Man and First Woman were made:

The gods laid one buckskin on the ground with the head to the west; on this they placed the two ears of corn, with their tips to the east, and over the corn the spread the other buckskin with its head to the east; under the white ear they put the feather of a white eagle, under the yellow ear the feather of a yellow eagle. Then they told the people[6] to stand at a distance and allow the wind to enter. The white wind blew from the east, and the yellow wind blew from the west, between the skins. While the wind was blowing, eight of the Mirage People came and walked around the objects on the ground four times, and as they walked the eagle feathers, whose tips protruded from between the buckskins, were seen to move. When the Mirage People had finished their walk the upper buckskin was lifted—the ears of corn had disappeared; a man and a woman lay there in their stead.

The white ear of corn had been changed into a man, the yellow ear into a

woman. It was the wind that gave them life. It is the wind that comes out of
our mouths now that gives us life. When this ceases to blow we die. In the skin
at the tips of our fingers we see the trail of the wind; it shows us where the
wind blew when our ancestors were created.7

A life lived in rhythmic time has some interesting differences from life lived in "linear time." In rhythmic time, things come around again. According to Gladys Reichard, the anthropologist who spent many years among the Diné, "Events of the lower world (for instance, the creation of First Man and First Woman) are remembered and certain episodes are acted out or represented in symbols to preserve the timelessness of power." This power rests in the fact that the past of the underworld is never really "done"; "From some viewpoints time is eternal, having no beginning or end. Once an event has taken place, its effects may be repeated at any future time; for instance, occurrences in the underworlds still affect this world and man."[8]

This sense of time is one key aspect of Diné ceremonies, where the power of the Holy People sets the individual, the community, and the earth back into mutual harmony.

It also plays out in daily practice. The benevolent wishes of the Holy People for human beings' benefit, the harmony that is the desired order of things, must be continually actualized, brought about through human agency and cooperation. It must be recreated through right thinking, and caring for the land and the sheep. This is the key to a harmonious life.

With the shining sun, the joy of hard work, the wind in the corn—it was almost possible to imagine that they had somehow managed to slip into this world of rhythmic time. It was almost possible to forget, however briefly, what Leroy and Adella's lives had become.

In fact, Leroy and Adella were caught fully in the torrent of "history." They found themselves locked in a struggle that encompassed their family, their tribal government, and countless outsiders. Their days had become an endless grappling with all the encumbrances of the modern world and were taken up by memos, resolutions, letters, and court rulings; by faxes, telephone calls, and endless hours of travel; and, above all, by the grind of contact with lawyers, government officials, environmentalists, and reporters. Together, as members of an organization they called "Diné CARE"⁹ they were engaged in a fight to protect the forests on their beloved Chuska mountains from the ravages of industrial logging.

■/

Those who are not familiar with the story of Diné CARE should not be too surprised to find that the organization's members sometimes frame their current predicament in terms of a centuries-old war against foreign colonialism. "By the simple and beautiful virtue of being Native American," wrote the artist T. C. Cannon (a quote used by Diné CARE in the first brochure they ever produced), "with the blood of mountain and bird motivation, we still have to be soldiers in our homeland."

For the Diné, this consciousness extends back to their very identity, in the stories of their origins. The oldest stories tell of how the first Earth Surface People, the people who came from the worlds below onto this present world, moved from place to place scratching out a meager living and always traveling in constant fear of the Nayéé', the Alien Monsters who once hunted them mercilessly and devoured them at will.

"This resistance has been part of our lives since the Monster Slayers, since the time of Changing Woman." Those words were spoken by John Redhouse, Leroy's most trusted counsel, to his fellow activists during one of their darkest hours. "This is just the way things are and the way things are intended to be. It's maybe not good to question this too much. It's just what we were born of and born for. It's part of our role as Diné, as keepers and caretakers of the land."¹⁰

Asdzą́ą́ nádleehé, "Changing Woman," the most beloved of all the Navajo Deities, gave birth to *Nayéé' Neizghání*, "Monster Slayer," who, along with his younger brother, Child Born of Water, rid the earth of the Alien Monsters. Monster Slayer's deeds are recounted in stories that form a key element in a vast and detailed corpus, including the Diné origin stories, and various important ceremonies.

Scattered across the homeland, a large number of sacred places provide a living reminder of the past struggles, tying these sacred stories concretely to the physical environment. *Tsoodził*—Mount Taylor—the sacred mountain of the south, marks the place where Monster Slayer and Child Born of Water killed *Yé'iitsoh*, the Big Giant. Shiprock, the giant basalt formation in northwestern New Mexico, is the place where Monster Slayer finally subdued the Monster Eagle. The land is covered with such sacred sites.

Now the landscape is dotted with a new class of Alien Monsters: oil rigs, coal drag lines, power plants, logging trucks, and uranium mines, to name but a few. These are a different breed. For one thing, they are only the contact points, the obvious evidence of monsters that are actually far more intractable, vast, and diffuse. Every mine and power line indexes a whole system, a complex infrastructure that includes not only mechanical, chemical, and electronic components, but social ones as well, including systems of labor, finance, and even ways of thinking. As technology historian Thomas Hughes points out, "the legacy of industrialism includes not only factories and mines but banks and brokerage houses."[11]

Industrial development has produced undeniable material benefits for a large number of people, especially in the United States. "Computers, automobiles, airplanes, VCR's, washing machines, vacuum cleaners, telephones, and other technologies—combined with mass production—give middle-class citizens of the United States degrees of material wealth—control over commodities, and the ability to consume services—that previous generations could barely imagine."[12]

It is partly the nature of these vast and complex modern systems of production that the costs associated with all this wealth building are often hidden, separated either by time or space from those who benefit. Sometimes, for instance, the costs emerge only gradually, as in the cases of ozone depletion or global warming.[13] Often, the environmental costs of these systems are visible only at the "margins" of a country or society, out of view of the mainstream. This trick of extracting costs from the marginal or politically less powerful has become as much a part of the political and social calculus of system building as the alignment of financing or labor. A growing awareness of this has given rise, over the past ten years, to a movement dealing with environmental justice.[14] As Deeohn Ferris, a leading environmental justice advocate, and member of the National Environmental Justice Advisory Council has put it: "We're all in the same sinking boat, only people of color are closest to the hole."[15] It is a story that is common not only on the American landscape, but globally as well.[16]

In the United States, American Indian people have been hit with some of the stiffest costs of economic development.[17] The Navajo Nation's coal, oil, uranium, and timber have been targeted for extraction for roughly a century. The Navajo homeland offers vast, relatively sparsely inhabited spaces which appear to outsiders as ideal places for dumping or burning toxic wastes that other communities have rejected. The Navajo Nation's coal mines and nearby power plants supply electricity for millions of people in the American Southwest and generate pollution that has been labeled a nuisance as far away as the Grand Canyon.

The Diné themselves do not typically enjoy the benefits of these systems. Despite the proximity of the power stations, for instance, and three major high-voltage power lines that cut across reservation lands, only about half of the households on the reservation have electricity. Even fewer have telephones.[18] An estimated 70 percent of Navajo homes lack indoor plumbing.

The population of the Navajo Nation, about 170,000, is scattered over an area of 26,000 square miles (approximately the size of West Virginia). There are about 8,800 miles in paved roadway on the reservation—about 10 percent of that in West Virginia. Travel between many points on the reservation is time consuming, difficult, and in rainy or winter months, dangerous or just plain impossible.

Unemployment rates range between 35 percent and 50 percent. At the end of 1997 there were four banks serving the entire twenty-six thousand square miles of the reservation. One of these was in a trailer home. The local joke was "who would be stupid enough to deposit money in a bank that is sitting on wheels?" Local economies are largely dependent on tribally run programs; there are few opportunities for entrepreneurial activity. The Tribe itself, desperate to support a large bureaucracy and a population that depends on it for jobs or other economic benefits, quickly seizes upon any economic opportunities that present themselves, often with striking disregard for adverse environmental and social costs on local communities.

Not only do people in such conditions often lack the political power to resist unwanted mining, cutting, or dumping, but as rural people, people whose livelihood depends on the integrity of the land, these effects can be more immediate than on people in urban settings. The extraction of Navajo mineral resources, or the dumping of toxic wastes or radioactive debris on lands thought to be "uninhabited" poses a very real threat to people whose livelihoods depend on the ability of the land to produce corn, melons, and other crops; grasses for the sheep; and herbs and medicines for cere-monial and daily uses.

Inseparable from the material effects, the Diné stand against the cul-tural effects wrought by development agendas. Degradation of the land has implications beyond aesthetics or economics. Earl Tulley, a founding member of Diné CARE and a gifted public speaker, continuously sought to find a way to communicate the Diné way of looking at their homeland:

> When you have different people coming in, when they enter the bound-aries of the four sacred mountains, they say "there's an energy field there. There's something there. I don't know what it is, but it's there."
>
> But we—those of us that have been in there, we know what it is, because it draws us back. We can go outside, and gain our education, and do what we need to do, but it's only when we come back, there's that burden that is, kind of, lifted from us. *Ei shimásání dóó shicheii*, "my grandmother and my grandfather" at that time when we come back, [they say to us] *sha'awéé,' shiyázhí* "my baby, my child." It never really dawned on me what we can lose until those people are no longer there that can greet you like that. But you know, like my mother tells me, through our relationships and our kinship, through the clans, we do have people that can take up those particular roles.
>
> This is hard for people to understand. They tell us that the trees are important because they make oxygen, they have some technical facts, but at the same time they really want to know about our spiritual her-itage as Native Americans, as indigenous people, Diné. They want us to show them where those spiritual connections are. Is it to a building? Is it to an herb? To something that is living, something that can be seen?
>
> This is our Jerusalem. This is our Zion between the four sacred mountains.[19]

But while their Diné traditions motivate their activism and give it shape, they are not simply "traditionalists" (as opposed to "progressives"—a dichotomy by which they are too often characterized). They do not regard development and Diné heritage as absolutely incompatible.

In fact, they don't really fit any of the labels that have been used on them. Leroy used to bristle, for example, whenever he was called an environmentalist. They are ordinary people, recognizable to any other American as middle-class professionals who have kids they'd like to see get a good education, aging parents to take care of, car payments to make. Leroy was trained as an engineer. Adella is a registered nurse. Others are health-care providers, building inspectors, and professionals of all sorts.

They see their struggle as one of *voice*, of whose perspective counts in the disposition of the land. Development can be managed, they contend, in a way that fits with a Diné philosophy and view of the land. "*Shimásání dóó shicheii*," Leroy once said, "the grandmas and grandpas, the people who live on the mountains, gather herbs, tend their sheep. They got something to say."

∎/

The day was about over. The sheep were all treated. Leroy, Eli, and the anthropologist returned home to a little duplex in the neighborhood of the Indian Health Service Clinic where Adella worked.

"Get cleaned up, *shiyáázh*," Adella called to Eli "We're going across the street for dinner."

"To Ben and Tom's?" Eli asked excitedly, referring to his best friends, two little blonde-haired boys whose parents were doctors at the clinic.

"No, not Ben and Tom's. Patty's."

Eli groaned and, as he was a four-year-old, did little to get himself ready.

Patty lived in a duplex that was (like every other house in the neighborhood) identical to Adella and Leroy's. She was a nurse from the state of Michigan. Her husband, a silver-haired man from North Carolina, taught at a nearby school.

"They are *soo* polite," nurse Patty said about Eli and the Bambina that night at dinner.

"You should see them at home," Adella said with a laugh.

Not long after they finished eating, Patty's husband pulled a stout wooden stool into the living room and sat down with his banjo. As he began to pluck out a tune, the Bambina, who had already begun to display some musical talent, eyed him carefully. She smiled at her parents a little awkwardly. Eli stared at his own hands and began to fidget.

Then the man started to sing.

Almost as soon as the first words came out of his mouth Eli and the Bambina were overcome by such an acute sense of social awkwardness that they actually seemed to be physically suffering. Eli dropped face first to the floor, laughing silently and hysterically into the carpet, pounding his fists and kicking his feet. The Bambina, also laughing silently in mortification, held her ears and closed her eyes. When her dad tried to playfully pull her hands from her head, she scrambled out of his grasp and hid behind the couch.

Their parents stared at them in disbelief, smiling a little sheepishly. Their host, undaunted, continued his performance.

Back outside in the cool of the summer night, crickets chirped lazily in all the yards. Adella couldn't stop herself from laughing.

"Why did you kids embarrass me like that? Didn't you like his singing or what?"

"It just made me feel funny," was all the Bambina could say.

Later that night, Leroy sat at the counter that separated the kitchen from a peculiar little room that he had converted into his office. Behind him was a large bookcase filled with technical forestry manuals, books on environmental justice and "green economics," histories of development in the Southwest, stacks of tribal documents, regulations, and Council resolutions. Next to the bookshelves a small filing cabinet was stuffed with timber sale documents, topographic maps of the forest, letters to tribal and federal government officials, more Council resolutions, minutes of the tribal sawmill's board meetings, and memos of all kinds. Across the room, on a little desk that had once been used only by the kids for coloring or homework, stood two rolodexes, one of which contained the names of Leroy's trading partners, the other crammed with phone numbers of lawyers, environmental activists, biologists, tribal, state, and federal government officials, news reporters, and a host of other contacts Leroy had made in his short career as an activist. Next to these was a large telephone/fax/answering machine, one of the first and most important purchases they had made after they began their forest activism. Theirs was without doubt one of the few private residences on the reservation so equipped. (Lori Goodman, Leroy and Adella's close friend and one of Diné CARE's founders, once reflected on this strange situation: "It's true that we walk in two worlds. We don't have any choice. No wonder we're a little schizophrenic sometimes.")

Adella stood leaning against the stove, not far away. She laughed as Leroy described Eli's brush with disaster. "I can't believe you almost got my son run over by a ram," she scolded him.

"It's good for him," he teased back. "Makes him tough. He was pretty hip, too—he got right up and hung in there. If you would have been there, he would have just been crying for his mom."

Adella just laughed and shook her head.

It had been, in their now hectic regime, a day of rare tranquility. By this time, they were no longer neophytes in the world of social and environmental activism. What had started as a part-time commitment had evolved into a way of life. They snatched moments of what had once been normal whenever they could get them. Tonight, at least, there were no urgent calls to return, no press releases to write, no dirty little tricks to respond to. Nothing in their behavior suggested just how crazy their lives had become. Nor was there any inkling of what was in store.

This is how the people arrived on the surface of this, the fifth world: It all started in the fourth world—the world just below the present one—when First Man and First Woman had a terrible fight. First Man took all the other men with him and crossed over a river, and for several years the men and women lived separately.

At first, both the men and the women found this arrangement to their liking, but before long, things grew worse and worse for them. The men grew lonely and the women's crops were failing. Finally, they all repented of their differences.

The men ferried all the women over, except for three, a mother and two daughters, whom they had missed. After dark, they heard the women's voices. "They begged to be ferried over, but the men told them it was too dark . . . hearing this, they jumped into the stream and tried to swim over. The mother succeeded in reaching the opposite bank and finding her husband. The daughters were seized by Tééhooltsódii, the water monster, and dragged down under the water.

"For three nights and three days the people heard nothing about the young women and supposed them lost forever. On the morning of the fourth day the call of the gods was heard—four times as usual—and after the fourth call White Body made his appearance, holding up two fingers and pointing to the river. The people supposed that these signs had reference to the lost girls."

The gods took a man and a woman with them, and descended beneath the water. Coyote followed them.

After some searching, "they beheld the water monster Tééhooltsódii with the two girls he had stolen and two children of his own. The man and the woman demanded the children, and as he said nothing in reply they took them and walked away. But as they went out, Coyote, unperceived by all, took the two children of Tééhooltsódii and carried them off under his robe. Coyote

always wore his robe folded close around him and always slept with it thus
folded, so no one was surprised to see that he still wore his robe in this way
when he came up from the waters, and no one suspected that he had stolen the
children of Tééhooltsódii."

—Derived from Matthews, *Navaho Legends*[1]

Just down the road from the winter home of Adella's parents, over the rim of Canyon del Muerto, stands a site called Massacre Cave. The roof of the cave bears the marks of dozens of bullets fired by Spanish soldiers, who had come down the canyon on a slave raid, perhaps, or on a punitive expedition in search of stolen livestock. It's said that the soldiers, initially unable to reach the cliff where several women and children had taken refuge, banked their shots off the overhang into the small crowd of people. Scraps of cloth and the skulls of children (crushed with rifle butts) were still in place when the first Anglo-Americans explored the cave many decades later.

Spanish influence on the Diné was certainly significant, despite the fact that, unlike the people of the Pueblos, the Diné were never subdued by Spanish colonials. They were too sparsely settled and too intractable for colonial rule. The early Spanish, incidentally, called the Diné *Indios Serranos* (Mountain Indians) and *Querechos* (Wanderers).[2]

The real effects of Spanish colonization were indirect: slave raids (by the Spanish themselves or by other tribes to sell to the colonists), the introduction of sheep and horses, and the ever shifting relations among neighboring tribes as a result of Spanish occupation. It is important to note that at this time the Diné did not view themselves as a single nation in the sense that they are recognized today. Linked through the clan system, with a common cultural and linguistic heritage, individual families nonetheless had variable relations with neighbors from other tribes, depending on which region, what neighbors, and other factors. After the Pueblo revolt at the end of the seventeenth century, for instance, when the Spanish returned to reassert colonial rule, many of the people of the Pueblos sought refuge among the Diné, as did many Hopi families who came to Canyon de Chelly during periods of drought. In contrast, the original Diné homeland was all but evacuated because of Comanche and Ute raiders during the Spanish colonial period.[3]

The most significant effects of foreign colonization on the Diné came later, in the middle of the nineteenth century, with the arrival of the Americans around the end of the Mexican-American War. In the increasingly complex relations with neighboring tribes and Hispanic and Anglo settlers, conflicts became more frequent, and often involved sheep (which, as mentioned, became an important part of the Navajo economy toward the end of the previous century). Vocal American settlers (those same symbols that seem to dominate America's nostalgia for both independence and a wilderness to conquer) called on Washington for protection from a tribe considered to be "hopelessly perfidious."[4]

The U.S. government deemed it necessary to establish a military presence in Navajo territory. Relations between the local Diné and the new Anglos suffered from misunderstanding and poor judgment almost from the very start. A contingency of Diné led by the prosperous elder Narbona, eager for peace with the newly arrived Americans, arranged for a meeting with Colonel James Washington as he approached from the east. After a short but apparently successful encounter, the Diné were taking their leave when one of Washington's troops reportedly spied a horse he claimed to have been stolen from him. Washington granted permission to give pursuit and, before long, Narbona, the most active advocate for peace among the Diné, lay dead on the ground, shot in the back.[5] The place where this happened is now alternately referred to as "Narbona Pass" or "Washington Pass."

Relations only went downhill from there. Within a few years, General James Carleton assumed the New Mexico command and ordered Colonel Kit Carson into the Diné Bikéyah, whereupon the military initiated a systematic eradication of the Diné from their homeland. Aided by Ute guides seeking revenge and livestock, Carson's troops conducted a systematic siege and pillaging of the Navajo homeland beginning in the summer of 1863. Crops were destroyed; scouts and military troops scoured the countryside.[6]

Thousands of people were rounded up or surrendered. The captives were marched fifteen miles per day to the Bosque Redondo (Fort Sumner) across the Pecos River in a barren region of southeastern New Mexico, over three hundred miles from the eastern frontier of the Navajo homeland. According to some accounts, elders, pregnant women, the sick, and others who couldn't keep up were shot on sight by the American soldiers. Some were snatched along the way by slave traders. Others died of famine and disease.

There were a few holdouts. The great warrior and leader Barboncito, for instance, managed to elude U.S. troops for nearly two more years. Still others—many families in what is now southern Utah and those living far to the west of the Diné Bikéyah—were never removed.

The first two thousand Diné arrived at the Bosque Redondo in the spring of 1864. Eventually, some seven thousand Diné were settled into an area of about forty square miles, along with captives from a few other tribes in the region. They ate canned food spoiled with maggots and drank water heavy with alkali. They were asked to farm arid, unproductive land. Under these conditions, the people were expected to learn the "art of peace" and the "truths of Christianity."[7]

In 1867 General Carleton was replaced by General William Tecumseh Sherman, who, though he had no reputation as a lover of Indians, was appalled at the conditions of life at the fort. Public awareness of the conditions caused an uproar in the nation's capital. Congressional leaders questioned the economic sensibleness of holding the Navajo people captive. Navajo leaders, including Manuelito and Barboncito, eventually persuaded Sherman to release the Diné. In 1868 the survivors—a few thousand in all—were allowed to return to their homeland, given a few sheep for each family, and granted a treaty under which they retained tribal sovereignty in exchange for the promise to cease their hostilities against their neighbors.

The Diné who returned from exile at Fort Sumner in 1868 resettled the land and rebuilt to the extent that, by the end of the nineteenth century, they were beginning to enjoy a degree of prosperity. Though times were still tough, the reservation boundaries were extended a handful of times, and the flocks began to multiply at an unprecedented rate.

Some have suggested that it was the Long Walk and Fort Sumner experience that first led the Diné to imagine themselves politically as "one nation."[8] However, it would still be decades before that view manifested itself in terms of political organization.

Despite their freedom, the Diné were by no means insulated from contact with the United States. By the early twentieth century, two external forces were at work on the reservation. First was a federal policy of integration—through such efforts as Indian schools (though these were established under the 1868 treaty, they were attended in the first few decades by very few Diné) and a system of administration that divided the reservation into five agencies, each under the jurisdiction of U.S.-government-appointed superintendents—predecessors of the current Bureau of Indian Affairs.[9] Some have regarded this arbitrary division of the Diné Bikéyah and an imposition of external rule as having a slowing effect on the evolution of the Navajo government,[10] but it did bring with it one important innovation: The agencies provided for local rule at the level of what were called "chapters." Chapters are local government entities of the Navajo Nation, handling the administration of grazing permits, housing permits and leases, some local employment, and other government services. According to some, the chapter governments "built upon what was already present." That is, some aspects of chapter government built on the tradition of local decision making and conflict resolution by "headmen" (local community leaders).[11]

A second force affecting the Diné was the growing demand for Navajo resources by outside commercial interests. Even as recently as the late 1890s, Washington Matthews was able to state: "Fortunately for the Navahoes, no mines of precious metals have yet been discovered on their reservation."[12] Within twenty years all that was changed as oil, gas, coal, and uranium were all found on Navajo lands. Organized assaults on the land by prospectors and mining and oil companies played a major role in initially forming and later shaping the Navajo Nation government.

The first attempts to get at Navajo resources met with limited success. A series of general councils in Shiprock and the Southern Navajo agency, for instance, were convened by the Indian agent "at the behest of persistent oil concerns."[13] These citizen councils granted the petitioning oil companies only marginal access to Navajo lands. At two such councils, proposed oil leases were rejected outright. Hoping to expedite the process of access, the U.S. government first tried to establish a three-man "business council" to represent the tribe as a whole in dealing resources to outsiders. This did result in the signing of a few initial leases, but a three-man business council "hardly could be construed as a legislative body truly representative of the whole tribe."[14]

Everything began to change in the 1920s. A series of bills passed between 1918 and 1920 opened a variety of Indian lands—including the Navajo Nation—to more resource exploitation.[15] In 1923, Indian commissioner Charles Burke issued *Regulations Relating to the Navajo Tribe of Indians*. This document established a "continuing body to be known and recognized as the Navajo Tribal Council with which administrative officers of the Government may directly deal in all matters affecting the Tribe," especially with regards to "oil, gas, coal and other mineral deposits, tribal timber, and development of underground water supply for stock purposes."[16] Thus was formed the first Navajo Nation Council.

In the late 1930s, a series of events led to the formation of the council as it is known today. It happened during a tumultuous decade during which occurred the infamous federal livestock reduction program—the Diné saw their growing herds forcibly reduced by government agents in the name of soil conservation. It has been called the most "devastating" chapter in Navajo history since the exile at Fort Sumner.[17] Livestock reduction was carried out under the supervision of Indian Commissioner John Collier, who, together with Superintendent E. R. Fryer agreed (in rather typical paternalistic fashion): "The future of the Navajo is in our hands. His very economy is dependent upon our successful solution of his land problems." (Tellingly, Fryer also likened stock reduction to "parents" treating sick children with the less palatable but ultimately more effective "castor oil" instead of "candy.")[18]

A bitter split ensued among the Diné—those who opposed stock reduction versus those who were willing to acquiesce in order to secure promised land grants in New Mexico and Arizona. According to the enlightened analysis of one senior federal official, those who opposed stock reduction suffered from any combination of four distinct conditions: "ignorance, blindness, laziness and dishonesty."[19] Things only got worse when, after the program was in full swing, promised land grants in New Mexico failed to materialize.[20]

The factional split led to a crisis within the old tribal council. For the next two years the Diné tried to work out what kind of government they wanted—were they a confederation of local groups with somewhat distinct identities, or were they to be a unified tribe with a powerful central government? In April 1937 a constitutional assembly gathered, out of which grew the current Navajo Nation Council.[21]

Today, the council is comprised of delegates from almost every single Navajo chapter (smaller chapters may share a delegate). As of the late 1990s, the Navajo Nation Council included eighty-eight delegates representing 110 local chapters.

Though the council was formed not so much by internal evolution as by external pressures, it would be inaccurate to say that the current Navajo Nation government is simply a rubber stamp for the federal government or other outsiders bent on access to Navajo resources. The council is an integral and highly active part of public life on the Navajo Nation, and many council members have brought perspectives and effective legislation to protect Navajo resources. A number of formerly active members of Diné CARE, in fact, have served either on the Navajo Nation Council or in other capacities in the Navajo Nation government, which now includes both an executive branch and a judicial branch as well. The council continues to be an important means by which the Diné work out issues of local economic development, of the general welfare of the People, and the relationship with the United States government.

Nonetheless, the Navajo Nation government does find itself in a continuously precarious position with respect to outsiders in the case of the disposition of the land and its effects on its citizens. The early council was induced to cooperate in granting leases through a "carrot-and-stick" relationship with the federal government—land grants to the Navajo Nation were frequently contingent on the approval of mineral leases to American industry, much the way the livestock reduction program was implemented.[22]

This "carrot and stick" relationship continued throughout much of the twentieth century in other disguises. In the late 1940s and early 1950s, for instance, post–Marshall Plan zeal for "economic development" swept both U.S. foreign policy and the U.S. Department of the Interior.[23] The goal of development policy was to establish a "rationalized" political and economic system in countries (and on reservations) where Western standards for education, health care, and perhaps more importantly, production and trade, were not being met. Like international development projects, development on tribal lands was typically approached with a threefold strategy of rapid industrialization, accumulation of capital, and participation in international markets.[24]

Development aid to the tribe during this time came mainly in the form of funding for large-scale resource extraction projects—timber production is the classic example of this. This has (both on the Navajo Nation and elsewhere) led to a cycle of spiraling debt and resource liquidation that eventually destroys environments and forecloses other economic approaches.[25] Large-scale industrialization came at the cost of any kind of promotion of entrepreneurial activity—most employment generated by such programs was in tribally run industries. The problem is, mines go dry, timber (especially when it is not replanted) disappears. "The net effect," Russell Lawrence Barsh points out, "has been to reduce the environmental assets of reservations without replacing them with industrial assets."[26]

That is one of the reasons that organizations such as Diné CARE often find themselves at odds with their own tribal government.

■/

After the two girls had been rescued from the Water Monster, a great flood came. It was the Water Monster pursuing the people through the fourth world. Though they retreated to the highest mountain, they could not escape the rising waters. They planted a piñon, which grew quickly but not high enough. They planted other trees and vines as well, but none grew high enough to help them escape. They finally managed their escape through a large reed that reached the sky of the fourth world. "Seeing no hole in the sky, they sent up the Great Hawk . . . to see what he could do. He flew up and began to scratch in the sky with his claws, and he scratched and scratched till he was lost to sight. After a while he came back, and said that he scratched to where he could see light, but that he did not get through the sky." Next the people sent up a locust, who made a small hole, then a badger, who made the hole larger. "When

Badger came back his legs were stained black with the mud, and the legs of all badgers have been black ever since. Then First Man and First Woman led the way and all the others followed them, and they climbed up through the hole to the surface of this—the fifth—world."[27]

Even in the fifth world, the waters continued to pursue the People. "A council was called at once to consider the new danger that threatened them. First Man, who rose to speak, said, pointing to Coyote:

'Yonder is a rascal, and there is something wrong about him. He never takes off his robe, even when he lies down. I have watched him for a long time, and have suspected that he carries some stolen property under his robe. Let us search him.'

They tore the robe from Coyote's shoulders, and two strange little objects dropped out that looked something like buffalo calves, but were spotted all over in various colors; they were the young of Tééhooltsódii [the water monster]. At once the people threw them into the hole through which the waters were pouring; in an instant the waters subsided, and rushed away with a deafening noise to the lower world."[28]

■|

Like the Navajo Nation itself, commercial logging on the reservation was the product of interactions between the Diné and the U.S. government.

The Chuska Mountains and Defiance Plateau are the two forest regions of the Navajo Nation that have supplied commercial timber to the people of the region. Although other areas of the Navajo Nation do have forest lands (e.g., Navajo Mountain in the northwestern section of the reservation, Black Mesa, and the Carrizo Mountains northwest of the Chuskas) these areas are considered too remote or too difficult to log. The Chuska Mountains, covering about 550 square miles along the northern Arizona/ New Mexico border, have been the site of the most timber cutting activity.

The composition of the Chuska Mountain forests, as mentioned, is primarily juniper and piñon below about seven thousand feet, giving way to ponderosa pine (the old growth is called "yellow pine") up to nine thousand feet. The highest elevations in the Chuska Mountains are home to a variety of other species as well. The name "Chuska" is an Anglo phonological adaptation of *Ch'óshgai*, a name that refers to the white spruce that grow in the upper elevations of the mountains.[29] Ponderosa pines are the primary target of logging on the Navajo Nation.

In 1888, the first sawmill on the Navajo Nation began operating on the Defiance Plateau, under the direct oversight of the Indian Agency Farmer. It supplied lumber for Indian Agency buildings such as schools, office buildings, missions, and agency homes. After about twenty years of small-scale logging on Defiance Plateau, logging began in the Chuska Mountains in 1907. By 1929, a number of small mills had been established in the *Diné Bikéyah* by the U.S. government, and lumber was already being sold to customers off the reservation. To manage these as a collective, the Indian Service established a Branch of Forestry for the Navajo Agency that covered the entire reservation.[30]

In spite of fires, accidents, and a variety of other setbacks, Navajo mills were producing about 1.7 million board feet annually by 1936, a number that continued to increase through World War II. Eight hundred thousand board feet of lumber, trees cut from Navajo forests and milled on the reservation, were used in the construction of work buildings and residences at the Los Alamos National Laboratories in New Mexico, about two hundred miles east of the forests.[31] (Besides the lumber, of course, Los Alamos used uranium mined on Navajo lands—the dangerous remnants of these mines continue to leak radiation onto Navajo lands to this day.) All throughout this early history of forestry on the Navajo Reservation, the sawmills and timber resources were managed by non-Indians, appointees of the federal Indian Agency.

In the late 1940s and early 1950s, the Department of the Interior funded studies for the expansion or creation of a variety of industries on the Navajo Nation, including a large-scale industrial timber program. The initial plan of operations had among its objectives: (1) to maximally utilize the Navajo Nation's forests—that is, to convert the forests to sustained yield timber farms; (2) to provide jobs for Navajo workers and develop skills among a new generation of Navajos who could then take over management roles; (3) to provide revenue for the Navajo Nation; and (4) to operate at a profit. Initial studies by the Interior Department recommended an annual allowable cut of thirteen million board feet to be taken from the Navajo forests.[32] Subsequent studies recommended the construction of a mill that could process up to thirty-eight million board feet annually (that projected volume was later expanded).

In 1958 the plan of operations for a new large-scale industrial sawmill was unanimously approved by the council. Navajo Forest Products Industries (NFPI), as the enterprise came to be known, was a huge and ambitious enterprise by tribal standards. The mill itself covered ten acres in Navajo, New Mexico—not far from the Navajo capital of Window Rock. The enterprise embodied an exuberance for industrial development that persisted throughout most of NFPI's history. In an annual report from 1978,[33] celebrating the first twenty years of operation, a photo depicts an unidentified logger taking a chainsaw to the base of a mature Ponderosa pine. The caption declares in no uncertain terms:

TIMBER IS A CROP

The goal of the forestry plan on the Navajo Nation was to integrate the Diné into the world economic community. The original board of directors was composed of a mix of Navajos and non-Indian lumbermen from California and the Pacific Northwest—"captains of industry" who, it was presumed, would provide knowledge and management skill and who could work together to share that ability with Navajo board members.[34] The mill was to be a wholly owned tribal enterprise, celebrated as a corporation that could boast (as one NFPI annual report stated) "each and every Navajo a stockholder."[35] This progressive-sounding plan was unfortunately little more than a figure of speech. Diné citizens did not directly participate as equity stakeholders in the mill—no shares were ever issued, and no system of direct public oversight was ever established. The Navajo Nation Council oversaw the operations of the mill, and while profits from the mill were reinvested in tribal programs (including the building of an infrastructure and high school in the mill town of Navajo, New Mexico) there was no control over this reinvestment at the grassroots level.

The mill was created as a tribal enterprise distinct from the Navajo Nation government. This carried a few implications worth noting—if only for the fact that they were routinely violated. First, it meant the mill would be required to purchase timber from the tribe (the payments are called "stumpage fees"). Second, the Navajo Department of Forestry, under contract to the Bureau of Indian Affairs (who is ultimately responsible for managing the forest) would be in charge of ensuring the health and sustainability of the forest, separate from the economic interests of the mill. As of 1980, all timber sales were supposed to be subject to a ten-year forest-management plan. The plan was to be accompanied by a comprehensive Environmental Impact Statement.

In reality, things didn't work as imagined. The parameters of the relationship between the mill and the tribe were vague and prone to conflict of interest. Members of the council's Natural Resources Committee, charged with making decisions that affected the lands of the Navajo Nation, have historically also served on NFPI's board of directors, and thus have found themselves in a position to materially benefit from granting NFPI liberal timber harvests.[36] Similar situations occurred on the council's Budget and Finance Committee, responsible for allocating development funds and loans to the mill, and for overseeing the billing process between the mill and the tribe.

The Navajo Department of Forestry, meanwhile, primarily served the needs of the mill—the department authorized an aggressive plan of harvest that continued mostly unabated for nearly three decades. From 1961 through 1982, the mill processed an average of over forty million board feet per year in timber from Navajo forests. From the early 1980s through 1992, NFPI's annual harvest from the Navajo forests fell to an average of about thirty-four million board feet, but this was still the most aggressive forest harvest activity among the major commercial forests in the region. By way of comparison, the Kaibab and Coconino forests in Arizona, both noted for an aggressive forest harvest policy, were logged at about 90 percent of the Navajo forest rate (as adjusted for size).[37] The Dixie and Santa Fe National Forests in New Mexico, by contrast, were subjected to timber harvest rates of a little over half of the Navajo forest. While the forests of the "sky islands" of the American Southwest are all fairly unique, this comparison gives a general idea of the aggressive harvest plan pursued on the Navajo forests.

Most of this timber was milled into dimensional lumber and sold at off-reservation markets. None of the lumber produced by the mill was ever used to build Navajo housing, nor was any of it used by value-added industries (for example, furniture making, which Zuni Pueblo has turned into a modestly profitable industry).

NFPI's beneficial arrangement with the tribe and easy access to cheap timber masked, for a while, its underlying weaknesses. As recently as 1980, some twenty years after its inception, the mill was regarded by some as a "prototype" for Indian enterprise.[38] Even as this pronouncement was being made, however, the mill's record of rapid industrialization, prolonged deficit spending, and failure to create any viable value-added industries had left it vulnerable to the forces of the broader marketplace.

At its peak in the late 1970s, NFPI employed over six hundred workers. Some of these were employed in an ill-fated particleboard-processing plant started by the mill in 1976 with a $10.5 million capital investment. That venture proved to be a crucial turning point in the fortunes of NFPI. After failing to produce a profit for eight consecutive years, the particleboard plant was sold to a non-Indian company called Ponderosa Products in 1984, and continued to lose money until its closure in 1991. The mill likewise suffered throughout the 1980s during a time of slow housing starts in the United States. The number of NFPI employees continued to drop from the late 1970s through the early 1990s. In 1991, at about the time that Adella and Leroy first began to question what was going on in the forests, the number of employees at NFPI was a little above two hundred. By 1995, NFPI was in debt over $20 million, including over $6 million owed to the Navajo Nation government in unpaid stumpage fees.[39]

NFPI's financial troubles were only part of the problem. The cycle of "resource dependency" engendered in the forest extracted a heavy toll. By 1980, the Navajo forests had been subjected to a hundred years of cutting—twenty of those years on a grand scale—without regeneration plans of any sort. In 1981, staff members of the Navajo Forestry Department prepared a series of "site condition reports" in anticipation of the first ten-year forest-management plan (required under the

National Indian Forest Resources Management Act—NIFRMA). In these reports, Navajo Forestry Department officials note a number of alarming issues:

- The age distribution of trees on Navajo forests shows a dangerous cumulative loss of new trees to replace those that had been cut. In "Navajo Forest Timber Resources: A Condition Report," Robert Billie (who would later take over as the head of Navajo Forestry Department), documented a "severe shortage of younger age classes" among the trees remaining in the forests of the Chuska Mountain and Defiance Plateau. Billie warned, "An under-stocked forest offers no insurance for the future. . . ."[40]
- Timber cutting had had a serious detrimental effect on area water quality. In a similar report discussing the health of the Navajo forest in terms of water quality, it was pointed out that "sedimentation from accelerated soil erosion is probably the worst water quality problem on the Navajo forest. Accelerated sheet erosion and deep gullies were reported at least as early as 1936 and were undoubtedly present much earlier. *These erosion problems have continued virtually unchecked.*"[41]
- The backlog of forest regeneration and replanting after a hundred years of cutting without mitigation, was nearly insurmountable. A third site report commented that "Reforestation backlog for the Navajo forest, both for planting and natural regeneration, is substantially large and keeps increasing annually." The authors of this report provided a grim assessment of the forest's sustainability: "Even if an extensive reforestation program is carried out on the Navajo and one thousand acres are each planted and site prepared annually, it will take 160 years to catch up with the planting backlog and 90 years to eliminate the site preparation backlog." The authors hastened to add that these numbers were purely academic; the Navajo Nation at the time had no reforestation plan, and, even if it did, one thousand acres per year was (and continues to be) impossible given the current circumstances, availability of funding, and so on.[42]

By 1991, the year that Leroy Jackson and Adella Begaye initiated their careers as activists, the forest had undergone ten more years of aggressive harvest, and none of the recommendations or cautions spelled out in the site condition reports had been taken seriously. Certainly, none had led to any operating or policy changes within the Navajo Department of Forestry. The mill, suffering from massive debts, clamored in front of the tribal council and its committees for easier access to Navajo timber, and the Navajo Nation Council seemed more than willing to grant it.

three

Over the course of my research there has never been a shortage of incidents, apparitions, dreams, and coincidences impossible to explain through the prism of Western science.

—Mark Plotkin, *Tales of a Shaman's Apprentice*

∎

At that time the first Earth Surface people were traveling from place to place. They journeyed towards the east, and after one day's march they reached a place called "White Spot on the Earth" and camped for the night. Here a woman brought forth, but her offspring was not like a child; it was round, misshapen, and had no head. The people counseled, and determined that it should be thrown into a gully. So they threw it away; but it lived and grew up and became the monster Déélgééd, who afterwards destroyed so many of the people.

Next day they wandered farther to the east, and camped at night at Rock Bending Back. Here was born another misshapen creature, which had something like feathers on both its shoulders. It looked like nothing that was ever seen before, so the people concluded to throw this away also. They took it to an alkali bed close by and cast it away there. But it lived and grew and became the terrible Tsé' naagháii, of whom I shall have much to tell later. . . .

All these monsters were the fruit of the transgressions of the women in the fourth world, when they were separated from the men. Other monsters were born on the march, and others, again, sprang from the blood which had been shed during the birth of the first monsters, and all these grew up to become enemies and destroyers of the people.

—Washington Matthews, *Navaho Legends*

■/

Early one morning in the summer of 1991, Adella woke up to the sound of singing. As she recalled later:

> It was early in the morning, still dark, but it was a warm night, so we were sleeping with the windows open. I was asleep, I thought, but I woke up to the sound of what seemed like a thousand voices singing. They were singing like—it sounded like a thousand medicine men, singing a song from a ceremony. At first it seemed like it was coming from outside, a long way off. I woke Leroy up. I said, "did you hear that singing." He didn't hear anything. Now I didn't hear it any more either. I went back to sleep.

It had been only a couple months since she and Leroy had first personally encountered the legacy of commercial forestry. On their first trip up to the family's summer grazing lands after the spring melt, they had been stunned by the specter of a cut they didn't even know had been planned. Technically, it wasn't a "clear cut"—as Adella pointed out, "they left about one tree for every twenty stumps." The great ridges that ran down from the mountains had once been undulating waves of green but were now mostly bare. A system of logging roads now crisscrossed the landscape. Some were poorly constructed and already showed trenches caused by unabated runoff from the mountains.

Shortly after they recovered from the initial shock, they decided to do something about it. That's about the time Adella had this vision.

> After I fell asleep I heard the singing again. It was like a Blessingway song,[1] but I haven't heard that song at any ceremony since then. I started to wake up, but before I was all the way awake I could see their faces, all the plants, all the trees on the Chuska Mountains. I could see each one of them. Each one of them like a different person. They were doing the singing. They were still in front of my eyes even after I woke up. I tried to wake Leroy up again, but by the time he woke up, the singing had stopped. He didn't hear it.

After that I didn't care if nobody supported me. I knew what I needed to do. And I knew we'd win this fight.

Adella did not offer up the details of this story lightly. She was certainly familiar with the skepticism of many bilagáanas, particularly academic types. Call it "physics envy" or Western materialist bias, but anthropologists have rarely been much good at understanding or reporting such experiences. "I think maybe White people are a little too . . . hard, on the inside, to have that kind of experience," Adella once reflected.[2] Perhaps the best thing an anthropologist *can* attempt to provide is an appreciation of how Adella interpreted her vision, which in turn contributed to the power it held for her. It was a result of this vision, after all, that she realized her commitment to the forests.

Even this more modest endeavor has its challenges. So much has been written about the Diné "spiritual connection to the land," that it borders on cliché. This large body of literature frequently leaves the Diné themselves largely unimpressed, at times even resentful. Like other Indian people from the American Southwest, they are very suspicious of attempts to "capture" traditional knowledge in writing or on tape.[3] They recognize that ceremonial knowledge and the language by which it is brought to life—spoken Navajo, *Diné bizaad*—is alive and powerful, a creative force. Attempts to "capture" this knowledge electronically or in written form, particularly in written form translated to some other language, represents a vain and possibly even dangerous undertaking—a somewhat foolish act of hubris.[4]

Earl Tulley, a close friend of Leroy and Adella, and one of the cofounders of Diné CARE, put it this way:

> The spiritual connection, they want that to become tangible so that they can put it in their books. That portion from us so that we can have some sort of a biblical account and put it in writing. They say that, "Now we've got the Navajo belief in a book. This is how they believe," and that's the part I have a hard time with.

A lifetime of learning, mostly from her own family, underlay Adella's understanding and commitment. Her education may have started with her mother's father, Curly Mustache. His portrait hung above the back door of Adella's little duplex by the clinic. It shows an elderly man wearing a large, flat-brimmed hat and a pair of heavy, framed spectacles. He has a tremendous, bushy, gray mustache; his long, gray hair is tied up in the traditional bun worn by Diné men. He has been called the "Navajo Aristotle." (A similar portrait of him hangs in the library of Diné College.) Several anthropologists relied for their own scholarly work on Curly Mustache's knowledge of Diné philosophy, history, botany, and other "religion" (as if those epistemological categories could be so neatly separated in a Navajo way of looking).

His knowledge of the medicinal uses of plants alone was encyclopedic—he knew the correct plants to use for a wide variety of conditions, from anemia to kidney infections. This amounted to far more than the simple categorical knowledge of "this plant is good for that ailment." Strict and often lengthy ritual procedures accompany the use of medicinal herbs. The appropriate prayers and songs must be known. The appropriate times to gather and the types of offerings must be honored. The plants are not simply "objects" one picks from the forest.

Trees, plants, animals, and all beings have *bii'gistíín*—inner form. Through breathing, all creatures share in *nítch'i*—Holy Wind—which binds them as relatives. Wholeness and harmony—the goals of a life lived properly—come from the awareness of one's relatedness to all things. The whole person is not merely a physical being, but interacts intimately with the bii'gistíín in other beings, and with the *Diné Diyinii*—the Holy People.

> There is fire in us . . . there is earth in us; everything has earth. There is water in us, there is air in us. So, in a sense, the trees out there, the plants, birds, animals . . . all these things, and we are the same. They are kin to us. They are our brothers, our sisters. And since we are both made of these elements, we are children of the earth and the sky. This is the way things are seen.[5]

Because animals and plants have their own spirits, their use requires acts of reciprocity no less than relations among humans. This is why Navajo herbalists make offerings to plants whenever they remove any from the land. This is also why people, when they are saying their morning prayers, make an offering of corn pollen on the tip of the tongue, to the spirit within.[6] The division among "social," "natural," and "spirit" worlds is an artificial one (and potentially destructive) from a Diné perspective. This orientation to the environment blurs the lines that most of us are accustomed to maintaining between economy and ecology, between "religious" and "secular" practice.

Underlying this orientation is an emphasis on living process—on change and motion—that is as evident in the language as it is in daily practice. "The Navajos' emphasis on motion is the foundation of their view of the world," writes anthropologist Trudy Griffin-Pierce.[7] Because all things in the universe are alive and in motion, the individual must continuously act to maintain harmony and balance—not only in ceremonies but through daily practice as well, particularly *hózhǫ́ ntsáhákees* (right thinking). The health of the individual, the community, and the world at large depends on an extended, dynamic, and highly complex pattern of interrelationships.

As she talked about her grandfather, Adella said that one of her biggest regrets was not listening to him more often or more carefully. "He always wanted to teach me things—songs, prayers, things about the plants in the forest. I only learned a little from him." She sighed, then laughed: "I was a typical teenager, it just wasn't 'cool.'"

Curly Mustache's daughter—Adella's mother—was an herbalist as well. She was tiny and hunched with age when the anthropologist first met her. In a life spanning eighty-some years, she had never lived in a home with electricity or running water. She spoke only Navajo. She didn't know how to read. Her eyes glistened with a fierce sense of independence that she retained throughout her life. Even Leroy, who took on powerful interests in the Navajo Nation government and the BIA, admitted to being more than a little intimidated by this woman. It was her land (Navajo inheritance is traced through the mother's lineage) on which the family's flocks grazed in the summertime.

With this heritage Adella grew up in the Chuska Mountains. Even when she was of the age to be shipped off to boarding school, she still spent her summers there, walking with the sheep—she once confessed that she preferred that to the alternative, cooking and doing dishes—always with a book in her hand. She was an avid reader, with a preference for true-crime stories. Despite the generational differences from her mother and grandfather, she knew the land in the kind of detail one can get only by wandering around on it by foot for many years. Later in life, she would move away several times, but she would inevitably return to her true home on the reservation, near the land she loved, and her family.

Across that landscape are strewn numerous sacred sites. Navajo sacred places are not clearly bounded by property lines or architectural structure. The hogan becomes a sacred space during a ceremony, then reverts to its mundane use when the ceremony has ended.[8] Outside the hogan, the entire Navajo landscape is infused with sacred meaning through stories, with offering places, with petroglyphs, with places where ceremonies are held. All of these sacred places tie the individual not only to the land but to history, the inherited traditions of the ancestors.

At some places life events are marked. When a baby is born, its umbilical cord is buried beneath the family land, attaching the new family member to a given place as home. Some sacred places are created by acts of nature: trees struck by lightning have power that must be respected. Sacred springs, the source of life-giving water that is so precious in the arid Southwest, can be found in the mountains. For springs to continue providing Mother Earth's life-blood, they must be given the same type of reciprocal acknowledgment that one's human relatives would receive.

Diné stories and a vast ceremonial corpus name hundreds of important places throughout the entire region as sacred. Because they don't have identifiable buildings and street addresses, many of the sacred places in the Navajo forest have never been formally documented or registered. Their identification, importance, and maintenance have largely been the domain of nearby families, or specialists such as herbalists or *hataałii*. Kelley and Francis point out that the Chuska Mountains are "likely to have a very high density of unrecorded sacred places," the vast majority of which still need to be documented and protected.[9]

More than this, however, the Chuska Mountain range itself, as a whole, "probably constitutes a single large sacred landscape as well." The Chuska Mountains represent the male deity in the Navajo tradition. There is a dualism in Navajo belief that divides things into male and female aspect.

Everything is seen in terms of male and female. Our right side, whether we are male or female, our right side is our female side. Our left side is our male side. Our left side is our aggressive nature, our right side is our gentle side. The left side is a warrior, the right side, gentle.[10]

This dualism forms a whole. Male and female, aggressive and gentle, evil and good are complementary aspects of that whole. It is impossible to imagine one side without keeping in mind the other. Harmony is achieved when elements are kept in their appropriate balance. Humans keep this harmony through participation in ceremonies, and through appropriate action in the course of daily life. When things are sent out of harmony, for instance, when illness or misfortune arises, corrective action must be taken. Things associated with "maleness" provide the patient with aggressiveness to combat that which can cause harm. Herbs coming from the Chuskas, because they come from the body of the male deity, serve an important role as a male component in various healing ceremonies. Sometimes, herbs from the Chuskas are combined with herbs from Black Mesa, which is the body of the female deity.

> So, it is necessary, if you are just going about with a peaceful nature, because there is harm out there, there is danger, wherever danger, evil lurks out there, we're going to succumb to that. You need to be a warrior, you need to be aggressive. You need to be "evil," this is how things respect us. This is how we combat illness, and anything that will harm us.[11]

Ceremonies are the application of sacred knowledge and power. They always involve an element of danger. Wrong attitudes, lack of preparation or other mistakes can bring harm. That is why a highly trained specialist— *hataałii* (medicine man)—is always used to perform a ceremony.

■/

Yé'iitsoh, the giant, was the biggest and most fearsome of all the alien monsters. He had a body made of flint, and he shot bolts of lightning. Yé'iitsoh had his home near Mount Taylor and Hot Spring (Grants). He would strike his victim with his club of dark, blue, yellow, and varicolored flint, then devour him. Déélgééd the Horned Monster ran at large over the country. His eyesight was keen and he would swallow his victims without chewing them.

At Shiprock the Eagle Monster had provided five black flint points and five blue flint points, the former along the east, the latter along the west ridge of the rock. He would drop a captured man on the dark flint points and then eat them. A woman victim would be thrust on the blue flint points so that they would be shattered and be devoured by the two (monster) children below; after that they would go on another raid.

The Traveling Rock would run his victims down four times, carry them home and eat them while reclining for a rest. Another monster called the Kicker-off-the-rock had his home on a rock shelf beyond which there was a field of sage arrows from which arrow(-shafts) were made. A single path led to the field. Here he sat with his hair grown into the rock and leaning against it with his right foot resting on his knee. If a passer-by inquired about the arrow-field, he was quite friendly and would explain that they were the finest in the country. But as soon as the person attempted to pass him he kicked them over the precipice where his two children were waiting. There was always a struggle for the eye, ear, liver and so forth of the victim.

There were many other monsters as well, including Tracking Bear, Two-crushing-rocks, Slicing reeds, and the Monsters-who-slay-with-their-eyes. In various other ways, these other monsters would similarly kill and devour their victims, the Earth Surface People.[12]

■/

The Diné have a sense about the power invoked in their ceremonies—practitioners may sometimes invoke that power, not to restore balance to the community, but for selfish gain or even for harm to others.

Like Adella, Leroy also had an unusual dream in the summer of 1991. He found himself in a strange city, walking down a street he had never seen before. He turned a corner and entered a shop—as it turned out, it was a barber shop. He was surprised to find there a number of people whom he knew, including a few high-ranking Navajo officials, plus several non-

Navajos, bilagáanas, all sitting around a table together. As he entered the shop, they all looked up at him silently, as if he'd startled them and interrupted something.

They were looking at a book on witchcraft.

He grew uneasy. "You shouldn't be messing around with those things," Leroy told the group. "That stuff will turn around on you." They looked at Leroy without saying anything. Then they went back to their book.

Leroy woke from the dream in a cold sweat, and mentioned it only to Adella, and much later, to the anthropologist. "Those Tony Hillerman books are OK," Leroy once remarked, "except all the stuff about witchcraft, like everybody's going around doing that kind of thing all the time."

Navajo witchcraft has long been a fascination of bilagáanas coming to Navajo country. One anthropologist, Clyde Kluckhohn, admits to making more than one local person uncomfortable with pressing questions about the topic, which as a rule the Diné would rather avoid discussing.[13] Fascination with the topic is unhealthy at best. As Adella once asked, "How come bilagáanas always want to know about witchcraft?"

Some have argued that the frequency of witchcraft allegations among the Diné has increased proportionally to contact with Anglo-Americans. The very values taught to children (directly or indirectly) in the boarding schools—competitiveness, independence, the importance of individual achievement—stand in direct contrast with important Navajo values of connectedness to place and family, of one's obligation and belonging in the clan system. Acquisitiveness, competitiveness, aggressiveness in daily interactions, these all appear to be the very type of selfishness that finds its ultimate expression in the evil of witchcraft. The worst thing a Diné can say about another is "she acts like she has no relatives."[14] From the perspective of many Navajo people, much of what bilagáana society offers in terms of economic opportunity seems to require behavior that looks suspiciously like acting "as if one has no relatives."

■|

Leroy traded in Indian arts and crafts, an industry estimated to have a worldwide market (mostly informal economy, at that) of between two and three billion dollars. On large, homemade shelves in a back bedroom of the duplex he kept his wares: rolls of soft, pale buckskin; stiff black leather belts strung with gleaming silver conchas; Hopi bracelets inlaid with intricate animal and symbolic designs; tin boxes full of beads, polished rocks, bits of precious stone—most prominently, turquoise—that would one day be worked into fine jewelry.

On the opposite wall was something quite different: a reprint of a portrait of a Mexican bandito. It was garish, almost a parody of itself, not unlike a velvet tapestry of Elvis with the beatific gaze, or dogs playing poker, which is maybe why Leroy liked it so much. The most striking thing about it, however, was that the man in the picture looked remarkably like Leroy. The same square jaw, the same fine, angular features. Except for the stubble, the string of bullets over the shoulder, and the slightly menacing grin that held a cigarillo in place, Leroy could have been that bandito.

"He keeps that because his buddies all say that macho bandito it looks like him," Adella once commented dryly. It is not inconceivable that Leroy could have had some Mexican ancestry in his background. There is even a Navajo clan called the *Naakaii Diné*, or "Mexican People." There are also clans for neighboring tribes—Apaches, Ute, some of the Pueblos. While conflict has always been a part of the region, these clan names trace a history of Navajo willingness to establish the bonds of kinship with their neighbors. Who knows? If the Anglo Americans hadn't come in the manner and the numbers which they did, perhaps today there would be a "bilagáana Diné" clan as well.

Like other kids from the Rez, Leroy spent at least part of his young life in Indian boarding schools. Those who attended BIA schools or many of the Christian mission schools share a common set of memories that have come to be called the "boarding school experience." The first Indian boarding school, established in 1879 in Carlisle, Pennsylvania, was designed to "kill the Indian to save the man," in the words of founder Colonel Richard Pratt.[15] (Sports fans may remember Carlisle for Jim Thorpe, one of America's greatest all-around athletes, and football coach Pop Warner.)

Pratt's basic formula became standard operating procedure at Indian boarding schools throughout most of the twentieth century. Children caught speaking their own native tongue instead of the required English ("the language of the greatest, most powerful and enterprising nationalities beneath the sun"[16]) would likely find their mouths washed out with soap or lye. Non-Christian ceremonies or prayers were strictly forbidden as the work of the Devil. Attendance at Christian services was mandatory. Beatings, often administered by older, more acculturated children, formed a regular part of the integration process.

According to Lori Goodman, a close friend to Leroy and Adella, and cofounder of Diné CARE, this integrationist philosophy is "cultural strip mining," and the underlying motivations are obvious. "The whole thing has been a way to get at our resources easier." Integrated Indians tend to be more compliant with development agendas that often call for a separation of the people from their land. (It should be pointed out that, despite this stark assessment of the system as a whole, she and other Diné CARE members frequently expressed a surprisingly conciliatory tone toward the actual people who staffed them: "They were good people," Lori once said. "They thought they were doing the right thing.")

According to one school buddy, Leroy "was a little guy, but he was stubborn, man. He was always taking a beating. He never gave in. He just kept coming out swinging, coming back for more." He graduated from Flagstaff High School in the 1960s, and not long after was drafted and sent to Vietnam.

Leroy never had much to say about that particular period of his life. "The thing about the military," he once said, "the reason so many *Indios* go into it and like it, is that in boarding school, you're taught that you're worse than the bilagáana, that you're not as good. You come out of boarding school, you don't belong at home anymore, and you're not good enough to be a bilagáana. You're nothing, you're the lowest of the low.

"Then in the military, they tell you that it doesn't matter what color you are. They break everybody down. It doesn't matter if you're red, black, or white, they tell you everybody is the same. All of a sudden, these poor Indios that have been told they're no good, they feel like they're as good as the next guy."

He didn't serve a full tour in Vietnam. He was dishonorably discharged, returned to the United States, and spent the next several years of his life wandering and battling alcohol.

"I was a hobo," he once said with what sounded like a hint of nostalgia in his voice. If such a hint was actually there, it was faint. He roamed the country—mostly the West—on trains, drinking, lost, dislocated from his family and his people. One day he woke up and found himself on the floor of a jail cell in Salt Lake City. He had hit bottom. He vowed to turn his life around. From that day he never took another drink. A friend got him into treatment in Salt Lake. Within a year he had enrolled in engineering courses at the University of Utah and began working as a substance-abuse counselor.

Only one subtle reminder of those days remains: On one wall of their house, behind the kitchen table, Adella still displays a priceless blanket that one of her sisters wove for Leroy. It is composed of row after row of small railroad cars, intricately and beautifully detailed.

Adella once recounted the first time she ever met Leroy, while they were both students at the University of Utah: "I had a good friend in school who knew this guy that worked as a substance-abuse counselor. He was Lakota. A lot of those Lakota guys are really nice looking, tall and hand-some. So, she wanted to go see this guy, but she didn't want to go over there by herself. She begged me to go along. I kept telling her 'I don't want to go to that place. Too depressing.' But she talked me into it."

Adella was a biology student at the university. She was younger than Leroy. "We were there, talking to this Lakota guy. She was flirting. Then Leroy came up to us—he worked there too—and told us to be quiet. 'There are people with problems!' he told us. 'Don't be coming in here flirting and giggling. This is a counseling center.'"

Adella smiled as she remembered that inauspicious beginning: "I thought, 'Sheesh who is this guy? He seems so serious!'"

Adella and Leroy married before she had finished college. He took a job at the San Juan power station, a coal-fired plant in the Four Corners area, quitting a couple years later when he realized that management at the plant had authorized the night shift to disable the scrubbers that are required by law to lower emissions of sulfur dioxide. (The power stations of the Four Corners area are notorious for their pollution; they've fouled the air qual-ity of much of the region, from Mesa Verde to the Grand Canyon.) A few years later, when their oldest child Michelle was still a little girl, they moved to Tucson, and Adella returned to school to earn her degree in nursing. When she graduated, they came back to the Rez.

■|

Their careers as forest activists started slowly, gradually, as they began to talk to other people in their community. They contacted friends in neighboring chapters. They realized that they weren't the only ones who were shocked by the remains of the timber cutting. They found out that many people in the mountains who herded their sheep, gathered sacred herbs, lived and performed ceremonies there had already expressed dismay at what the Navajo forestry program was doing to the Chuskas. Nothing the people said had ever seemed to make a difference, however.

They organized a handful of neighbors, clan relatives, and others in the mountains, and formed a little group they called the Diné bi Wilderness Society. As Leroy put it: "We didn't want to put an end to forestry, we just wanted these guys to be accountable. To stand up and say 'Hey. You people have to answer to the people that live on these mountains.'"

Neither he nor Adella had ever received formal education in the specifics of technical forestry, watershed management, or any of the other aspects of the forest that they would come, over time, to learn about from a wide variety of sources. They didn't have strong connections in the federal or state governments, they knew no one in the environmental-activist community, they were not even well connected at the Navajo Nation government or its Department of Forestry (though, over time, they would develop all these relationships). They just knew they had to do something. Leroy laughed as he recalled much later, "I thought I'd spend a month, maybe two, getting this thing settled."

Their goal was to work within the existing system to bring about change and greater accountability from the mill and the tribe. They knew they needed to start locally, at the level of their own chapter house. They decided that the best way to get the attention of the Navajo Nation government was to pass a chapter resolution, a resolution voicing the concerns of the community to the council, and requesting reform.

On a sunny Sunday afternoon in October 1991, after waiting patiently for several hours at the Tsaile-Wheatfields Chapter House as the biweekly chapter meeting trudged through its routine business of grazing permits, HUD housing business, and community work projects, Leroy got up and gave a talk to the people of their chapter to take a stand and demand some accountability from Navajo Nation forestry, NFPI, and the Tribal Council. It was not an impassioned plea. It was, in fact, a fairly low-key presentation. The community responded overwhelmingly. A resolution was drafted and approved calling for an immediate end to all timber cutting, until reforms to the process, especially in terms of local oversight, could be implemented.

Theirs was the first of an eventual fourteen Navajo chapters to approve resolutions supporting forestry reform. Ironically, their home chapter would also be the only one to have a subsequent resolution passed that rescinded that support. Sam Yazzie, their own council delegate, was both a member of the Navajo Nation Council's resources committee and a member of NFPI's board of directors. Before Leroy and Adella came along, no one thought to publicly question whether this put Councilman Yazzie in a position of conflict of interest, perhaps because, before Leroy and Adella, no one from outside the tribal government had taken a good hard look at the situation.

Councilman Yazzie clearly did not appreciate the new scrutiny. At a "special chapter meeting" that he convened some months later, attended by a select group of mill workers, loggers, and others with economic ties to NFPI, a "counter-resolution" was drafted and approved that instructed the council to disregard the previous chapter resolution, along with the "environmental group" Diné CARE that had introduced it.

But by this time, the voices of those calling for a reform in the forestry program were too loud to ignore. And by now, Leroy, Adella, and their allies in the community had been encouraged by the support of the organization they helped form, known as "Diné Citizens Against Ruining our Environment."

four

The first Earth Surface People now removed to White Standing Rock, where, a few days after they arrived, they found on the ground a small turquoise image of a woman; this they preserved. Of late the monsters had been actively pursuing and devouring the people, and at the time this image was found there were only four persons remaining alive; these were an old man and woman and their two children, a young man and a young woman. Two days after the finding of the image, early in the morning, before they rose, they heard the voice of the Talking God, crying his call of 'Wu'hu'hu'hú' so faint and far that they could scarcely hear it. After a while the call was repeated a second time, nearer and louder than at first. Again, after a brief silence, the call was heard for the third time, still nearer and still louder. The fourth call was loud and clear, as if sounded near at hand; as soon as it ceased, the shuffling tread of moccasined feet was heard, and a moment later the Talking God stood before them.

He told them to come up to Spruce Mountain after twelve nights had passed, bringing with them the turquoise image they had found, and at once he departed.

On the morning of the appointed day they ascended the mountain by a holy trail, and on a level spot, near the summit, they met a party that awaited them there. They found there the Home God, White Body (who came up from the lower world with the Diné), the eleven brothers (of the Bear Maiden), the Mirage Stone People, the Daylight People standing in the east, the Blue Sky People standing in the south, the Yellow Light People standing in the west, and the Darkness People standing in the north. White Body stood in the east among the Daylight People, bearing in his hand a small image of a woman wrought in white shell, about the same size and shape as the blue image the Navajos bore.

Talking God laid down a sacred buckskin with its head toward the west. The Mirage Stone People laid on the buckskin, heads west, the two little images—of turquoise and white shell—a white and a yellow ear of corn, the

Pollen Boy, and the Grasshopper Girl. On top of all these Talking God laid another sacred buckskin with its head to the east, and under this they now put Nílch'i (Holy Wind).

Then the assembled crowd stood so as to form a circle, leaving in the east an opening through which Talking God and Home God might pass in and out, and they sang the sacred song of Hozhǫ́ngisin. Four times the gods entered and raised the cover. When they raised it for the fourth time, the images and the ears of corn were found changed to living beings in human form: the turquoise image had become Changing Woman, the white shell image had become White Shell Woman; the white ear of corn had become White Corn Boy, and the yellow ear of corn, Yellow Corn Girl. After the ceremony, White Body took Pollen Boy, Grasshopper Girl, White Corn Boy and Yellow Corn Girl away with him; the rest of the assembly departed, and the two divine sisters, Changing Woman and White Shell Woman, were left on the mountain alone.

—Matthews, *Navaho Legends*

■|

A summer storm rolled up over the Mogollon Rim, onto the high plains and buttes in the southwestern portion of the Navajo Reservation, the place the Diné call *Chézhintah* (Lava Butte Land). In these wide open spaces, such a storm could be disastrous for the sheep. Thunder and lightning can drive a flock for miles, tiring them out far from home, where they're vulnerable to coyotes.

Robert Joe slipped into a windbreaker and put on his cowboy hat. He grabbed the keys to the pickup. This was a man who was wholly self-sufficient and at home in multiple worlds. He was as comfortable diagnosing a troubled engine or installing a solar battery as butchering a sheep. As a younger man, he had provided for his family by working for the railroad. He was fluent in Navajo, Hopi, English, and Spanish. He was both a "traditionalist" and a "progressive."

"Do you want some help?" the anthropologist asked him.

"It's up to you," was his answer. This was classic Diné. *It's up to you.* One thing Diné traditionally never do is presume to speak for another, or to assume that a person can, purely through some sense of obligation, be forced to do something he or she does not want to do. "The Navajo phrase which fuses both autonomy and consensus conceptions," writes anthropologist Louise Lamphere "is *t'áá bee bóholníih,* which has been translated as 'He is the boss' . . . but is more accurately rendered by, 'It's up to him to decide,' 'It is his business,' or 'It's his area of concern.'"[1]

They climbed into the pickup and started up the long, dirt road that led from the house to the highway. The sheep were already out of sight. They stopped at a ridge still well away from the main road, and Robert scanned the horizon. "There," he said, pointing by pursing his lips in their general direction. The anthropologist strained and squinted, but could see nothing that stood out from the sagebrush.

The sheep were perhaps two miles from the house. They had wandered down the plain in a wide arroyo that emptied out into a large depression near two massive and perfectly conical buttes.

"Just stay to the outside of them," Robert told the anthropologist a few minutes later, as the latter stepped out of the truck. "The lightning makes them want to run."

Throughout the rest of the afternoon, the sheep led the anthropologist slowly back toward the house, up and down the undulating ground, through old washes where, if one looked closely enough, tiny pink shards of Anasazi pottery could be found mixed with the similarly colored gravel. Years had worn their edges and fractures smooth, but their thin, gently curved surfaces gave them away.

Hundreds of years after the Anasazi had occupied this place, when Kit Carson's raiders led the assault on the Diné, many people found refuge in the vast, forbidding terrain of the Western Navajo homeland. From the Lava Butte Lands, up through the area now called the Painted Desert to Navajo Mountain, many families from this region were spared the misery of the Long Walk. As one elder from Navajo Mountain put it:

Those from here, that didn't happen to them. People were taken from over at Huerfano Mountain and Mount Taylor [in the eastern part of Navajo land] and further on. All along the way the people suffered. Those that were captured—the women, their children—for them those who were still here, the

men, performed prayers. It's true that the Navajo stories and prayers are
sacred . . . Prayers were made there [at a shrine to the Warrior Twins on
Navajo Mountain], prayers called repeating prayers.[2]

It was their prayers more than anything else, the Navajo people say,
that led to their eventual release from imprisonment at Fort Sumner and
their return to their homeland.

■/

Later that evening, Robert Joe and the anthropologist sat on the colon-
naded front porch of the Joe family home, a handsome ranch house made
of brick—unusual in these parts both for its style and its size. It boasted,
among other things, multiple bedrooms, a spacious kitchen, and separate
living and dining rooms. But for all its modern-ness, this was without
doubt the home of a Diné: out front stood a hogan, its six sides built of the
same red brick as the house. Not far from that stood a small, whitewashed
cinder-block cabin, now used for storage, that for many years had been
their only dwelling, five hundred square feet for a family of ten.

The storm had passed. To the west, the buttes gave way to a broad plain
across which *Dook'o'oosłííd*, the sacred Navajo mountain that forms the
western boundary of the homeland, could be seen silhouetted against the
yellow sky. The mountain's Navajo name refers to the fact that the snow
on its summit never melts, despite the fact that the lands surrounding it
can be merciless in summer time. Very often the summit of *Dook'o'oosłííd*
will have clouds clinging to it, even when the rest of the desert sky is clear;
it intercepts the moist air sailing over the western deserts.

The Hopi people, many of whom live on Second Mesa just north of
Lava Butte Land, likewise regard this mountain as sacred. They say the
Qatsinas come from that mountain when they bring the precious rains. The
bilagáana people have named that mountain the San Francisco Peaks, built
a ski resort on it, and mine it for pumice.

It hadn't been much of a storm as far as rain goes. It was mid-July and
all around them the land was dry and sparse. In the old days, Robert told
the anthropologist, there used to be a lot more grass in the summertime.

Now, the chapter officials would have to begin hauling in hay and water for local livestock.

They sat in silence and watched the buttes catch fire with the glow of the setting sun.

"I bet you saw some Anasazi pottery," Robert said to the anthropologist in the hush of the evening breeze.

"How did you know?" asked the surprised anthropologist.

"It's all over the place." He waved vaguely toward the south. "We started to build our first house further down that way," he said. "While we were working on it, the sand blew away and some skeletons of Anasazis were buried there. So we built our house further up this way instead."

The Joe children used to depart every Sunday night from their original one-room cinder-block cabin for another week at the Indian boarding school in nearby Seba Dalkai. Robert Joe was a pragmatic man, and he insisted on his kids getting their education. His hopes for them didn't go unfulfilled. They have grown up to be successful in a wide variety of professions—one is a lawyer, two are engineers, one has been a council delegate, another is an accountant, and yet another is a college instructor.

His kids learned to succeed in the American economy, like him, without forsaking their own Diné heritage, an accomplishment that doesn't just come naturally. Lori Goodman, who would eventually become a key member of Diné CARE, recalls: "Every Sunday night it was the same thing: my brother used to cry . . . he just hated being shipped off to school. For me it wasn't such a big deal, it was more of a party. All of my cousins were there . . .

"In school they made us choose a Christian religion. They told us we were heathens if we believed in the Holy People or attended Navajo ceremonies—we would go to hell. I had no idea what the difference was, so I chose the Catholics.

"On the day of my baptism and first communion, I was so excited, so happy to know that I wasn't going to go to hell after all. But then I'm there in the church and I'm looking all around, and my parents didn't show up. I couldn't understand that. I was really upset.

"Later I just asked my dad. 'Why didn't you come to my first communion?'

"He sat me down. 'Well, that's something that you have to do to get by.' For him it was like taking a math class or passing an English exam."

■/

It was here in the midst of Lava Butte Land, in the community of Dilkon Navajo Chapter, that Diné CARE was born (originally simply as CARE— "Citizens Against Ruining our Environment"). In 1987 a handful of representatives from a company called Waste-Tech approached the office of Navajo Nation President Peter MacDonald with a proposal. Waste-Tech was a Colorado-based division of the Amoco Corporation specializing in the construction and operation of toxic-waste incinerators. Its management wanted to build a huge incinerator and storage facility, a $40 million project that would bring in toxic wastes from all over the region for treatment on the Navajo Nation.

Why Waste-Tech chose the Navajo Nation is perhaps impossible to say for sure, but not hard to imagine. By this time, the "NIMBY" ("Not in my back yard") movement was alive and well in the United States. Beginning with Rachel Carson's *Silent Spring* (first published in 1962) and gaining momentum with the first Earth Day in 1970, widespread resistance to toxic dumping found its real catalyst in 1980 at Love Canal, the now (in)famous blue-collar suburb of Buffalo. Lois Gibbs, one of the Love Canal residents who organized the local movement, drew national attention to the problem of toxic waste in American communities and crystallized "[a] new class of activist—the angry mother."[3]

In selecting the Navajo Nation as a site, Waste-Tech likely anticipated less organized resistance: Here was a place with a poor communications infrastructure, a population not heavily connected to mass media and mainstream educational systems, high unemployment and perhaps most of all, a friendly tribal government and a federal agency (the Bureau of Indian Affairs) exerting little or no environmental oversight.

Waste-Tech hired MacDonald's own son Rocky as their official liaison, and recruited Dilkon council delegate Manuel Shirley to help promote the project. Before long, the project had been "railroaded" (in Lori's words) to approval in a chapter vote.

At the time, Lori Goodman was living with her husband and four boys several hours from Dilkon, in the southwest corner of Colorado. One afternoon her sister (who lived in the same town) called with the news: "She heard it on National Public Radio. 'They're putting a forty-million-dollar garbage dump in at Dilkon,' she told me."

"It's true. We're getting a new garbage dump," her dad said later over the phone. "The chapter has been talking about it now, for three or four chapter meetings. It's going to be worth forty million dollars. It's supposed to bring a lot of jobs to Dilkon too. It will be a regional landfill." (Lori recalls, "This was his Navajo understanding. I'm sure they didn't say 'regional landfill.'")

Even those few people who were initially suspicious were strongly discouraged from organizing opposition. "They were being told by our council delegate that the decision had already been made in D.C. Of course, these were lies told to our community people. That it was going to be approved, we can't do anything about it. People were scared to speak up because of their jobs and other types of intimidation."

But a few people decided to do something about it. Local activists (now local elders) Abe Plummer, Jane Yazzie, and James and Sista Paddock joined with the Joe family to organize opposition to the dump. Anna Frazier, the Joes' "next door" neighbor (two miles away down the gently sloping prairie) joined them as well. Together they formed CARE, and made Lori's brother Al—who lived in Dilkon—the president.

As Lori recalled, "Al was picked as the president of CARE, more because he didn't receive water, hay, a job, anything from the tribe. Because he wasn't dependent on the chapter or the tribal government, he had nothing to lose so he became the key spokesperson. He could speak the truth without fear of real retributions." She added with a laugh, "I have to say that my dad probably volunteered Al somewhere along the way. He always stressed our duty to our people. Help and share where we can. He was always coming back from meetings, and we would learn which one of us he had volunteered for something. He was always telling us that 'it was said' in stories, The Kiyaa'áanii[4] were a selfish clan, just to shame us into it."

Regarding her own involvement in the early days of CARE, she commented: "I was maybe the last person you would have thought would get involved in something like that. I was a total stay-at-home mom. I was the kind of person that couldn't even say no to people selling magazine subscriptions at my door. After my youngest was born, I hardly came out of the house for a whole year."

It was the fall of 1988. She had no idea about the "NIMBY" movement. She had never heard of Waste-Tech. "Mostly what I was doing was clipping pictures of toxic waste from *National Geographic*."

The tiny group had one thing working in their favor: The MacDonald administration was caught in the middle of a major scandal. Senator Barry Goldwater had been pursuing MacDonald mercilessly on charges of graft and corruption. Factionalism within the tribe had erupted into unprecedented intratribal violence. There were riots in the streets of Window Rock. All of that, according to Lori, "gave time for us to pull our act together."

Abe Plummer managed to get in contact with Greenpeace. Within a month, Bradley Angel, Greenpeace's community toxics representative, showed up at the chapter. Lori remembered it clearly: "What he had to share about scope of toxic waste was something the community knew nothing about. All of a sudden they saw the real danger they found themselves in.

"He showed us that this is happening all over the country where poor people of color live, the health effects to people and animals. He basically scared everyone into action." One of the major concerns, then as always, was the effects to the sheep. Could contaminated soils or groundwater affect their grazing lands? What would happen then?

Called to action by their new education in toxic wastes, they enacted an education and community-action campaign, both in their own chapter and in the neighboring chapters of Leupp, Teesto, and White Cone. It took almost a year, but they managed to get the dump proposal in front of the community for a second referendum. Surprised by this sudden opposition, Waste-Tech launched a series of frantic trips back to Dilkon to try to shore up their eroding support. They were too late. In March 1989 the Dilkon chapter rescinded its previous approval with a vote of 99 to 6 opposing any toxic-waste treatment in the community. A Greenpeace videotape[5] captured the moment when the crestfallen Waste-Tech officials officially decided to "pull the plug" on the whole incinerator idea.

Al Joe became council delegate for Dilkon Chapter at the next election—

a post for which he never campaigned. Lori soon found herself teaching children and families how to eliminate toxic substances from their households.

"We were just happy to save our own little community. We didn't know that other native people across the country were facing the same types of things," Lori recalls. The group of activists were soon being contacted by other communities both within and beyond the Navajo Nation. As a result, in the summer of 1990, CARE sponsored the first "Protecting Mother Earth" gathering.

There weren't many of them, but the indigenous activists who attended that first Protecting Mother Earth event came from as far away as Minnesota and North Carolina. They gathered, held their meetings, and camped out in the Dilkon rodeo grounds, where howling summer winds drove dust into every tent and every item of food, clothing, and drink. Thus was spawned the Indigenous Environmental Network, a national coalition of grassroots native organizations that now includes members from Canadian first nations as well. IEN provides one mechanism by which communities who may be at odds with both outside interests and their own tribal governments can begin to find the political and legal clout to make their voices heard. The Protecting Mother Earth gatherings have been held every summer since that first one in 1990.

■|

Changing Woman and White Shell Woman grew very fast. They spent their early years on Travelers' Circle Mountain. One day, Changing Woman said to White Shell Woman: "It is lonely here; we have no one to speak to but ourselves we see nothing but that which rolls over our heads (the sun), and that which drops below us (a small dripping waterfall). I wonder if they can be people. I shall stay here and wait for the one in the morning, while you go down among the rocks and seek the other."

In the morning Changing Woman found a bare, flat rock and lay on it with her feet to the east, and the rising sun shone upon her. White Shell Woman went down where the dripping waters descended, allowing them to fall upon her.

Four days later, White Shell Woman said to her sister: "Elder Sister,

I feel something strange moving within me; what can it be?" And Changing woman answered: "It is a child. It was for this that you lay under the waterfall. I feel, too, the motions of a child within me. It was for this that I let the sun shine upon me." Soon after the voice of Talking God was heard four times, as usual, and after the last call he and Water Sprinkler appeared. They came to prepare the women for the approaching delivery."

Changing Woman's child was born first. Talking God took it aside and washed it. He was glad, and laughed and made ironical motions, as if he were cutting the baby in slices and throwing the slices away. They made for the children two baby-baskets, both alike. The foot rests and the back battens were made of sun-beam, the hoods of rainbow, the side-strings of sheet lightning, and the lacing strings of zigzag lightning. One child they covered with the black cloud, and the other with the female rain. He called the children "Grandchildren," and then left, promising to return at the end of four days.[6]

■/

CARE soon expanded within the Navajo Nation as well. In October 1991, in the middle of a freakish early snowstorm, the members of CARE convened a meeting of "concerned Navajo citizens" in Gallup, New Mexico. Gallup lies at a Southwest crossroads that has bred its own unique but recognizable mix of border-town boom and misery. The main highway into Gallup from the north brings Diné families by the pickup load as they run the gauntlet past a barrage of fast food, a sizable shopping mall, and the inevitable Wal-Mart. From the south, the road brings the people from Zuni. From east to west Interstate 40 tears through the town as well, bringing people from a couple nearby Pueblos, or, more commonly, tourists and passersby on their way to or from California. From the freeway one can make out the sad remains of Route 66, including a couple of the old hotels that once housed the beautiful people who came out on the trains early in the twentieth century.

Gallup calls itself the "Indian Capital of the World." Like other border towns, and the forts and trading posts that preceded them on the Western frontier,[7] it's a strange place that one local writer described as "somewhere between reality and rationalization and between benevolence and predation."[8] It started as a railroad paymaster's quarters. It once attracted Hollywood stars via the railroad.

Its real economic engines, however, are driven by the flow of dollars from the nearby reservations. One "surprising and little known fact" about Gallup: it boasts, according to a local visitors' guide, the largest per capita population of millionaires in the world. As the guide points out, "Most of these people, *some of whom are Native American,* have made their fortunes in the commerce of Indian art."[9] Much of this wealth has been driven by the economy of cash pawn, "a unique form of bank and art gallery rolled into one," the guidebook cheerily reports:

> when Indians convert their creations or possessions to income for life's necessities such as groceries, medical bills, tuition, mortgages and car payments. Pawn can also be items from antiquity, heirloom pieces of handmade jewelry or craft passed from a family into the public marketplace.[10]

It's not just the pawnshops that prey on misfortune and lack of information. Some local merchants—car dealerships, for instance—have profited from the combination of geographic isolation and the poverty of Navajo Nation residents. Local car dealerships and other big-ticket suppliers have charged prices and interest rates that are out of line with competition at more distant, urban areas such as Albuquerque or Phoenix. A flyer found in Gallup not long ago addressed to "the Navajo People" declared, "This town feeds upon us!"[11] As recently as 1987, the Navajo Nation Council was forced to pass a resolution requesting that Gallup vendors open their restrooms to Navajo customers. In the summer of 1994 a group of Diné marched in protest of a local truck stop and motel featuring a "teepee village," complete with a captive, malnourished bison covered with some sort of painful-looking skin disease. The place symbolized, to the marchers, the willingness to perform any act of degradation and desecration for the sake of a dollar.

Nothing in Gallup has spawned more misery and controversy, however, than alcohol, which has been part of the town's legacy from the start. Since the Navajo Nation is a "dry" reservation, Gallup in particular became "the principal supplier and established a reputation for illicit liquor sales and a considerable display of public drunkenness." As early as 1939, "the major concern of the Navajo police force had shifted to cases involving alcohol,"[12] a situation that persisted virtually throughout the twentieth century. Alcohol was continuously implicated in deaths related to pneumonia and exposure, homicide, and motor vehicle accidents. Navajos were dying both in the streets and, sometimes, in their jail cells.[13]

Three of those present at that first gathering—Earl Tulley, Sylvia Clahchischilli, and Anna Frazier—had been active in a campaign to bring some change to this situation. In February of 1989, despite a well-funded opposition by local bar owners and drive-through liquor merchants, Earl, Anna, and Sylvia had organized a group of about forty Gallup residents—mostly Diné but also including some non-Navajos—on an eleven-day march some 240 miles from Gallup to the New Mexico capitol in Santa Fe. They were led out of town on the first day of their walk by Gallup's mayor at the time, Eddie Munoz. Their efforts resulted in a liquor tax in Gallup that helped fund cessation programs, a treatment center, and educational campaigns.[14] Three years later, Earl Tulley led a group on horseback back to Santa Fe, on a campaign to close the drive-through liquor windows in Gallup and surrounding McKinley County.[15]

■/

People came to that first meeting in Gallup from throughout the Navajo Nation, from communities facing a variety of environmental-justice issues—oil and gas drilling that had polluted southern Utah, uranium mining, asbestos dumping, and a variety of other issues, including forestry.

"It was like meeting lost family," according to Lori Goodman. "There was this instant recognition that here was a group of us who had survived the boarding-school experience. That wanted to do something about what was facing our communities." That shared past proved significant not just in providing them with a common experience. Life off the Rez had confirmed for them the importance of their heritage, and at the same time, provided them with the education and skills they needed to negotiate the demands of the "outside" world that inevitably accompanied the life of activism. At that meeting, Diné CARE was officially formed as a reservation-wide organization.

From the very start, they shared a vision of how they wanted to operate. Years later Lori Goodman would describe their mission as providing logistical and technical support to local activists, while leaving them free to control their own endeavors in their own communities.

But while they shared a tacit understanding of what they wanted to achieve, they struggled in the attempt to put that in terms that outsiders— for example, funding organizations—could understand. Such discussions as the following occurred at a number of their early meetings.

"All I know is hard words," said Adella with a laugh.[16]

Anna Frazier agreed: "That's right. Hard Navajo words *(more laughter)* 'Kinship' and 'Reciprocity.' If you talk about culture, that's too deep. It's impossible to capture that."

(Adella) "But what I see when we say 'culture' is, our culture really means conserving. Not really preserving. Preserving means something that you freeze, and nothing ever changes. That's impossible. But you can conserve, like our elders, you know they only use what they need, but they know how to conserve for future generations."

(Anna) "Things change. Our culture is going to change. We know that. Our job is to make sure that our elders are heard and respected."

(Lori Goodman) "I think what draws us together is that vision, of consulting the local people, the grassroots people, grandmas and grandpas. We want their voice to be heard. I think that's what we're asking. When we worked with the asbestos and this other stuff, it was all centralized, it's all in Window Rock. The people at the bottom aren't consulted . . . we're saying give power back to the people, let the people be heard."

Leroy Jackson thought about this in terms of the forestry dispute in which he was immersed: "Well, the thing I see with the forest is that, okay, Dexter Gill[17] comes out there and gives us all these formulas, and all these plans, the Navajo forestry, things that he's learned at NAU and from the Forest Service and how this is a healthy forest . . . turning it into a tree farm. And that might be fine for a place you designate as a tree farm. But there are people living there, and that's the most important thing he's leaving out, is that there are people there. The true guardian, the true environmentalist is the *shicheii* ('grandfather') *shimásání* ('grandmother'). And they know what's going on in the forest. Nobody ever goes and asks them what they think, what their opinion is. . . . So that is what I would like to see. More input from the elders.

"The elders, a lot of times they don't want to come out and say things, because they've been conditioned to thinking that what they think is not important, it doesn't make a difference. Even though they have a lot of valuable things to offer. But now, recently, the things they said, 'you shouldn't harm that,' *díí kwe'é* ('this here') you know, the water, the streams, those kind of thinking. Now we're finding out that . . . what they were saying really does have a value."

Anna agreed with Leroy about barriers facing elders: "The people don't—they're intimidated, even by me. I mean they feel intimidated by me because I speak both languages, and I know how to write, because they see me as a writer. They say 'we're not educated,' you know, 'we haven't been to school . . .'"

Lori added, "So I think what Diné CARE is about is empowering our people, to, say it's OK to stand up. Because they were like that originally, before they were conditioned. So we're saying, it's OK and then, you know it could be a real movement. so we're empowering them, so that they can determine their own destiny."[18]

◼/

The model of providing logistical support to the locals was worked out more in on-the-ground activism than in discussions at meetings. An early example of this occurred in the community of Huerfano.

In 1990, a company called Insulation Contractors Unlimited (ICU) a company specializing in the abatement and disposal of asbestos, applied to the New Mexico State Land Use Commission for a permit to locate a 160-acre asbestos dump on lands near the Navajo community of Huerfano. The land here forms the eastern frontier of the traditional Diné homeland. Some of it is outside current reservation boundaries. Much of the land south of Huerfano is "checkerboard" land, the product of an original allocation created by a congressional land grant to the Atlantic and Pacific

Railroad in 1866. Railroad plots were alternated with public-domain lands in a program to promote settlement throughout the American West. Much of the public-domain land was eventually allotted to individual Navajo families (between 1908 and about 1920), but much of the nearby region is under the control of the Bureau of Land Management.[19]

Despite the zoning, the entire area is rich in places of historical and religious importance to the Diné (many of which, incidentally, are under threat on a number of fronts).[20] Some of the oldest stories are set in this area. Place names mark many events from the stories about the Emergence People, stories "of wandering and hiding to escape monsters, of a quest for food meagerly rewarded, and of incredible loneliness."[21] There are petroglyphs and *pueblitos* here, sacred springs, and offering sites. In one part of this land, not far south of Farmington and just east of New Mexico Highway 44, stands the sacred mountain *Dził Ná'oodiłii*.

The name *Dził Ná'oodiłii* is translated into English as (roughly) "travelers circle mountain." It forms the axis around which the ancestors wandered. Most importantly, it was the one-time residence of *Asdzą́ą́ Nádleehé*, Changing Woman, "the most revered of all Navajo deities,"[22] "the benevolent goddess" whose diminishment in winter is followed, year after year, with her rejuvenation in the spring. "According to the Plan of the Earth, *Ch'óol'į'í* is the pulsating heart of our sacred Ground-Mother and *Dził Ná'oodiłii* is the breathing center of the Navajo world."[23]

Dził Ná'oodiłii is not a high mountain; it has no timberline or year-round snowfields. Its broad, level summit is now covered in a race track for off-road recreational vehicles and an "orgy" of microwave towers, cell-phone repeaters, and other communications equipment.[24] At every installation of this equipment, the Diné Spiritual and Cultural Society (formerly known as the Medicine Man's Association) asked the New Mexico state government to cease the continuing desecration of one of their holiest mountains. Each time, they were ignored.

Lucy Charlie, who would become one of Diné CARE's founding members, led local opposition to the asbestos dump. She was joined by the Diné Spiritual and Cultural Society, and the tribe as well. "ICU told the state that there were only a few weekend camps [in the vicinity of the site]," recalled Lucy. "That was news to us. My mom and most of her family lived there."

Beyond local habitation, there were other issues. The dump site contained Anasazi artifacts and Navajo herb-gathering places. An archaeological report prepared by ICU had not mentioned any grave sites or other sites of cultural importance.[25] The site also adjoined grazing lands, and drained to Blanco Wash, which ultimately drained to the San Juan River, a major water source for all of northwestern New Mexico. Most important, however, was the proposed site's proximity to *Dził Ná'oodiłíí*.

Initially, local opposition to the dump meant letters to the editors of area newspapers, and appeals to the Navajo Nation Council and Navajo legal aid. It's worth noting that in this case the tribe (by that time under the administration of Peterson Zah) and the locals were united in their opposition. The Navajo Nation government retained an outside law firm and put its own environmental protection agency and historic-preservation-department staff to work to document the importance of the land.[26]

By late 1991 Lucy and Lori Goodman were working closely together. Lucy coordinated the local effort by contacting the locals, educating them about the proposed dump, identifying those interested in opposing it, and gathering statements to submit to the appropriate agencies in the New Mexico state government. Lori then handled much of the administrative overhead, including getting the statements in shape to submit to the appropriate government agencies, contacting state bureaucrats by telephone, dealing with the press, and serving as liaison with tribal legal people.

What Lucy remembers most about those days were the endless hours of travel. "It seemed like I was driving all the time," Lucy says with the same clear, unhurried calm she always uses when speaking. "I would get off work and head down there to find out what was going on. On weekends I usually spent time gathering official statements from the residents, so we could send them in to the state."

To get the statements into the state land-use board, Lucy sent her own hand-written notes, or the handwritten statements contributed by locals, from a fax machine at a print shop in Bloomfield (at a cost of two dollars for the first page, a dollar per page for all subsequent pages) to a fax machine at a print shop in Lori's hometown, where Lori paid similar rates to retrieve them. Lori then typed up the statements, brought them back to the print shop, and sent them in to the state, again paying by the page. This type of labor-intensive, inefficient, and expensive operation is actually quite typical of poor communities facing outside challenges. Lacking the tools for communication and documentation themselves, they are forced to rely on individuals in more urbanized areas to mediate much of their outside contact.[27]

Thus, partly because of her location in a town with the necessary infrastructure, and partly because of her own experience in Dilkon, Lori found herself in a position that she continues to occupy to this day: She was Diné CARE's hub and primary access point to the outside world. With money she "borrowed" from her own kids' college tuition fund (her oldest was still in high school) Lori bought Diné CARE's first piece of information-age technology, a thermal fax. "The fax machine has been probably one of our most important tools," Lori once commented.

In the spring of 1992, at the Huerfano Boarding School gymnasium, the state convened hearings on the proposed dump. By all accounts the event was a study in contrasts not unlike the last encounter between Waste Tech and the people of Dilkon. ICU brought a cadre of lawyers and experts, as did the tribe. The locals brought their passion for the land and enough mutton stew for everyone.

Lori laughed about it later: "Here are these Navajo grandmas going around giving out mutton stew and sandwiches to everybody, the people from the state, even for the people from ICU. Those lawyers didn't know what to think."

Lucy added nonchalantly that "That's just how Navajo people treat their guests."

"We told the people from the state what we knew, that these weren't weekend camps, we lived there, and that was sacred land," Lucy said of the ensuing hearing. By the time the local people finished stating their case, ICU was already defeated. They never even argued their side. According to one account, the hearing "produced such an outpouring of indignant testimony from local Navajos and many others that, before the Navajo Nation's lawyers had a chance to parade all their expert witnesses, ICU asked for a break while they tried to find another site."[28]

The case brought early attention to Diné CARE and issues of environmental justice on Navajo lands outside reservation boundaries. Peterson

Zah, then president of the Navajo Nation, pointed to the *Dził Ná'oodiłíí* case while testifying before the Senate Select Committee responsible for modifying the 1978 American Indian Freedom of Religion Act.[29]

Their success in Huerfano wasn't final—none of Diné CARE's victories ever have been. In 1997 ICU once again filed plans with the state to store asbestos in the area.[30] And, as with all of Diné CARE's other victories, success in Huerfano extracted high personal costs from local activists.

The children of Changing Woman and White Shell Woman grew quickly. Changing Woman and White Shell Woman made rude bows of juniper wood, and arrows, such as children play with, and they said to the boys: "Go and play around with these, but do not go out of sight from our hut, and do not go to the east." Notwithstanding these warnings the boys went to the east the first day, and when they had traveled a good distance they saw an animal with brownish hair and a sharp nose. They drew their arrows and pointed them toward the sharp-nosed stranger; but before they could shoot he jumped down into a canyon and disappeared. When they returned home they told the women what they had seen. The women said: "That is Coyote which you saw. He is a spy for the monster Déélgééd."

The following day, although again strictly warned not to go far from the lodge, the boys wandered far to the south, and there they saw a great black bird seated on a tree. They aimed their arrows at it; but just as they were about to shoot the bird rose and flew away . . . "This was Raven that you saw," the women told the boys later. "He is the spy of the great winged creatures that devour men."

On the third day the boys wandered to the west, where they saw the Buzzard, spy for He Who Kicks Men Down the Cliffs.

On the fourth day the boys went toward the north. There they saw Magpie.

Finally the women scolded them: "Alas, what shall we do to save you? You would not listen to us. Now the spies of the alien monsters in all quarters of the world have seen you. They will tell their chiefs, and soon the monsters will come here to devour you, as they have devoured all your kind before you."

The next morning, while baking a corn cake, Changing Woman saw Yé'iitsoh, the biggest and fiercest of the alien monsters approaching. White Shell Woman ascended a nearby hill, and she too beheld many of the monsters hastening in the direction of her lodge. She returned speedily, and told her sister what she had seen. Changing Woman took four colored hoops, and threw one toward each of the cardinal points—a white one to the east, a blue one to the south, a yellow one to the west, and a black one to the north. At once a great gale arose, blowing so fiercely in all directions from the hogan that none of the enemies could advance against it.

Next morning, fearing for their own safety and the safety of their mothers, the boys got up before daybreak and stole away. They snuck away on the holy trail . . .

—Matthews, *Navaho Legends*

■|

Leroy Jackson sat facing the rest of Diné CARE's "Core Group" (they hadn't yet formalized into a board of directors) in a modest-sized Albuquerque hotel room. They perched on bedsides, squeezed into chairs, doubled up on a small bench seat and sat on the floor, roughly forming a circle around the perimeter of the room. Outside the fifth-floor window, a heavy wet snow was falling. Downstairs, their kids were enjoying the one tangible and immediate benefit of their parents' new life of activism: these frequent trips to the city meant meals at McDonalds, movies in real movie theaters, and best of all, motels with swimming pools.

Through newly formed contacts in Window Rock, Leroy had learned that the tribe was preparing a new timber sale contract for an area known as Whiskey Creek and Ugly Valley. The contract was well on its way to approval despite the fact that it fell outside the mandatory ten-year forest-management plan, which had expired at the end of 1991.[1]

As mentioned earlier (chapter 2), ten-year forest-management plans are supposed to be accompanied by Environmental Impact Statements. Now the tribe was proposing a timber sale outside any ten-year plan— which created a bit of a political liability. To make up for this, various tribal agencies were put to work preparing an "Environmental Assessment"— a sort of mini–Environmental Impact Statement. Their conclusion: what is known as a "Finding of No Significant Impact." Despite the fact that none of the problems described in the (by then, ten-year-old) Site Condition

Reports had been addressed, nor did Navajo forestry or any of the tribal oversight committees have any idea about how to address such problems, the conclusion was that the Whiskey Creek timber sale would not affect the forest. The tribe seemed to be proceeding as if everything in the forests was just fine.

Leroy put it bluntly to the rest of the group: "NFPI is a runaway train," he told them. "They're going to take the whole forest down with them. We've been hitting it in spurts so far [e.g., with the chapter resolutions]. Maybe this is the way to do it. Maybe we just have to be patient, just be persistent, eventually we'll get there.

"See, I'm not that experienced in these things. But I was thinking, maybe we need to get a little more aggressive, maybe go for a lawsuit. These guys, NFPI, the council delegates, Natural Resources, they won't listen unless we hit them with the legal. Then, then will they listen."

John Redhouse sat on the floor in a narrow opening between a bed and the wall at one corner of the room. This, it turned out, was his usual way of situating himself. Always hidden behind a pair of sunglasses and a baseball hat, he would locate himself somewhere on the periphery of Core Group meetings, or near the door, from where he was able to make quick and silent exits.

His voice was deep and resonant. He agreed with Leroy that Diné CARE needed to pursue legal action. "Just as the great Navajo warriors of the past," he told the group, "the Navajo leaders Manuelito and Barboncito, had to learn to use the white man's guns to defend our land, so we have to learn the white man's laws." Probably few men have knowledge of the geopolitics of the American Southwest, especially with regards to native lands, as complete and encyclopedic as John Redhouse. He not only assists Diné CARE, he has provided consultation to groups from a number of tribes of the region. His vision of the struggle facing the Diné and their neighboring tribes is uncompromising.

His public life began in the early 1970s in Farmington, a tough mix of reservation border town and oil industry boom town in northwestern New Mexico. The local teen pastime of "rolling drunks" (which meant drunk Diné, a practice long tolerated by authorities both in Farmington and Gallup) spilled over into a series of incidents in which three local white teenagers brutally tortured, sexually mutilated, and murdered three Navajo men, who because of their intoxication were defenseless. These murders, and the way the subsequent investigations and prosecution were handled (the boys did minimum time at youth facilities), finally ignited the smoldering resentment of the Diné in the Farmington area.[2]

John was twenty-one at the time of the murders. He helped organize the rallies that crystallized the local Navajo community. It was about this time he made the decision to pursue a life of activism regardless of the consequences. Even at that age, he was aware of the sacrifices that such a life would involve. While various former AIM members, people whom John knew and worked with as a younger man, have "made it"—as movie stars, touring the lecture circuit, or otherwise—John has lived on subsistence wages directing a variety of human rights organizations, researching and writing on subjects including water, energy, land, and resource rights affecting not only the Diné but other tribes of the Southwest as well.

Throughout much of this time, he and his family were subjected to surveillance and borderline acts of harassment by the U.S. government. Not long ago he retrieved his FBI file through the Freedom of Information Act. Two-thirds of the fifty-page document were blacked out to protect the identities of informants or for "national security" reasons. "The FBI has always employed a strategy of 'divide and conquer,'" he once said.

Despite his many years of hard-won experience, he rarely attempted to influence the other members of the Core Group. He only spoke, in fact, when pressed. Only once did the anthropologist hear him explicitly state his vision of Diné CARE's work—it's clarity was chilling: "It is," he said, "inextricably tied to a Navajo view of the universe that comes from our origins here within the four sacred mountains, from our relationship to the land which is rooted in Beauty and Harmony. Our vision is nothing less than a vision of a return to that pristine harmony, and that includes getting the white man off our land."

Other communities and citizens' groups were successfully filing appeals against timber sales on U.S. public lands. Their situation was different, however. The Chuska Mountains were on reservation lands, held in trust by the U.S. government, but not administered by the same agencies as forests on public lands. Ordinary Navajo people were caught in a weird state of limbo with regard to their status as citizens both of the United States and of a sovereign indigenous nation.

Another problem was finding reliable legal representation. Leroy had already contacted an organization called "Forest Trust" in Santa Fe. The organization's biologist, Lane Krahl, had even prepared a short statement on Leroy's behalf challenging the environmental assessment. Through Forest Trust, Leroy made friends with Bruce Baizel, an environmental attorney. Leroy trusted him right from the start, and was eager for him to get involved as Diné CARE's lawyer. However, Forest Trust director Henry Carey had hired Mr. Baizel to build a coalition of environmental groups in the Southwest, not to provide legal services to Diné CARE.

Bruce Baizel recalls about that time: "It was clear that Diné CARE needed legal help more than anything, and I felt like that was what I was trained to do. It was a real conflict for me. I knew it was a conflict for me because at one point I broke out in a rash all over my body." It was only months later that Baizel would quit Forest Trust and go on to become one of Diné CARE's closest and most trusted allies.

In the meantime, there was a hole to be filled. Into that gap—and into that cramped motel room in Albuquerque—walked Sam Hitt. The son of a forester, Hitt had first gotten involved in forestry issues in 1980, during a time when the national forests in northern New Mexico were undergoing an aggressive pesticide treatment for the spruce budworm. The treatment was saving merchantable timber at the expense of the rest of the forest inhabitants. In 1986, after a long and often bitter struggle, Hitt's organization—which he called Forest Guardians—prevailed on the government to end the spraying program. After that initial victory, Hitt went on to pursue a decrease of commercial timber cutting on public lands in New Mexico. He soon became widely known as a "mill buster."

Hitt, it turns out, was actively interested in Leroy and Diné CARE. "I had been to the Chuskas," he told the members of Diné CARE that afternoon in Albuquerque, "and I know that the logging in the Chuskas is the most destructive in the whole Southwest, but, it's not a national forest so there's nothing I could do about it, it's not public lands. So I was delighted at the opportunity to get involved."

It was the start of a stormy relationship.

■/

*Monster Slayer and Born for Water, having accidentally betrayed their moth-
ers' hiding place from the Alien Monsters, had left their home on the path of
the Holy People, the trail of the rainbow. For some time they traveled without
seeing any sign of haven or refuge. Finally, they noticed a thin wisp of smoke
coming from the ground. As they approached it and peered down that smoke
hole, they saw an old woman—it was Na'ashjéii asdzą́ą́, the Spider Woman.*

*"Come in shiyáázh (my sons)" she told them. They set foot on her ladder
and began their descent. "Who are you, and why are you following the trail
of sunbeams?" She asked them.*

*Several times she asked them. Each time, the boys told her little. They told
her only that they were the sons of Changing Woman and White Shell Woman,
and that they were fleeing the dreaded Nayéé'.*

*Spider Woman, though she was old and her voice was raspy, welcomed
the boys with a warm embrace. She fed them, and allowed them to sit by the
fire and warm themselves. Then she explained everything to them:*

*"Your father is Jóhonaa'éí, the Sun, and he lives in the sky far above us
all," She explained to them.*

*Spider Woman further told them they must go to find their father the sun.
She told them they would have to pass through four dangerous places just to
reach their father, past the rocks that crush travelers, past the reeds and the
cactuses that cut wanderers to shreds, and past the boiling sands. Spider
Woman gave them a talisman to survive these dangers.*

*She also told them that their father, the Sun, may not be happy to see them,
that he would subject them to all kinds of punishments and trials, that they
must endure these if they were to save their people.[3]*

■/

John W. Sherry

It was early spring, 1992. Leroy headed south through Crystal, New Mexico,
to the turnoff for Narbona Pass, the shortest route over the mountains. Well
before they reached summit, there were already patches of snow and ice in
the road. The alternate route, north through Mexican Water and Teec Nos
Pos, was more likely to be easy driving, but the drive was a lot longer.

Since the first meeting of Diné CARE, Sam Hitt had quickly moved in to establish his presence in the forest conflict. He pushed the group to go for a timber sale appeal. Many locals, however, were naturally suspicious of getting themselves involved in non-Navajo legal wrangles about which they had little understanding. Leroy and Adella thus became legal liaisons on the Navajo Nation. They were charged with the task of gathering and documenting the stakeholders, keeping potential appellants informed of all progress in the case, conveying documents between the appellants and the legal team, and handling all the tasks of translation, explanation, and education that come with helping people who have little prior exposure to the legal system. They willingly pursued this end of the partnership with Forest Guardians, even though they were never paid for it.

Leroy's destination that particular day was the home of an elderly couple, an herbalist, and her husband, who was a member of the Diné Spiritual and Cultural Society, once called the Medicine Man's Association. He was a hataałii, a "singer." They were concerned about the part of the forest that would be affected by the upcoming timber sale, but they had no idea how to stop it. These weren't the kind of people who felt empowered or comfortable driving into Santa Fe to find themselves a good lawyer. It was for people such as these that Leroy—and particularly Adella—felt motivated to act.

The couple lived somewhere along the eastern base of the Chuskas near Sheep Springs during the winter. They had no electricity, phone, or indoor plumbing (certainly no fax machine or E-mail.) To talk to them for any reason, Leroy needed to drive. That's what he spent most of his time doing in 1992. The anthropologist used to tag along with Leroy on trips such as these. It provided him a way to pepper Leroy with any number of questions.

The road at the summit of Narbona Pass had been sanded so the driving was easy. Their talk—Leroy's and the anthropologist's—turned to technology. Not long before, they had met an activist from northern California who was using sophisticated Geographic Information Systems to assist in community planning and forest restoration. When the anthropologist asked Leroy what he thought about computers in Diné CARE's efforts, he thought for a moment, unconsciously rubbing the back of his neck. "I can see that they're real helpful in writing letters and that kind of thing, and that's important. But for me, the real work is up here in the mountains, at the homesites of the grandmas and the grandpas. And at the chapters. Because that's the part that the forestry people don't have a handle on." It was thus that Leroy defined the "real work" of Diné CARE.

They descended the pass and reached New Mexico Highway 666. The snow was completely gone now, and the sky was beginning to clear. They were in the precipitation shadow of the mountains. To the east the land stretched out brown and barren. The smog from the San Juan power station hung in the air in the distance, drifting off over the original Diné homeland.

Not too much later they arrived at a muddy road, followed it for a quarter of a mile, then slid and careened to a stop. Next to a trailer home stood a small hogan where smoke could be seen, the sign, they hoped, that someone was home. Out behind the hogan was a corral. A flock of perhaps twenty sheep huddled together. Leroy stopped the engine and sat out in front of the hogan for a few seconds, waiting to see if someone would come out (it is not considered polite, on the Navajo Nation, to stride confidently up to someone's door and give a big hearty knock). Some moments later an elderly woman opened the door and gave them a kind of brief once-over. She must have recognized Leroy. Without saying a word, without a wave or any other motion, she turned and went back into the hogan. But she left the door open behind her. That was all the invitation they needed.

The door frame wasn't exactly square. The floor was packed dirt. The space inside was small but definitely not cramped or stuffy. It was, as all hogans were, somehow very inviting. The warmth of the stove (in the center of the space, as always) carried the smell of green-chili stew and coffee. The woman was home alone with a young girl, perhaps her granddaughter, no older than nine years old, who was off to one side on a cot covered with wool blankets.

The old woman had already begun washing a couple bowls in a basin off to one side. Her hair, which was barely visible beneath her scarf, was not yet entirely white, but her face was weathered with age. She was a tiny woman, made even tinier by her slightly stooped frame, but her black eyes glistened with that same fierceness that Adella's mother had. Leroy took her hand silently in a customary manner that was more like a brief and gentle clasp than a firm, extended, and vigorous "handshake." The anthropologist followed suit.

"*Yá'át'ééh shimá*," he said tentatively as he took her hand.

"*Ao'* (yes) *yá'át'ééh shiyáázh*," she replied.

She immediately returned to the stove, and completed washing the bowls. She then served them. "Who's the bilagáana?" she asked Leroy in the Navajo language as she handed him his bowl.

"He's helping us with the appeal," he answered, also in Navajo. "He's a lawyer." He turned to the anthropologist, laughing. "I just told her you're a lawyer." For some reason Leroy thought this answer was great fun. The members of Diné CARE always tolerated the anthropologist's presence with grace and hospitality. However, they sometimes found it difficult to explain to others what this bilagáana was doing following them around wherever they went.

The green chili stew was piping hot. The coffee, to which she had added canned milk, was thick, sweet, and potent. Before long the anthropologist felt himself breaking out into a sweat. His nose started running.

The old woman asked Leroy a few questions about the weather up in Tsaile. She laughed when he told her he came across Narbona Pass in his van.

Off to the side, her granddaughter sat near a television and VCR with the sound turned down low. It wasn't receiving any kind of remote signal—this was in the days before small-dish, satellite TV was common. It was really just a videotape-watching appliance.

After the first short exchange, they settled into their stew in silence. No one, it seemed, was in a hurry to "get down to business." After some time Leroy mentioned the timber sale appeal. She nodded, not saying a word.

She looked out the window, for a moment, then her gaze returned to the inside of the hogan, at seemingly nothing in particular. Suddenly, unprompted, she began talking about her sheep. As the old woman spoke, Leroy listened intently, his head down and his eyes looking at the ground, not at her. He made no attempt to reply, to acknowledge her utterances with an American "uh huh" or "I see." As she spoke he remained completely silent. (This posture can be confusing to speakers of standard American English, who sometimes mistake it for inattention.)

She was concerned about the health of her flock. Her husband and son were off getting hay. She commented that it seemed they were hauling hay much more than they ever used to. Despite the fact that this winter was a good one for snow, things seemed to be getting worse every year. Their grasses weren't growing as they once did, either in the mountains or down below.

Her talk continued unabated for perhaps fifteen or twenty minutes. Occasionally she would pause for five or ten seconds. The anthropologist fidgeted and shifted awkwardly in his seat, trying not to draw attention to himself. His poor grasp of the language, and his inability to discern the relevance of the words he did understand, were further complicated by the effects of the coffee.

Much as this situation may have felt like a rather lengthy "chat" it was certainly nothing of the sort. Her message was pointed and serious. Leroy, of course, understood this. Fifty years ago, anthropologist Gladys Reichard observed how Navajo people respected "the finality of an older person's decisions. . . . The principle, though verbally unformulated, is thoroughly binding in practice."[4] In fact, the authority of elders extends well beyond decisions. Their words demand one's attention and respect, one's serious consideration. In most families it seemed to be simply taken for granted that an older person's talk (no matter how "rambling" it might seem to an ignorant outsider) did have a point, and did merit close attention. It is up to the listener to figure out just what that relevance is. This is perhaps why Diné children are, as Adella once pointed out, taught just to listen, to observe, and not to talk so much. Mastering a language involves much more than syntax and grammar, it involves vastly different types of knowledge about how to "process" and understand, to interpret, and to behave.

The woman was talking about her sheep, about the weather (lack of rainfall), about hauling hay and other apparently mundane issues, but her point, as Leroy explained later, was that she feared that commercial timber cutting in the mountains had created a situation of imbalance. Her concerns were not merely issues of mundane practicality, but an expression of alarm that the entire Diné homeland was dangerously out of harmony. She was concerned by the fact that the Diné had abandoned the ways given to them by the Holy People, in favor of the convenience of modern life. The surest sign of this lack of harmony was the drying up of the rain and snow. This was why she had agreed to participate in the timber-sale appeal. This was why Leroy was at her home that day.

This was what Leroy meant by the "real work."

six.

When the forest is harvested in accordance with a thoroughly researched, scientific program, it not only produces a consistent harvest each year, but a better crop as well.

—Navajo Forest Products Industries Annual Report, 1974

■|

Don't we realize that that mountain is a deity?

—Leroy Jackson

■|

The hero brothers left the home of Spider Woman and made their way along the Holy Trail, encountering, just as Spider Woman had said, many trials, obstacles and Monsters. First they encountered the Crushing Rocks. As they approached, the cliffs parted, as if to greet them. The boys walked almost to within their reach, then stopped short. The rock walls slammed shut to crush them, but the Warrior Twins managed to trick them.

This continued several times. "Who are you?" the rocks finally said. "Where do you come from and where are you going?"

"We are children of the Sun," the Twins replied. "We are from Dził Ná'oodiłii, and we seek the dwelling of our father in order to bring him a message."

"What is the message?" demanded the rocks.

The boys took the talisman given them by Spider Woman, the hoop of feathers of the giant eagles, and, staring fearlessly at the rocks, recited the chant that Spider Woman had taught them.

"Continue your way," said the rocks, now docile. "Long life is ahead. Happiness is ahead."

The boys passed by the rocks, and soon encountered the other threats just as Spider Woman said they would. Each time, using the magic she had given them, they subdued these threats on their journey to the house of their father the Sun.

—Berard Haile, *Upward Moving and Emergence Way*

■|

Adella's sisters, Angie and Janet, sat outside an old hogan up in the mountains, tending a campfire. They leaned forward with long barbecue forks, turning pieces of roasting mutton on a big iron grill. Angie skewered a small amount of sizzling meat and offered it to the anthropologist. It was fatty and full of flavor; hot juice ran down his chin.

"What is it?" he burbled.

"It's *'ach'íí*," they told him—roasted sheep's intestines.

"A-chu-eeh," said the anthropologist.

"No, *'ach'íí*," said Angie, correcting him.

"A-chu-eeh," said the anthropologist again, providing the sisters with some amusement. Besides the fact that his mouth was still full, he found it almost impossible to produce the right combination of sounds without inserting an extra syllable. It's very hard: it involves uttering what phonologists call a "palatal fricative" (the 'ch' sound) followed by a "glottal stop," which has no letter in English but can be heard as the stop deep in the throat in the expression "uh oh."

"A-chu-eeh," he said again, this time a little more quietly. Once again Angie and Janet heard him and began to giggle.

"A-chu-eeh, a-chu-eeh, a-chu-eeh," repeated the anthropologist to himself with a mouth full of chewed intestines, as Angie and Janet began to laugh openly. It was like the sound of a mechanical pump.

"People are always saying that our language is hard to learn," Adella once commented. "What's that supposed to mean, anyway? That our language doesn't make sense or something?"

The fact is, many English speakers do seem to have a terrible time learning Navajo—and the unfamiliar combinations of sounds are only part of the reason. Another is the fact that the *Diné Bizaad* is a tonal language. Rising and falling tones change word meanings (the diacritic above the final "e" in the word Diné, for instance, marks a rising tone). Non-native speakers often have a terrible time remembering these, since in English, rising and falling tones have much less precise usage.

But without doubt the most difficult aspect of the Navajo language is its grammar. Compared to, say, English or Spanish, the Navajo language depends heavily on a highly elaborated verb morphology for encoding meaning in sentences. Roughly speaking, detailed sentence meanings are encoded into each and every prefix and suffix in Navajo verbs—and verbs can contain affixes in as many as ten different positions relative to the verb stem. Nuances of action, of motion or stasis, of who is doing what to whom and the relationship between them, of quality, of duration, and many other aspects of meaning are encoded in an array of verb morphemes, all of which are deeply interdependent.

Quite often the very names of things make heavy use of this detailed encoding in verbs, producing lengthy descriptions of behaviors or activities. Computers, for instance, have been called *béésh doo biyooch'įįdí* "the machine that doesn't lie."[1]

It's a . . . curious name. "When something new comes along," Lori's brother once explained to the anthropologist, "the elders will take a look at it and see how it fits in with our lives. Then they'll come up with a name for it." One can only suspect that these elders, perhaps more than the bilagáana people, have a keen appreciation for irony in their naming of technology.

The poetic imagery enabled by Navajo verb morphology is particularly evident in Navajo place names. The original Navajo name for Wheatfields, for instance, is *Tó Dzís'á*, meaning "strip of water extending away into the distance." Keams Canyon is *Lók'aa' Deeshjin*: "a black streak of reeds extends." It's more than just poetry. Such names provide a powerful means by which the Diné (like many other native people of the Americas) have situated themselves into their landscape. They create a concrete image that allows people seeing a place for the first time to recognize it just from the description.[2]

That's not the whole story, however. The act of naming in Navajo storytelling binds different places into an organized unity and binds the people who occupy the land into a relationship of significance with these places. Navajo people "tell stories about the landscapes that teach, guide, and justify various activities in various parts of the landscape."[3]

As Kelley and Francis point out:

These stories are about all kinds of things—the origins of the present world, the Navajo and other peoples, Navajo customs; family chronicles; encounters, both hostile and friendly, between Navajos and other Indians and non-Indian colonizers; interactions, both long ago and recent, between particular Navajos and the immortals who inhabit the land, and so forth. They define, "construct" the landscape by telling, explicitly or implicitly, about different places on the landscape and how each relates to the whole. The stories map the place and the landscape onto a dense structure of powerful cultural symbols, images and beliefs that give meaning to that landscape and place.[4]

Keith Basso, an anthropologist who has worked for many years among the Western Apache people (whose language is so closely related to Navajo that they are mutually intelligible) has similarly noted this power of naming and its role in storytelling. "The land is always stalking people," seventy-seven-year-old Annie Peaches told Basso. "The land makes people live right. The land looks after us."[5]

In storytelling, in prayers and ceremonies, in the very act of naming, land and word are united. For the Diné, language is not seen as simply a way of talking about the world—language plays a vital role in creating the world.[6] And both word and land are tied inextricably to Holy Wind itself. "The relationship between speech and breath—and thus, the life principle—makes the speech act sacred."[7]

As Navajo elders have explained, Holy Wind, the same Wind that breathed life into First Man, First Woman, and Changing Woman, the same Wind that came to the aid of the twins during their trials at the home of the Sun, and which stands within all beings, unites the act of speech with the sacredness of life: "We breathe by it (Wind). It moves absolutely all of our blood vessels, it moves all parts of our body. We live by it, it moves all parts, even our heart." Another elder added, "It is only by means of Wind that we talk." A third pointed out, "the one called Holy Wind and Wind *álílee naagháii* stands within us. This same one . . . turns this (Earth) . . . it turns water, everything. It alone is our Holy One. Really, only it is our prayer."[8]

Land, wind, and word are thus intimately connected in the Navajo way of looking at the world. Once, when asked by a non-Navajo at one of their meetings what they valued most about their heritage, nearly every one of the members of the Core Group mentioned their language. Anna Frazier put it most succinctly: "I love the language, our beautiful Navajo language."[9]

This was a mildly astonishing comment. With the possible exception of a few poets, it is almost inconceivable that speakers of "standard American English" might regard or speak about their language this way. At least since the early twentieth century,[10] most of us (particularly, it seems, most scientific types and certainly most linguists), tend to regard the function of language as purely utilitarian, simply the means by which we "represent" the world that is both "out there" and separate from the words used to describe it.

But whether we admit it or not, all language use is loaded with ritual, and those rituals help create the world around us. In this respect, the Diné view of language is perhaps a little more honest than that which prevails in the technoscientific world of "the West." The ritual creation of our world is as much a part of scientific and legal discourse as it is of Navajo place names. From the metaphors that identify the world and all its creatures as machines or other objects to be exploited,[11] to the rules of engagement whereby some opinions count more than others, even the most "rational-ized" uses of language are loaded with rituals that build up particular views of the world, result in relations of power and prestige, and privilege particular voices at the expense of others.

■|

From a 1992 report to Congress titled "Assessment of Indian Forests and Forest Management:"[12]

- Section 1: Tribal members emphasize different visions and goals for their forests than do BIA forestry employees.
- Tribal members value resource protection most. Yet BIA forestry employees place relatively less emphasis on these goals and more on the forest's economic benefits.
- The forest's scenic beauty is much more important to tribal members than to BIA forestry employees.
- Tribal members emphasize that an integrative, holistic approach be taken in managing all forest resources, recognizing a multiplicity of use and values. Through funding, staffing, and approach, the BIA has tended to emphasize commercial timber production.

■/

In late 1992, the Navajo Nation Department of Forestry scheduled a series of "scoping sessions," public forums designed to gather citizen input on the tribe's ten-year forest-management plan.[13] One of them was held in Aneth, Utah. Aneth is definitely not timber country. The ground is flat and treeless for miles. Beneath this ground, however, lie most of the Navajo Nation's oil fields. The local residents are no strangers to conflicts over resources. Leroy attended the scoping session in Aneth, as he did most of the other half-dozen or so similar events held during a two-month period.

The intent of scoping sessions was ostensibly to bring the Navajo Forestry Department, the BIA, and the mill more into line with the interests of tribal members. Sadly this was not to be the case. None of the sessions were well attended, and Aneth was no exception. Of the few locals who were present, not many were elders. Even the Navajo Nation forestry staff expressed disappointment with the turnout. And, though they were designed to "gather public input," a number of factors conspired (whether inadvertently or by design) to mostly stifle local opinion.

It started with the very way individuals were given turns to talk at the events. In the back of the chapter house was a clipboard with a piece of paper on it. Anyone who wanted to talk was supposed to sign up as they entered. One old man, upon arrival, took a look at the sheet with what appeared to be a certain amount of puzzlement, looked into the hall, then looked back at the sheet. He hesitated for a minute, then simply turned and left.

A few of the elders who came into the hall apparently failed to notice it. When a Navajo forestry representative stood up and convened the meeting, and mentioned the sheet, they looked a little insulted. This was clearly not a situation in which elders were given their positions of traditional respect or "the last word."

It went beyond the allocation of turns at talk, of course. The Navajo forestry representative continued with the introduction. After welcoming the attendees, he told the audience:

> Federal law mandates that the Navajo forest be managed under sustained-yield principles. That means a sustained flow of wood coming from the forest for whatever purpose the Navajo Tribe deems necessary.

And thus, with this simple invocation of federal law, a whole framework was set for all that followed. The uncontestable "purpose" of the forest was to provide a "sustained flow of wood."[14] All subsequent discussions of the forest are, from the perspective of Navajo forestry and the BIA, limited to questions of how much and in what manner.

Considerable though the mandate of federal law may be, the invocation of "science" may have carried even more weight. After all, Navajo people have a long history of well-placed mistrust in the federal government, but science makes claims to objectivity and impartiality that are considered beyond the interests of any individual.

After a few of the speakers had taken their turns, Eddie Richards, general manager of NFPI, stood up to speak. He set out to convince the locals that their forest was healthy.

> The health of the forest from my perspective looks to be pretty good. The forest looks to be pretty vigorous and pretty healthy. I think the growth numbers that I've seen from the last inventory data are in excess of what was expected.

One attendee, although he expressed feeling a little intimidated by his own lack of technical competence, nonetheless attempted to raise some doubts about whether large-scale commercial timber cutting was the best course of action for the Navajo forests:

> My concern is that perhaps we need to slow down on some of the timbering, because it doesn't appear to be really a, a profitable operation anymore. Maybe it's run its cycle. And this is something I'm concerned about. And as I am not a forestry person, so I don't really know what all this talk about uneven growth, even growth, you know, but, what I see, I see [he pauses] I can tell, you know, what happened to the forest.

But Mr. Richards, who held a degree in forest management, quickly dismissed such concerns as "visual effects" that have nothing to do with the "objective" state of the forest's health. He thus offered and simultaneously discounted an alternative that would have improved visual results but decreased "objective" results:

> In light of that I think that perhaps it would be wise if you would look at perhaps managing some of your lands on an uneven-aged basis. I think, perhaps the visual effects might be a little bit more pleasing to you . . . There are some drawbacks, the cut per acre will be reduced for industry. There may be some genetic high grading that occurs inadvertently, I think, as a result of that method. But I think overall the visual effects might be more pleasing to you.

The late Carl Sagan admonishes: "One of the great commandments of science is, 'Mistrust arguments from authority.'" He hastens to add that scientists, being "primates, and thus given to dominance hierarchies, of course do not always follow this commandment."[15] He neglects to point out that, in many situations, science itself is used as a weapon of argument, a claim to authority.

In such objectifying tools as technical reports, mathematical models, computer simulations, and all kinds of documentation, science produces various representations that seem to lie "outside" any particular time and place. "Scientific" evidence (despite how shoddy or biased the underlying research may sometimes be) takes on the patina of authority by the very fact that it looks "objective." The "numbers" speak for themselves (or so it would appear); the "experts" are just the mouthpieces. Those who are not initiated into a scientific discipline must then rely on experts to interpret these disembodied representations.[16] This approach to knowledge all but ensures that nontechnical locals have little standing in any disputes over either the "purpose" or the "health" of the forest.

Computers, the ultimate arbiters or authority, *béésh doo biyooch'į́į́dí* (the "machine that doesn't lie") are deeply implicated in this construction of authority. The "numbers" to which Mr. Richards referred were from a computer-generated model created by members of the forest management program at Northern Arizona University, under contract to the tribe. This model (perhaps not surprisingly) predicted that the forests could sustain an annual harvest of thirty-eight million board feet of timber. Dubious assumptions about tree growth rates, rainfall, stand data, soil conditions, and a host of other information, entered into a computer, became almost unassailable evidence about the true health of the forest.

Perhaps even more than paper documents,[17] technological artifacts such as computer models put technical ways of talking out of the reach of challenges by removing all the underlying assumptions from public scrutiny "and endowing them with a misplaced concreteness"[18] The computer model, like the formal document, represents institutional authority and a whole set of disciplined practices. If such artifacts say the forest is "healthy" who can argue? Such digital or printed facts seem to come from above.

Most of all, computers and their associated artifacts help to remove from scrutiny the assumptions about what "counts": "TIMBER IS A CROP" said the NFPI annual report; at the scoping sessions this view of the nature and value of timber was unassailable. Only the technical details were apparently up for grabs, and then only to those who had access to "the numbers."

Some have grown to accept new institutions such as scoping sessions:

However much one might like to avoid the irony of new social forms to "preserve" Navajo landscapes and the stories and customs that go with them . . . these new forms are a fact of life. . . . The struggle to keep Navajo culture alive isn't limited to perpetuating the extended family's role in passing down the stories and protecting the associated landscapes. The modern social institutions are also involved in public discourse about keeping Navajo culture and landscapes alive.[19]

Problems arise, however, when such modern social institutions fail to provide local people with an opportunity to make their voices heard.

This is not the first analysis to make that observation, of course—any number of social scientists have made similar observations.[20] However, there is more to this story.

Many of the critiques that point out how science lays claim to authority have sometimes erred in their assessments of exactly how unassailable its objectivist claims may be. Despite the fact that scientific discourses, computers, documentation, and a host of other devices may lay claim to authority, they are not, as some seem to suggest, entirely unassailable. In fact, the experience of Diné CARE suggests that there are "ordinary people" who can and have pierced this veil.

When his turn to speak came, Leroy rose slowly and went to the front of the room. He started off casually, almost conversationally. The first thing he did was question the computer-based forest models.

It looks great in a computer. You come out with forty million board feet [the requested timber sale amount] and everybody says "Yeah, Yeah that looks great." And they take out people and say "Looky here. This is what we got. Forty million board feet it's all there on paper." But we question that. This is not 1957.[21] This is 1992. There are some Navajos that know what's happening.[22]

He then took issue with the very foundations of forestry as a technical discipline, questioning the "flow of wood" philosophy by reminding the audience of the mountain's status in Navajo belief:

Don't we realize that that mountain is a deity? That it provides the rainfall? The runoff provides—sustains a livelihood for people on both sides of the Chuskas? Isn't that called living? Don't people farm that? Don't they use the water? Isn't the fact that the animals that live there, the biodiversity, mental health? Isn't that what we're all about?

In chiding the foresters for their forgetfulness of the mountain as a deity, he pointed out the intimate relationship between humans and the land that technical forestry professionals have neglected.

> We're concerned about the wildlife. I don't know if you understand that, but that's part of being alive, that's part of living. It's part of thinking. It's part of your emotional, physical, and mental health. It's those animals. The biodiversity. You can't just plant and cut and plant and cut because that's not your job. It belongs to the turkeys and the squirrels and the bears. They provide the biodiversity. And you're part of that system. The most important part of that mountain that they left out is the American Indian. The Navajo.

This close connection between humans and the land was central to Leroy's critique of forestry as a professional discipline. He challenged a fundamental assumption that seems to lie at the very heart of many Western technical disciplines, the clean separation between the human and nonhuman worlds.[23] Leroy's greatest concern was the simple fact that there were people living in the mountains, and that forestry had failed to account for them.

(Ironically, many Western environmentalists have fallen into the same trap while drawing different conclusions, calling for the elimination of all human activity in certain "pristine" ecosystems. This stance has often created barriers between urban environmental groups and the indigenous communities that have occupied such "pristine" environments for centuries or even millennia. This is probably another reason why members of Diné CARE routinely resisted the title "environmentalists.")

The forest is neither a place to be set aside and preserved in a pristine state nor a "crop" for industrial management. Echoing a charge usually leveled at economists, Leroy accuses the forestry professionals of knowing "the price of everything and the value of nothing."

When are we going to get a Navajo management professional team that
know what they're doing? That shows respect for Navajo life? Navajo
mountain, beliefs, trees?

He then makes a play on the meaning of "professional" to turn it from
those who have earned technical degrees to those whose knowledge of the
forest derive from Navajo traditions and a lifetime in the mountains.

You talk about professionals, the real professionals are the people that
have been living there for years. They got something to say.

■|

Leroy's work at the scoping sessions provides an interesting view on Diné
CARE's complex relationship to science and technology. With a phone, a
fax machine, and later a computer, Leroy managed to reach many of the
people on whom he relied for on-the-fly educational sessions in technical
forestry, not to mention any number of other activists and allies from
throughout the region. Without the impromptu and highly specific training these technologies made possible, he would not have had the technical information he needed to go to scoping sessions and raise many of the
issues he did.

At the same time, Leroy's challenges weren't just on technical grounds.
His strongest positions were based on a thoroughly Diné perspective.
There is little doubt that Leroy's influence at such events (which was
widely recognized) would have been impossible if he had lacked either
element. By routinely treading between the "two worlds" both on and off
the reservation, Leroy and the other members of Diné CARE may have
risked becoming "schizophrenic sometimes" (as Lori Goodman put it), but
they were also enabled to critically examine both their own and others' systems of knowledge. Which, not surprisingly, further strained his already
adversarial relationship with Navajo forestry and NFPI.

Leroy returned from one scoping session laughing to himself. "I'm not
sure what to make of that guy [mill GM Ed Richards]. He's a little bit of a
clown, always joking around. He came right up to me after the thing and

said 'Well, you may have done pretty good at this one, but we'll get you in the end.'"

It was mildly ironic to hear Leroy talk about Mr. Richards like this. Humor, even clowning, seemed to be a strategy Leroy himself used to disarm his opponents. Even in the most serious situations he had a strange habit of peppering his speech with incidental mispronunciations (he consistently said "stragedy" instead of "strategy," for instance), and with nonsense words like "gobbledygook," or other unusual expressions that dropped so casually from his lips you were never sure if you heard him correctly. Maybe it was an old trick he had learned from his days on the street, to let people think he was a joker, a harmless *Indio*. This is probably what led Dexter Gill, the non-Indian director of Navajo Department of Forestry, to insist that Leroy was "just a mouthpiece. He didn't have the ability or understanding to do much. His wife was basically the brains behind that pair."[24]

Ed Richards, incidentally, simply took exception to the fact that Leroy was a charismatic speaker. "He just gets up there and talks like a damn preacher," Richards once said. "He's a rabble-rouser."[25]

For his part, Jim Carter, the old-school bilagáana forester who worked for the BIA, just couldn't seem to believe that Leroy would go to such lengths purely on the basis of his beliefs. "Leroy was pretending the trees were sacred so he could create an issue that would enable him to run for office," Carter told one interviewer.[26]

"Who's paying you to do this?" Carter used to ask Leroy. "What's your angle?"

It was a thinly veiled challenge that Leroy would hear on many occasions. In the coming months, this mutual suspicion would turn into open hostility.

seven

It is said the Sun's dwelling was made of turquoise and that it was a square house, like the Pueblos. It stood on the shore of a great body of water. When Monster Slayer and Born for Water found their father's house, they found the Sun's wife and some of his children living inside. These hid the warrior twins until the Sun returned in the evening.

"I saw two strangers from the Earth Surface come this way," said the Sun angrily to his wife when he returned to his home at the end of the day. "Where are they?"

"No, there was nobody came this way," she said.

"Have I no eyes?" he asked in fury. "I saw somebody come this way, I tell you. Why do you conceal them? Who are they?"

"Strange," she said. "Someone always boasts of his honesty. One never commits adultery, he insists. And yet here two persons arrived, saying 'where is our father?' Perhaps you know them," she added. (Some of the elders say it was at this time that jealousy started).

The Sun's wife uncovered the boys from the bundle where they were hiding. He immediately seized them and began to beat them and abuse them, throwing them against spikes of shell and rock, in all four directions he threw them, but each time they were protected by the talisman—the living feather—given them by Spider Woman.

"I wish it were true they were sons of mine," said the Sun in exasperation.

—Adapted from Paul Zolbrod, *Diné Bahane':*
The Navajo Creation Story

■/

"What do you kiddos think about your mom bringin' home all the bacon?" Leroy asked Eli and the Bambina one afternoon. Clearly it made no difference to them. As far as they knew, their mom had always worked. His tone of voice was ambiguous; maybe he was putting the question to himself as much as to his kids. Leroy had by this time almost entirely abandoned his trading business. They were dipping into their savings to finance their life of activism, to pay for travel, long-distance phone bills, and the countless other incidental expenses.

They found themselves entangled with this new lifestyle in ways they had never anticipated. When they first started, it had been a fairly diffuse community effort. When the confrontation escalated, however (beginning with their own chapter delegate), and as Leroy began to talk about legal action, possibly involving outside courts, some members of the community balked. "Leroy was very aggressive," one community member commented later. "He didn't always do things the Navajo way." Leroy and Adella found themselves carrying more and more of the local burden in order to keep their forest reform effort alive.

Late in the spring, Sam Hitt secured the services of Aletta Belin, a lawyer from New Mexico who had experience in timber-sale appeals. Belin and Hitt intended to challenge both the contract and the environmental assessment's "Finding of No Significant Impact" (FONSI). Given that the timber sale fell outside any ten-year planning process (which was, at least in theory, supposed to govern all timber-cutting activity), they felt that they had solid legal grounds for the challenge.

That confidence was quickly shattered. In the early summer, the BIA approved the Whiskey Creek/Ugly Valley timber-sale contract. NFPI was so desperate for timber that they sent their loggers into the forests immediately after the BIA's signature. This *should* have been to Diné CARE's advantage. Once the BIA area director signs off on a sale, loggers are supposed to wait a minimum of thirty days before beginning to cut trees until all potential appellants have come forward.

Diné CARE and their lawyers needed to act quickly. Belin hastily filed the timber-sale appeal with the Interior Board of Indian Appeals. It did temporarily bring the timber cutting to a halt. As soon as the appeal was filed, the IBIA issued a stay of operations pending its outcome. That was the good news. The bad news was everything that followed.

Bruce Baizel, forced to watch the entire process unfold from the sidelines, later pointed out that Diné CARE was swimming in completely uncharted waters. He also noted that "no one in the Interior Department really knew what to make of the appeal." No community group had ever filed an appeal of a timber sale on Indian lands based on environmental concerns.

Eddie Brown, undersecretary for Indian Affairs, summarily dismissed the appeal, citing the hardship conditions facing the Navajo Nation's forestry enterprise (NFPI was by this time millions in debt). At the same time, Brown noted that the timber sale was technically unauthorized, falling as it did outside the framework of a forest-management plan. He stipulated that the dismissal was a one-time exception, and that the Navajo Nation needed to get its house in order on future timber sales.[1]

Leroy appeared to shake off the bad news, but it was clear that he was disappointed. Probably more than anything, he was beginning to feel the strain of the work of activism, which at one point he had thought would be only a temporary chapter in his life. Bruce Baizel and John Redhouse, however, both agreed that Brown's dismissal still left open the possibility for a lawsuit. "It seems to me it could have been a slam-dunk case," Baizel recalled later. "Diné CARE had a very strong case, particularly with NFPI going into the woods before the thirty-day waiting period had expired."

Unfortunately, the lines of communication between the Rez and Forest Guardians were never very strong. Neither Belin nor Hitt provided information back to the community about what was going on with the case. Diné CARE and the families who had decided to sign on found themselves with little to do but wait and speculate. After Brown's rejection of the appeal, Belin chose not to pursue a lawsuit, but did not inform Leroy or anyone else on the Rez about her reasons. "I don't know what their reasons were," Baizel later commented, when asked for an attorney's point of view. "Maybe they had sound ones, maybe not. The worst thing is, they didn't let anybody else in on their reasoning either."

The worst blow to relations between Diné CARE and their legal team came when Anthony Aguirre, of Navajo Nation Department of Justice, proposed a meeting with Hitt and Belin in Santa Fe. Without the advice or consent of Diné CARE or the appellants, Hitt accepted. Behind closed doors at the offices of Forest Guardians in Santa Fe, Belin and Hitt met with Aguirre, NFPI general manager Eddie Richards, and Navajo Forestry director Dexter Gill. None of Forest Guardians' clients was included.

"It got totally out of our control," John Redhouse said. "We had a situation where there was absolutely no accountability between the lawyer and clients, no sense of responsibility. They took it upon themselves to make decisions and enter into negotiations without consulting us."

It may be that Forest Guardians considered this within the bounds of proper legal counsel, or perhaps they were desperate to salvage something from the failed appeal. Maybe they assumed that the locals did not want to be bothered with the details of a settlement. Whatever the reason, their lack of communication may have been one of the worst mistakes Hitt's organization could have made with respect to Diné CARE. As mentioned, something that most Diné virtually never do is to speak on behalf of another without having permission.

"We speak for ourselves," says the Indigenous Environmental Network slogan. It has been a rallying cry for many community-based groups with whom Diné CARE has come in contact. Hitt's presumption to enter into negotiations "on their behalf" without any consultation was, to the members of Diné CARE, an inexcusable breach of trust.

■|

By summer, the forest dispute had turned far uglier than Leroy or Adella had ever imagined it could. It's not that it caught them entirely by surprise. It built up fairly steadily at first. There were letters to the editor, mostly from the mill's board and management. These letters talked about the "handful of troublemakers" and "puppets of outside environmental groups." But those letters had been more than offset by a far greater number—from residents of the mountains, from medicine men, even from Navajo outfitters and tour guides—supporting Diné CARE, calling for a reform of forestry. Many of these people Leroy and Adella had never met.

NFPI's board meetings also showed an increasing willingness to use Diné CARE as a scapegoat. Minutes of board meetings prior to 1992 show NFPI management regularly complaining about slow housing starts, the tribe's inefficiency in its approval of timber sales, and the lack of timber to run the mill at full capacity. NFPI's workers and logging contractors (who were also all Diné and operating constantly on the edge of bankruptcy), were likewise feeling the stress of a declining industry before Diné CARE even came into existence. But from 1992 mill management became increasingly vocal about "special interests" inhibiting timber-sale progress, and displayed a growing concern about "managing public perceptions."

But the letters, the comments in board meetings, and the public forums seemed trivial compared to what Adella saw when she opened the paper one morning in the summer of 1992. When she looked up and showed it to Leroy, her face looked as if it had lost all its blood. There, on the front page, were pictures of loggers and mill workers, gathered at a rally organized by NFPI in the mountain community of Crystal.[2] Hand-painted signs, carried by workers or posted on the doors of trucks, read: "Leroy Jackson, will you pay for my truck?" "Leroy Jackson wants to take your job." They showed angry workers making speeches against Diné CARE and the other "puppets" of the Santa Fe attorneys. Worst of all, the article contained a chilling description of the effigy of Leroy that was ritually hung, then set on fire as the high point of the rally. No one in Diné CARE had been prepared for this savage outpouring of animosity. But if any of this bothered Leroy, he didn't let it show. As he looked at the paper, he laughed that laugh of his.

"Sheeuh," was all he said. Later he commented: "They just got those guys brainwashed," he said. "They got them thinking that's all they can do, is to cut down trees to make a living."

And, in fact, he seemed to step up his pace—he traveled to the neighboring chapters even more, he lined up interviews (often with Lori's help) on local TV stations in Gallup and Farmington. He made radio appearances. As the most active and visible Diné CARE member in the forestry dispute, Leroy Jackson was constantly depicted and quoted in the local papers. The issue also received attention in Phoenix and Albuquerque newspapers, as well as in papers covering broader regions, such as *High Country News* and *Indian Country Today*.

He also went to work on the phone. He intensified the process of educating himself on the legal and technical aspects of forestry on Indian lands. He routinely talked to his contacts in Navajo Forestry, to Bruce

Baizel, to John Redhouse, and to Sam Hitt, whom Leroy continued to work with despite the recent breakdown in communications.

Locally, Leroy and Adella set about finding ways to mobilize the community to speak out more forcefully for a new way of managing the forests. In the summer of 1992 they therefore convened the first Diné Spiritual Gathering at a homesite high on the Chuska Mountain slopes.

■|

On the morning of the gathering, they sat in the predawn chill, huddled around a fire at the summer campsite belonging to Ray and Liz Redhouse.[3] It was astonishingly cold for the month of July in Arizona, but they were close to eight thousand feet above sea level, after all. The sky above was dazzling—the anthropologist had never seen so many stars. It's no wonder the Southwest tribes have such extensive astronomical knowledge. This knowledge plays an important role in the cultural and spiritual life of the Diné. Sand paintings in a wide variety of Diné ceremonies, for instance, are full of constellations, some corresponding closely to Western ones, some completely different.[4]

Ervin's wife McQueen was nearby, making coffee and fry bread. She was clearly irritated. She slapped the dough savagely as she prepared it. Finally, she couldn't hold it in any longer. "You need to talk to that father of yours," she scolded Ervin, "and tell him to show some respect!" Earlier in the night, while they were all gathered in the hogan during a ceremony, Ray had been telling one of his boys something while the *hataałii* was singing—the rough equivalent of talking in church. Even after a couple sharp looks from McQueen, Ray had continued talking quietly.

Ervin began to laugh. "What do you want me to do about it?" He asked her. He turned to the anthropologist, almost apologetically, and explained. "Ray doesn't really mean to be disrespectful. Sometimes with these old guys, what can you tell them? They just do what they want." McQueen just rolled her eyes. Ervin noticed this and laughed again.

Ray and Leroy were brothers through the Diné clan system; Ray was a little older than Leroy. At the camp in the hills, or at Ray and Liz's house in the HUD projects down below, over the mandatory cup of strong black coffee (a standard part of all social visits on the Rez) Leroy would confer with Ray, share what he had learned from his various contacts both within and outside the Navajo Nation, and solicit his opinion and advice. Ray would sit quietly and listen to Leroy, hearing him out all the way through before saying anything. After a short while, Ray would offer his opinion: "You know, the way I see it . . . " These seemingly languid consultations might last for a few minutes or several hours.

They were a standard part of Leroy's routine. He had a growing network of individuals on whom he relied for information, for advice, for input. Some of these involved what were from a Navajo perspective rather "foreign" ways of interacting—brief, to-the-point telephone calls to lawyers or technical experts, for instance—and some involved more "traditional" Diné modes of conduct: sitting together in near silence over a cup of coffee, letting meanings settle in, thinking carefully about what needs to be done. Both forms of consultation were deeply evident of a truth that often seems lost in early twenty-first-century enthusiasm for computing and communications technology: information is a social process. Even highly trained technical experts have "trusted" sources on whom they rely for consultation.[5] That trust is built through relationships. "Leroy never made a move," Adella once commented, "without consulting at least three people first." His hours on the phone, his personal visits and consultations with Ray or other locals, were as important for building a community of opposition to the timber cutting as they were about "access to information."

The whole Redhouse family, but particularly Ervin and McQueen, had joined in challenging the forestry program. Ervin and McQueen brought their youth and energy to Diné CARE. They also brought a knowledge of their cultural traditions that was considered unique among people their age. They were particularly effective in assisting Diné CARE with an ingenious strategy of public outreach. Although most Diné households may lack electricity or running water, one would be hard put to find even the most modest hogan without a portable transistor radio. Every morning between 6:30 and 7:30 A.M., a large portion of the Navajo Nation tunes into KTNN (based in Window Rock) for the morning news broadcast in the Navajo language. Elders, especially, were a large and regular audience for these broadcasts. KTNN boasts a signal strong enough to reach virtually all parts of the reservation. On clear nights, one can pick up its signal as far away as Tucson, several hundred miles to the south. These radio broadcasts have become Diné CARE's tried and true method of spreading messages to the people of the Navajo Nation.

McQueen and Ervin together produced a series of five-minute talks, which McQueen recorded on tape. Diné CARE then purchased ad time during the morning news. These talks publicly challenged NFPI and Navajo Forestry, and encouraged local people to do the same. (One talk was entirely devoted to a discussion of the value of the forests in ceremonies and stories of the Diné. This talk in particular had a big effect on the listening audience. "Who is that young woman who speaks the language so beautifully?" Lori's mother asked one day in Dilkon.) Largely by virtue of the radio ads, the turnout at the Spiritual Gathering was impressive.

As they prepared the camp for the coming crowds, Ervin and the anthropologist walked up into the woods to gather firewood. They scoured the ground for downed limbs of old oaks, which make nice, hot, long-burning fires.

"Some friends of McQueen's came out from New York last summer," Ervin said suddenly. "One girl found a piece of rock that she thought was pretty. She had no idea what it was. I told her 'Oh, man! Are you ever lucky. That's a special rock to our people. You gotta hang on to that one!' She put it in her jacket and carried it around for the rest of the day.

"When she brought it back to show McQueen and my folks, she was so proud of it. I thought McQueen was going to kill me . . . " at this point he was laughing so hard he had to pause. "It was a cow pie."

Ervin was still laughing about his story as they scrambled up a steep bank, climbed a short, rocky ledge and reached a flat summit. The sun was already beginning to warm them up. The ground was covered with the decaying pine needles. A few cactus and tufts of dry grass poked out through them. To the northeast, a well-graded gravel road stretched into the distance, rising and falling through the peaks and valleys of the range. It had been built for the log trucks.

"My brothers and I used to run around up in these hills for days at a time in the summers," he said. "We could get everything we needed up here. We could fish and hunt . . . Just in the time since I was a kid, a lot has changed. We don't see any bear anymore, or beavers. There used to be all kinds of beaver ponds up in these hills. Now I only know where one is, and I don't even know how long that will be around. We hardly ever see the wild turkeys. I keep thinking, what will be left when my son is old enough to explore these hills?"

They spent the rest of the morning collecting firewood in silence. When they returned to camp a couple hours later, the crowds were beginning to gather. Many of them were elders, often too old to drive themselves, accompanied by sons, daughters, and grandchildren, who patiently brought them to a comfortable place to sit on the ground, or opened lawn chairs under the shade of the pines. Even though it was not an "official" tribal event, that first Spiritual Gathering proved to be an important forum, one that the Navajo Nation government could not help but acknowledge. There were council members, Navajo Forestry Department staff members, reporters, and many others there.

The guests of honor, however, were the elders. One after another they got up to speak into the generator-powered PA system in front of the crowd. They talked about the way the forest used to be. They talked about the herbs that grow in the forest. They talked about the animals that have disappeared. They talked about sacred places—hogans where ancestors died, trees struck by lightning, sacred springs—that have been desecrated by timber cutting. One after the other they vented their frustrations with their tribal government, they challenged their children to be more proud and self-sufficient. One after another they came up, all day long.

"We couldn't get the microphone away from them," Lori joked later.

■/

Thereupon the Sun told his older children to go out and prepare the sweat house. When the winds heard this, they said "He still seeks to kill his children. How shall we avert the danger?" The sweat house was built against a bank. Wind dug into the bank a hole behind the sudatory, and concealed the opening with a flat stone. Wind then whispered into the ears of the boys the secret of the hole and said: "Do not hide in the hole until you have answered the questions of your father."

The boys went into the sweat-house. The Sun called out to them: "Are you hot?" and they answered: "Yes, very hot." Then they crept into the hiding-place and lay there. After a while the Sun came and poured water through the top of the sweat house on the stones, making them burst with a loud noise, and a great heat and steam was raised. But in time the stones cooled and the boys crept out of their hiding-place into the sweat house. "Are you hot?" The sun asked them again, hoping to get no reply; but the boys still answered: "Yes, very hot." Then he took the coverings off the sweat house and let the boys come out. He greeted them in a friendly way and said: "Yes, these are my children," and yet he was thinking of other ways by which he might destroy them if they were not.[6]

■|

As the day wound down, members of the Core Group sat around a picnic table taking stock. Ervin's son Lymon was nearby, tasting soda pop for the first time in his young life. He lifted the cup up to his face and immediately withdrew as the carbonation squirted him in the face. He tried again, quickly dispatched it, and held the cup out.

"More!" he said.

He received another ounce or two, gulped it down, and put the cup out again. "More!" he said again.

"No more," McQueen told him.

"More!" he said sternly, with a slightly menacing glare. Lymon was sporting a neat row of stitches on his forehead. Ervin, who at the time worked as a paramedic for the Public Health Service, had done them himself after the boy had run headfirst into the edge of a picnic table. "The clinics were all closed" he explained. "Not a bad job, though, eh?"

"More!" his son repeated once again to McQueen's back. When she didn't respond, he simply gave up, put his cup down, climbed onto the table, then ran to one end and jumped off into the dirt. McQueen turned around quickly, but he was already off running. She laughed and shook her head, and turned back to the fire.

"Feisty little guy isn't he?" Ervin laughed.

The elders had all returned home to tend their sheep. Ervin and his brothers took the anthropologist down toward a creek where Ervin's grandfather had built a sweat lodge (the "sweat" they called it) years before. It was a small dugout hut, made only of earth and timber, into which about six grown men can fit. Several large wool blankets covered the small entrance. Ervin's brother Nathan had built a huge roaring fire out front. Into this fire they placed several rocks, each about the size of a small pumpkin. These would be heated and placed inside the sweat.

They sat outside the sweat, waiting for the rocks to heat up. Ervin pointed (actually indicated, by pursing his lips and jutting his chin in the Navajo way of pointing) to a ledge high above them, across a ravine and the logging road, hidden in the shadows of the late afternoon sun. "See that ledge up there?" He said to the anthropologist. "One night there were a bunch of families up there, they were having a *Yé'ii Bicheii.* Kit Carson's raiders snuck up on them while they were having the ceremony and jumped them. Killed them all, even the grandmas and the little children."

His tone of voice was not emphatic. He was not trying to impress the anthropologist, or to elicit a reaction. He pointed it out the way he had pointed out many other things—local landmarks, constellations in the night sky, and so forth. He pointed it out the way someone might point out the house in which his grandmother was born, for instance.

As they sat staring silently at the fire, Ervin's brother Nathan talked about the value of the sweat—which despite its appropriation by "men's groups" and other New Age wannabes is not just a "men's thing," like watching football or playing cards in bilagáana society.[7] "My grandfather taught us about the sweat, as a means of promoting our health," he said. "It is important to be close to the earth. You look at this sweat, it is dug down into the earth. And it is made out of the earth, out of sticks and ground. That is how we stay close to our Mother. Some of the northern Indian people, they make portable sweats. They cover them with tarps, sometimes nowadays they use these plastic tarps that have who knows what kinds of toxins in them. That's not good."

As Nathan talked, he tore small narrow strips of rags and distributed them to the younger men and the boys in the group. They rolled them between their hands, or chewed on them, making them into strings. "Do you know what these are for?" Ervin asked the anthropologist. He was smiling.

"I have a pretty good idea," joked the anthropologist weakly, his mind racing with a million ridiculous doubts and questions the likes of which are nothing one prepares for in graduate school.

"The old men tell us we better wear these things if we want to have children," Ervin clarified, smiling even more broadly.

The inside of the sweat was cramped, completely dark, and of course, very hot. The air was humid and smelled like earth and the ferns that covered the ground. Ervin and Nathan had told the boys "This is not a macho thing. If it gets too hot, just go out. No one will care." The anthropologist thought about this as he began to feel a painful throbbing in his right temple.

After sitting in the darkened sweat for what could have been several minutes or several hours (by now he was so disoriented that time had lost all meaning) they emerged and drank ice-cold water drawn from the creek. Ervin lit a small cigarette he had rolled from wild tobacco plants his mother had picked on the mountain. The smoke was very sweet. The anthropologist was not an ethnobotanist, nor did he have the presence of mind to quiz Ervin about the plant.[8] He did, however, soon find that the pounding in his temple was gone. They entered the sweat a second time. This time, the anthropologist felt more in control of his faculties. Ervin sang a song about the sacred mountains. The other men knew the refrain. It was a stunningly simple and beautiful song. The anthropologist found himself lulled along by the singing, by the glimpses of recognition, ephemeral in the darkness, of names and words he could recognize . . .

> Sisnaajinii, Eastern mountain, mountain of daybreak, mountain of Spring, mountain of white shell;
> Tsoodzil, Big Mountain, mountain of the South, mountain of the blue sky of daytime, turquoise mountain;
> Dook'o'oosłííd, the Western mountain, mountain of twilight yellow, autumn mountain, abalone shell mountain;
> Dibé Ntsaa the Northern mountain, night time mountain, mountain of jet, mountain of winter . . .

Anyone lying awake later that night might have heard the anthropologist, somewhere through the trees, retching and groaning as the emetic effects of the sweat (so he was told later) caused a swift and thorough evacuation from what felt like every possible route from his body. He was still green the next morning as the rest of the campers chatted among themselves. No one else seemed to be hurting, he noted with mild resentment. Ervin teased him gently: "You've been living on Big Macs and cheap beer for too long."

Ray was even more amused by it all. In the coming weeks, on every chance encounter, he'd ask the anthropologist the same question—always in complete deadpan: "Want to go sweat?"

■/

It was the summer of gatherings. At one, Leroy was hung and burned in effigy. At another, elder after elder stood up, emboldened by the activism of the younger generation, and nearly commanded Leroy, Adella, and the rest of them to push on with their efforts. Despite the mill's attempts to foment broad-scale opposition to the "handful of troublemakers" known as Diné CARE, events like the Spiritual Gathering established the young organization as a positive force on the Navajo Nation. On the streets, in the trading posts, and at the homesites of the elders, Diné CARE members were greeted with words of encouragement and admonishments to keep pushing.

By early autumn, their notoriety had spread throughout Navajo Nation. At the Navajo fair in Tuba City (far to the west of the Chuskas) Diné CARE was named collective Grand Marshal. This was quite a statement. The Navajo fairs are big deals. The Tuba City fair is one of three main fairs held on separate weekends in the fall (Window Rock and Shiprock are the other two main sites). Thousands gather for parades, races, outdoor markets, food, games, and ceremonies.

On a warm October Saturday in Tuba City, a wide-open and windswept place, dozens of elders, children, and everyone else who claimed sympathy with Diné CARE scrambled onto the back of a big flatbed truck—their organization's "float." There wasn't enough room for everybody who wanted to be a part of it. Those who were able—Lori, Earl, Anna, Leroy, and Adella—walked behind it. Lori's mother, who had come to ride with her daughter, decided she did not need to take up room on the truck, and quickly began taking off her best jewelry, including expensive silver and turquoise necklaces and a bracelet, to hand it to another elderly woman who was on the float.

"Mom what are you doing?" Lori asked her. ("That jewelry was precious!" she said later.)

"She needs to have this if she's going to be up there."

"You don't even know that woman!"

"She'll get it back to me. Don't worry."

One month later, Lori was invited to Washington, D.C., where Ralph Nader presented Lori with an "outstanding citizen" award. Like Leroy, Lori had been all over the media, first about the asbestos dump at Huerfano, and then about the forests. At the end of 1992, Lori was named "Navajo of the Year" by the Flagstaff (Arizona) weekly *Navajo/Hopi Observer*, for her efforts both with the original CARE group as well as for the organization's activities in Huerfano and now in the forests. Lori was a little embarrassed by all the attention, but Adella and Leroy, Anna, Lucy, and Sylvia all bought up stacks of the local papers and photocopied the articles when they ran out.

The group accepted these honors insofar as they helped them publicize many of the issues facing their constituent communities, and to build a sense of confidence that ordinary people can make a difference on the Rez. Still, they found both the positive and negative attention to be a little puzzling. They considered themselves to be simply representatives of a much broader group of people, not the "handful of environmentalists," as the mill and much of the local media made them out to be. They continually pointed to the resolutions from the fourteen area chapters calling for a change in forestry practices on the reservation. They also attempted to remind the press that there were many people living in the timber-sale area who were opposed to commercial timber cutting. "We've never been a membership organization like bilagáana organizations," Lori explained to the media and funding organizations (who, as a result of the activity, were beginning to take an interest in the little group). "Diné CARE is anyone who takes initiative in protecting their community."

The appeal and other activities had also gotten the attention of the

John W. Sherry

Navajo Nation government. Up until the time of the appeal, Navajo Nation President Peterson Zah had all but ignored the requests of Diné CARE. Suddenly, however, the wind had changed. Zah, recognizing the rising groundswell of support for forest reform, called for a special meeting at his office in Window Rock, to be attended by "all forest stakeholders." Diné CARE met this announcement with guarded optimism. Maybe the heavy price they had paid for the appeal wasn't completely wasted. Maybe it had served its purpose after all—to get the tribe's respect.

Bruce Baizel had been forced to stay out of the appeal by the terms of his employment at Forest Trust. When it came to advising Diné CARE in more direct community organizing or other local participation, however, he was able to participate openly. Leroy thus called Bruce to Window Rock when Zah proposed the meeting. When he got there, however, it was now the president's turn to keep him out of the action. "His aides wound up kicking most of us out of there," Bruce recalls. "I found myself standing outside in the hall with Dexter (Gill) and Eddie (Richards). It felt like we were kids who had been kicked out of class. Pretty soon we just had to laugh. So we sat and exchanged a little small talk, and waited it out."

Inside the meeting, Diné CARE presented a list of concerns to President Zah. They said they would reserve the right to pursue litigation on any future timber sales unless the following conditions were met:

- The Navajo Nation should not pursue any more timber sales until a new ten-year forest-management plan had been duly drafted and approved. In addition, unlike the previous ten-year plan, the new forest-management plan should be conducted according to NEPA (National Environmental Policy Act) and NIFRMA (National Indian Forest Resources Management Act) regulations, which require the completion of an Environmental Impact Statement prior to the adoption of any plan.
- Replace the non-Indian head of the Navajo Forestry Department (Dexter Gill) with an individual who is knowledgeable of Navajo history, religion, and culture, and who is not an "old-school" (maximized harvest) forester.
- For timber sales occurring before the next ten-year plan that have

already been approved, thorough environmental assessments should be conducted, and the results shared with forest communities for input.

- A review of NFPI's operations must be conducted, including a financial audit of the mill, and replacement of NFPI board members who are also council delegates, or who sit on committees that review and approve timber sales. This request was intended to eliminate what Diné CARE members regarded as a clear case of conflict of interest.[9]

A few days later, President Zah's office produced a classic example of political equivocation, calculated to placate Diné CARE and keep the timber sales rolling at the same time. The president recommended that no more timber sales be approved without a new ten-year plan. At the same time he directed the Tribal Council committees to find a way to expedite the timber-sale-approval process so that three new contracts could be approved—in advance of the next ten-year plan.[10] For all their work, recognition, and support, the activists of Diné CARE realized they still had a long way to go.

eight

Finally, convinced that the boys were his children, the Sun asked them: "Now you must tell me why you have come here."

"We dwell in the place where Nayéé,' the Alien Monsters, stalk our people. Where we dwell those creatures devour flesh like the grazing herds devour grass.

"Yé'iitsoh the Big Giant devours our people, and Déélgééd the Horned Monster devours them. Tsé nináhálééh the Bird Monster feasts upon us, and so does Bináá' yee agháni, who kills with his eyes."

Now Yé'iitsoh, the Big Giant, was the Sun's own offspring as well. The Sun revealed as much to the Warrior Twins. He sat and said nothing for a while. "Even so," he said finally, "I shall help you."

The Sun gave the Twins chain lightning arrows. He gave them sheet lightning arrows. He gave them deadly sunbeam arrows, and he gave them fatal rainbow arrows. He also gave them each the hard flint knife, and the broad blade knife.

Thus armed, they set out to slay the alien gods, the monsters that threatened the Emergence People.

—Adapted from Berard Haile,
Upward Moving and Emergence Way

■

As Leroy and Adella had done, Lori converted a room of her house into a Diné CARE office, gradually displacing just about everything in the entire space with a couple filing cabinets, a PC desk, and a second desk on which stood a massive fax machine that endured an amazing amount of traffic. Over time, Lori would have a second, then a third, phone line installed in the house.

A huge desk calendar lay on the floor, scribbled with lines and short place names in multiple colors ("Earl in Wash DC" in red, "Lucy in Ship-rock" in brown, "Anna in St. Louis" in blue). An early version of Quicken[1] was running on the PC. Lori was trying to correlate all of Earl's receipts, by date, with the places he'd been. From this information, she could gradually reconstruct what he had been up to when he incurred his expenses. This was how Lori prepared the reports that would be required of her and her organization.

Buried in the third drawer of the small filing cabinet next to Lori's desk (a much bigger filing cabinet stood across the room), were dozens of grant applications, letters of intent, preproposal application forms, rejection letters, acceptance letters, completed proposals, and countless other bits of evidence of this activity she had inherited.

On top of the desk, a rather typical-looking funding application lay open and scattered, half completed. On page 6 of the application instructions (out of a total of ten) is the Application Checklist. At the top, in bold capital letters, is the admonishment:

DO NOT PLACE APPLICATION IN BINDERS OR FOLDERS

The contents of the checklist are as follows (all bold text was likewise in bold in the original):

- Did you complete the Application Form?
- Did you complete the Board information for both the Board of Directors of your organization and the Policymaking Board of your Project, if applicable?
- Did you complete the Proposal Narrative?
- Is your narrative no more than 10–15 double-spaced typewritten or laser printed pages (please, no dot matrix printers)?
- Do you have 7 copies of your Application Form, 7 copies of your Proposal Narrative and 7 copies of all attachments?
- Are all of your materials, including any addenda, on **8½" by 11" white paper?**
- Is a copy of your Application Form stapled to the front of each of the 7 copies of your Proposal Narrative?

- Have you included the resumes of key staff?
- Did you **mail all 7 copies of the Application and narrative in one package?** No faxes will be accepted.
- If your organization is composed of institutions or organizations, did you include a list?

ATTACHMENTS
- Did you attach the following financial information:
- Last year's financial statement (audited, if available)?
- Current income and expense statement?
- List of sources and amounts of funds raised
- Current year budget,
- Attach a copy of the motion approving the submission of this proposal
- Attach the organization's articles of incorporation
- Attach the organization's letter of 501(c)(3) determination as a non-profit organization by the Internal Revenue Service, or, if the organization is a sponsored project of another organization, attach the letter of fiscal sponsorship
- Attach sample news articles

In addition to the ten-page form, the application requires a seven-page narrative ("typed or laser printed, double spaced, no dot matrix printers, please"). In it are sections required for describing (a) the organization's history, purpose, and community it serves; (b) the structure of the organization—how membership is designated, who the policy-making board is, how staff will be recruited, trained, and compensated; (c) *measurable* goals and expected outcomes for the grant year plus specific *measurable* long-range goals (emphasis added); (d) specific organizational strategies to achieve the measurable goals and outcomes; and (e) budget and fundraising information, including a "3-year fundraising plan to raise funds from diversified funding sources such as dues, raffles, ad books, special events, foundations and corporations, major donors, direct mail, canvas."[2]

This was what Lori's life had become. Mostly by virtue of the fact that she lived in a house in an actual town with telephone and power, she slipped into the job of unofficial, unpaid executive director—which meant she was the point of contact in what she dubbed "the funding game." It was a job she never wanted, never enjoyed, but endured, because she knew that they could not continue to operate spending their own families' savings, as she, Leroy and Adella, and other members of the group had done up through 1993. That is also why she went out and bought her first computer.

Telephones and fax machines had obvious benefits for organizations such as Diné CARE, as tools for communications among themselves and with distant allies. Computers, however, were different. Their primary use, particularly in the early years, was to allow them to respond to the needs of outside institutions that claimed to want to help local grassroots organizations, but strangely, treated such organizations as if they occupied well-equipped urban offices. By requiring "laser printed" applications, audited financial statements, and such evidence of formalization as by-laws and articles of incorporation, the foundations were (inadvertently or otherwise) biasing against the very types of organizations they claimed they wanted to help.

In a detailed ethnographic study of navigation, Edwin Hutchins has noted something that might as easily be said of the funding game: "It is really astonishing how much is taken for granted in our current practice. . . . Only when we look at the history can we see just how many problems had to be solved and how many could have been solved differently in the course of development of the modern practices." He adds a point worth emphasizing: "A way of thinking comes with these techniques and tools."[3]

The structures that pervade the "funding game"—an emphasis on financial metrics, for instance, or a reliance on bureaucratic forms as a way of connecting people and institutions—are all products of a fairly long history of solutions to very particular problems. These adaptations have become pervasive in Western society—so much so that even new technologies such as computers make far more use of them than is typically acknowledged. These structures are so common and feel so "natural" to most of us that we rarely notice them, unless they arise in a situation (such as the funding game) where they just don't work.

Of course, the very roots of writing lie in such bureaucratic activities as accounting for tribute, taxes, and large-scale employment projects (e.g., in Mesopotamia five thousand years ago).[4] The history that concerns us, however, is a little more recent—about three hundred years or so—beginning with the time when the feudal and sovereign power that had long governed Europe began to give way to what Michel Foucault calls *disciplinary power*, "exercised by surveillance rather than ceremonies, by observation rather than commemorative accounts."

Disciplinary power emerged in many places, in a variety of domains—in the classroom, in the medical clinic, in the prison, in the ordered ranks of the military, and eventually on the factory floor. Discipline, enabled by tools of surveillance, is "a modest, suspicious power," constituted in the use of "simple instruments, hierarchical observation, normalizing judgment and their combination in a procedure that is specific to it, *the examination*."[5]

The examination was and is the key to disciplinary power. It may be, as Foucault claims, "a slender technique" but it is a little bit awe-inspiring just how pervasive the examination has become in modern life. From the moment we enter school we encounter ordered rows of seating (often arranged alphabetically) and take standardized examinations; examinations follow us—or, rather, precede us and guard our passage—through virtually every institutional encounter our lives may require, from the acquisition of a driver's license to the application for work to the paying of taxes, to every medical examination and even the filing of a death certificate. For all their mundanity, each examination reveals "a whole domain of knowledge, a whole type of power."[6]

The examination has been no less instrumental in defining modern work practice. Many historical accounts have emphasized the importance of technologies of energy conversion and mechanics (steam, the internal combustion engine, electricity) in the explosion of industry in the nineteenth century. Fewer have examined the organizational and representational technologies that paved the way for the Industrial Revolution. "As the machinery of production became larger and more complex, as the number of workers and the division of labor increased, supervision became ever more necessary and ever more difficult."[7]

Added to that was the need for metrics of organizational health and accountability. Balance sheets evolved, for instance, as a way for potential lenders (primarily banking interests) to gauge a firm's liquidity. Similarly, income statements became particularly important in the 1920s in the

United States, as firms turned from borrowing capital to the practice of issuing corporate stock in order to finance expansion. This trend spurred a greater separation between capital ownership and the actual management of operations, requiring new modes by which capital investors could oversee operations without actually being on-site.[8]

All that surveillance created new types of jobs, new forms of management, and required new forms of record keeping. In the latter part of the nineteenth century, "a veritable revolution in communication technology took place,"[9] and bureaucratic forms were in the middle of it all. The typewriter, carbon paper (and duplicators), and vertical filing—three innovations still recognizable today—were developed to deal with the demands of this explosion.

So successful were the innovations of discipline and cost accounting that they have become a standard part of American life. It is therefore perhaps not too surprising that virtually every incorporated American institution relies heavily on these very tools—standardized observations, routinely gathered through bureaucratic forms, financial metrics of organizational health—as a means of regulating themselves and interacting with other organizations. This pervasiveness and apparent naturalness can be a problem, however: the examination can sometimes be applied to domains where it simply doesn't belong. Such was the case, Diné CARE members felt, with the funding game, where "the bottom line" was not the issue, and written representations were not the point.

Earl Tulley once tried to make this clear as he explained the group's situation to a grant maker:

> We are an oral people. For us our word is everything. That's why we prefer to speak to each just right here [hands motioning in front of him] without anything written down, without contracts or legalese, even without notes or what have you. In that particular manner we know that we are speaking from our hearts.[10]

Diné CARE members argued that funders, like other institutions, placed far too much emphasis on representations (their bureaucratic forms and financial statements) and not enough on the people being represented.

Hutchins (with respect to the navigation problem) has called this tendency "a passion for measurement and a tendency to take the representation more seriously than the things themselves."[11]

> Most of our activists have heard this at least several times: "Wow! The work you do here is great! Just send us a 10-page proposal, along with last year's financial statements and next year's budget, a copy of your IRS letter of exemption, and a diagram of your organizational structure, and we'll be glad to fund your work."[12]

By relying on their own familiar Western tools, grant makers inadvertently undermined their own intentions. Most grant makers really *wanted* to put their money in the hands of local communities—at least they said they did. But the "bottom line" approach, it seems, does not apply as well to organizations whose goals are qualitatively different from making money.[13] As one community organizer put it, the funding game forces grassroots organizations to act like "little businesses."

"By the time [local Navajo activists] get the funding game right," Lori once complained, "they're corrupted too. They're not themselves anymore, they've learned to become these self-perpetuating organizations that exist just for the sake of getting money."

Faced with this bind, many local Navajo communities, and many grassroots organizations worldwide,[14] have thus been forced to turn to outsiders to mediate their relationships with grant makers and other resources. The result has frequently been forms of exploitation that sometimes verge on the criminal.

Larger urban groups with access to computers and laser printers, groups familiar with the representational rituals of grant writing, look much more "accountable" on paper. Many of these organizations have prospered by writing grants in which they claim to be doing the work of environmental justice on reservation lands. But while they were getting all the money they were actually doing little or nothing to help local Navajo people.

> [A]llong come the urban environmental groups. They live a little closer to the reservation. They know who our activists are. . . . They bring our

elders to the cities and sit them in front of panels to tell their stories. "We were glad to be of assistance to you," they tell us. "Now could you please give us a letter for our files, officially requesting our help. It's just a formality."[15]

Once local activists have their "brains picked" the urban organizations know what to write on their grant proposals. They now not only have the printer and the paper, they have the right story to tell as well. "Meanwhile, another mine is being dug, another forest is being cut."[16] Diné CARE has encountered this situation over and over in their work.

With this situation on her mind, in early 1993 Lori dropped her first bombshell on the funding community at a national gathering of grant makers in Houston, Texas, by declaring to horrified funders and infuriated urban activists: "The system currently in place for funding grassroots work simply is not working. Local people—the people who are in a position to make a difference—aren't getting the support they need. In the meantime, the wrong people are getting the money."

■/

Ronald Reagan once commented that "more than armies, more than diplomacy, more than the best intentions of democratic nations, the communications revolution will be the greatest force for the advancement of human freedom the world has ever seen."

"Computers promote heterogeneity, individualization, and autonomy," claims Kevin Kelly.[17] "No one has been more wrong about computerization than George Orwell in *1984*."

"[J]ust as our culture is moving from the printed book to the computer, it is also in the final stages of the transition from a hierarchical social order to what we might call a 'network culture.'" The old powers will crumble. Many-to-many forms of communication will precipitate direct democracy that our ancestors could barely imagine. "[A]ll of the monopolies and hierarchies and pyramids and power grids of industrial society are going to dissolve."[18]

Environmentalists themselves have occasionally seemed seduced by these utopian technological fantasies. One summer afternoon, the fax machine in the little study at Adella's house near the clinic disgorged a memo. It was an older-style fax machine, the kind that required long rolls of thin, shiny thermal paper. The sheets, after being printed and clipped, rolled themselves up and tumbled among the usual clutter—the rolodex cards, notes, messages, file folders, pens, and crayons. Buried in these rolls of memo was the following prediction:

> Based on what is happening currently in information processing, the grassroots network of the future will be a virtual organization with virtual members. It will exist in cyberspace—everywhere and nowhere. Its currency will be information, and its location a collection of E-mail addresses and fax numbers. Its leadership will be in constant flux, self motivated, self selecting, opportunistic and situational.

This was an astonishing prediction—not so much in its content as in its origin. Its author did not come from the towers of Madison Avenue or the sunny glow of Silicon Valley; he was hidden in the mists and Douglas firs of the Central Oregon coast. He was an actual on-the-ground environmentalist. The very presence of the fax seemed to be proof of its own veracity. But yet, for the poorer, rural communities such as most of those found on the Navajo Nation (and certainly many, many more worldwide), the fantastic prospects of a technological conversation are as remote as ever.

It is mildly ironic. As many Americans enjoy greater access to broadband connectivity, with all its promise of digital entertainment and real-time stock quotes, the hottest political issue surrounding the Internet seems to be consumer privacy. All that access, it appears, comes with a price: digital surveillance. The examination, that slender technique of power and knowledge, has been automated and distributed over database systems, web forms, and other means in ways that seventeenth-century Europe could never have imagined. George Orwell wasn't entirely wrong—it may not be Big Brother who's watching you, but Amazon.com and Citibank sure are.

While those with access become "too visible," people from poor, rural, and minority communities who lack access to technology are rendered even more invisible.

Think of a stretch limo in the potholed streets of New York City, where homeless beggars live. Inside the limo are the air-conditioned post-industrial regions of North America, Europe, the emerging Pacific Rim, and a few other isolated places, with their trade summitry and computer-information highways. Outside is the rest of mankind, going in a completely different direction.[19]

Technology does not cut out the middleman or empower the powerless—if they want to be seen, local organizations must either rely on outsiders such as the urban environmental groups, and thus open themselves up to exploitation, or, if they are lucky, find someone like Lori Goodman. Lori took on the role of facilitating outside contact partly by virtue of her location, and partly out of the desire to let the local activists stay focused on the "real work." "I'm willing to corrupt myself," she once half-joked, "for the sake of the group."

It's a position with which she has never been entirely comfortable, in part because it quickly became her own prison. Beyond the merely mind-numbing routines of book keeping, reporting, proposal writing, and filing, the funding game requires constant "schmoozing" with grant makers, traveling extensively for coalition and funding organization meetings. She's also forced to monitor more closely than she would like to the activities of all the other members of the organization. On top of this, she has a family to attend to, a family that, before the toxic waste company ever came to Dilkon, had known her primarily as a "stay-at-home" mom. She continuously struggles with near exhaustion. On a few rare occasions she's even questioned out loud why she stays with it.

In the midst of this struggle, the rewards have come gradually and painfully. Some of Diné CARE's first grant money came from the Citizens Clearinghouse for Hazardous Wastes (CCHW), whose director, Lois Gibbs, started her life of environmental activism at Love Canal. Perhaps united by the bond of one "angry mother" to another, Lois Gibbs has turned out to be a longtime supporter of Lori Goodman and the rest of Diné CARE.

Diné CARE leveraged this initial vote of confidence to pursue its own solution to the problem—increasing the personal contact between funders and local communities in need of funds. Lori's relentless efforts in this regard have definitely paid off—but only after extensive travel to New York, Washington, San Francisco, and many other places. Some of their solutions have been unique (and sometimes rapidly copied). On many occasions, Lori, Anna Frazier, Earl, or other Core Group members have personally driven funders to remote local communities, just to be sure that the local people have a chance to make an impression. In 1994, Diné CARE hit on an even more innovative solution. With the help of Albuquerque-based air transportation company Lighthawk, the group arranged for representatives from several major funding organizations to take an air tour of environmental "hot spots" on the reservation.

Of course, the larger environmental groups weren't about to take all this sitting still. Within months, organizations from Albuquerque and Phoenix, and even one from Washington, D.C., were trying to do air tours of their own. The competition for funding remains tight and contentious to this day.

The Sun spread a streak of lightning; he made his children (Monster Slayer and Child Born of Water) stand on it—one on each end—and he shot them down to the top of Tsoodził [Mount Taylor].

They descended the mountain, and soon heard thunderous footsteps, and beheld the head of Yé'iitsoh, peering over a high hill in the east; it was withdrawn in a moment. Soon after, the monster raised his head and chest over a hill in the south, and remained in sight a little longer than when he was in the east. Later he displayed his body to the waist over a hill in the west; and lastly he showed himself, down to the knees, over Tsoodził in the north. Then he descended the mountain, came to the edge of a lake, and laid down a basket which he was accustomed to carry.

Yé'iitsoh stooped four times to the lake to drink, and, each time he drank, the waters perceptibly diminished; when he had done drinking the lake was nearly drained. The brothers lost their presence of mind at sight of the great giant drinking, and did nothing while he was stooping down. As he took his last drink they advanced to the edge of the lake, and Yé'iitsoh saw their reflection in the water. He raised his head, and, looking at them, roared "What a pretty pair? Where have I been hunting [that I should have missed these]?"

"What a great thing has come in sight!" responded Monster Slayer. "Where have we been hunting?"

The brothers then heard Wind whispering: "Beware! Beware!"

—Matthews, *Navaho Legends*

■|

When she was still very young the Bambina developed the practice of close and careful observation—scrutiny, really—on anyone who was willing to sit still for it. If she caught you while you were watching TV, it was all over.

Leroy made the perfect subject as he sat on a tattered bar stool at the counter that separated the kitchen from his office. He was occupied on the phone. She crawled up onto the edge of the counter. Her tiny bare feet clung to the edge of Leroy's seat.

She studied the way he bent his neck to pin the phone between his ear and his shoulder. She watched his hand closely as he scribbled some cryptic notes on a legal pad. She looked at his face and examined his teeth while he talked. She peered into his free ear. What possible purpose she had in conducting this painstaking ritual was a mystery.

"What are you doing?" asked the anthropologist, unable to contain his own curiosity.

"I'm just looking," she said as she flashed him a brief but stern glare. The impertinence of these anthropologists!

Leroy was so deeply involved in the conversation he hardly noticed. She leaned over closer, squinting, and stuck a tiny finger in his ear. He brushed her hand away, gently and absent-mindedly, without interrupting his conversation. When he finally hung up the phone, he looked glum and tired. For a moment he sat still and slowly rubbed his face with both hands. Then he noticed the Bambina, seemingly for the first time. He quickly rotated her on the spot and put his arms around her from behind. He picked her up in a bear hug, and swung her dangling feet back and forth.

"The Baaammmbina" he said in a loud voice. "She's gonna be a doctor when she grows up." He laughed as he held her. She giggled and wriggled out of his arms.

The phone call had been from Lori. She and Leroy were talking at least once a day during that time, often more, as part of Leroy's routine of checking in with his many contacts. This time it was bad news. Lori had been informed by one of Diné CARE's sympathizers in Window Rock that the council had, with a swift impunity, extended the (then expired) ten-year forest-management plan to an eleventh year. The move cleared the way for more timber sales, the first of which was to be carried out in the Wheatfields area, not far from Leroy and Adella's home. It was approved by all tribal authorities and the BIA area director within a matter of a few weeks. By the time Leroy got his hands on a copy of the contract, the loggers were already in the forest oiling their chainsaws.

Bruce Baizel, who had left his job at Forest Trust and was now free to act as Diné CARE's legal counsel, drafted a letter to the BIA, pointing out that the extension of the ten-year plan was in violation of federal environmental regulations,[1] and that the loggers were violating additional laws by going into the woods without waiting a mandatory thirty days for potential timber-sale appeals to be filed.[2] He also protested that Diné CARE was never given notification of the pending sale.

The acting BIA area director responded a few weeks later with a curt dismissal of these objections, arguing that Diné CARE did not merit notification since they had no legal standing. "Without a specific showing by individuals, that their interests are adversely affected, I cannot assume that Diné CARE has standing to appeal the approval as an interested party."[3]

Nature intervened where local officials would not. A series of winter storms blew across the Chuskas, leaving the logging roads in an impassable state of snow, mud, and slush. This temporary moratorium provided the members of Diné CARE with just enough time to consider whether or not to take more formal action. The events of the previous summer—especially the loggers' rally in Crystal and the disastrous representation they had gotten from the Santa Fe legal team—had shaken them all, whether or not they were willing to admit it. None of them was eager to get involved in more legal action.

Meanwhile, Earl Tulley, who was as skilled a diplomat as Diné CARE would ever find, and the group's eyes and ears in Window Rock, told his companions about a conversation he'd had with Andy Morgan, the head of the Navajo Nation's Department of Natural Resources. "Andy told me 'just give us this one timber sale. We can get NFPI out from under its debt, and then we can start doing things right.'"

They all wanted to believe it. It wasn't just a matter of cold feet. There were serious obstacles to overcome before they could mount another appeal. They did not have a lawyer or any money. Even Sam Hitt advised against pursuing any legal action.

So they waited and hoped for the best. As the roads of the Chuskas began to dry out in the spring, however, Morgan's promises proved to ring hollow. From local residents they learned of places where cutting had violated "buffer zones" around sacred sites, or ignored cultural-resource management recommendations altogether. In some places, stands had been cut that were not even listed in the timber-sale document. One dense old-growth stand was conveniently diagnosed with a mistletoe infestation and thus cleared "to protect the overall health of the forest."[4]

It was also becoming obvious that "just one more timber sale" was never going to pull NFPI out of its financial tailspin. General Manager Eddie Richards had once boasted, "During my travels to various meetings and conferences, people were always envious of NFPI because we could cut our own timber and not have to compete with anyone."[5] Now, even monopoly access to Navajo timber wasn't enough. Faced with mounting losses, mill management hit on the idea of persuading the tribe to forgive millions in debt and provide cheaper timber in the future.

Recall that, as a separate legal entity, the mill was required to purchase its timber from Navajo lands—called "stumpage fees." In a special hearing before the council,[6] NFPI's management proposed changing the way stumpage fees were reckoned, from fair market value for the timber they cut, to simply a percentage of their own profits after milling. What's more, NFPI wanted to make the new pricing system retroactive, thereby eradicating a roughly six-million-dollar debt owed the tribe for unpaid stumpage fees.[7] Mill management argued that special interests, especially "environmentalist concerns" (that is, Diné CARE) had made their operating environment so hostile that the tribe "owed" them this special consideration.

At that same hearing, Leroy leveled a scathing critique at mill management. "NFPI can no longer compete in the marketplace," he told the council finance committee at a hearing convened at NFPI's request. "Why is the tribe subsidizing this inefficient and costly enterprise? First it was the particleboard plant, then it was the housing slowdown in the eighties, and now it's suddenly Diné CARE's fault. When is NFPI going to accept the blame for its own mismanagement? Diné CARE has bent over backwards to give NFPI and Navajo Forestry time to comply with the law. Despite our efforts, we are made the scapegoat for NFPI's problems."

Much to everyone's surprise, somebody was listening to Leroy and Diné CARE this time. With additional testimony from the Navajo Nation controller supporting Diné CARE's position, the council rejected NFPI's proposal. There was no restructuring of pricing and no debt forgiveness.

But while Diné CARE may have won that battle, they still felt as though they were losing the war. By the end of May, before cutting on the Wheatfields sale was complete, a new timber sale was already in the works. This one was scheduled for the Tó Ntsaa region, south of Adella's homesite, over the summit on the eastern slopes of the mountains.

Once again, they heard the same old promises from the same old people in the council's natural resources committee and tribal forestry. "Just give us this one timber sale," they said. "This time we promise. We'll get it right."

"They've been using us," Leroy said to Adella. "They're playing us for fools."

So, once again, the steady flows of correspondence began. As a precautionary measure in the event of an appeal, Bruce Baizel sent the Navajo Nation Forestry staff a critique of the Tó Ntsaa sale's Environmental Assessment.[8] The letter opened on a conciliatory note, congratulating the Navajo Forestry staff "for their efforts to bring Navajo forest management practices into the 20th century." But it also objected to the fact that there were no meaningful alternatives to the "even aged" (clear cut) management prescription for the forest. The letter complained of a "complete lack of data upon which to base any analysis of environmental consequences." The prescribed timber harvest was simply unsustainable.[9]

Diné CARE received no response from the Navajo Forestry Department—they never expected one. But it was clear their relentless pressure was beginning to have some effects. Anderson Morgan (head of Navajo Natural Resources Division) called for the resignation of Dexter Gill from the Forestry Department. It was clearly a move designed to placate Diné CARE, a response to one of the original points they had requested from Peterson Zah over a year earlier.

Dexter Gill resented this bitterly, and without doubt held Leroy responsible. This was clearly evident in a June 24 memo he penned called "Forestry Issues—The Crisis Is Here—What to Do?"

"As a non-Navajo I apparently have no credibility in todays [sic] political climate," Gill wrote in the opening of the memo, "so I hope that my leaving the Directorship will assist someone to open their eyes and deal with the true issues." Echoing his long-standing position, Gill asserted that

The Navajo Nation has apparently submitted to the direction of the larger surrounding society by allowing (possibly requesting) the "Forest Trust" and "Forest Guardians," a couple of non-Navajo radical environmental activist groups from Santa Fe, to set the stage to have the Navajo forest be managed like they want. The result was the establishment of a Navajo environmental clone of the outside Santa Fe interests . . . A general attitude had been generated that economic benefits to the Navajo Nation is contrary to the Navajo culture. Further, that business profits are evil . . . the termination of the non-Navajo Forestry Department director was to be necessary as he promoted economic use of the forest and support for the Enterprise.[10]

When Leroy saw the letter he could do little more than laugh.

Gill's replacement was Robert Billie, who had prepared the 1981 Site Condition Report that sounded the first alarming note on the health of the forest, and who had been one of the few people in the department who had been responsive to Diné CARE's perspective. It appeared to be a hopeful sign that the tribe was willing to do things right. As the weeks went by, however, Billie showed no signs of changing the scope or the schedule of the Tó Ntsaa timber sale.

■|

Yé'iitsoh hurled a lightning bolt that passed over the heads of the brothers. He hurled a second, they bent the rainbow on which they were standing, while the bolt passed beneath their feet. With the third, they descended again and let the bolt pass over them. When he threw the fourth bolt they bent the rainbow very high, for this time he aimed higher than before; but his weapon still passed under their feet and did them no harm.

He drew a fifth bolt to throw at them; but at this moment lightning descended from the sky (sent by the Sun), hitting the giant in the head. He reeled but he did not fall. Then the elder brother sped a chain-lightning arrow; his enemy tottered to the east, but straightened himself up again. A second arrow sent him toppling toward the south; a third toward the west, and the fourth arrow sent him toward the north, where he fell to his knees, raised himself partly again, fell flat on his face, stretched out his limbs, and moved no more.

When the arrows struck him, his hard-flint armor was shivered in pieces and the scales flew in every direction. The elder brother said: "They may be useful to the people in the future."

They cut off the Giant's head and threw it into the hills, beyond the summit of Tsoodził, the Giant Mountain. A torrent of blood began to flow down the valley. That blood fills the valley at the foot of Tsoodził to this very day.[11]

■|

It's true. Along Interstate 40 there is a stretch of highway at the foot of Mount Taylor where deep red-black lava lies frozen, heaving and churning all along the side of the highway. Only a few scattered weeds grow out from the fissures in the hard rock. The scene is an impressive reminder of the cataclysm that created it.

Leroy and Adella passed it on their way to Santa Fe one beautiful summer morning. Leroy was at the wheel of the old Jeep they used to own until one strange day when it managed to start itself up at a gas station in Winslow and nearly ran down the frightened young man at the pump.

Adella looked in the back seats at the Bambina and Eli. They were both awake but quiet, looking out the windows.

"Do you know what that is?" she asked, indicating the lava.

"Ummm," Eli said.

"Yé'iitsoh's blood!" shouted the Bambina.

■|

Later that day in Santa Fe, Sam Hitt sat behind his desk in a sunny little office, explaining to Leroy the terms by which he might be able to raise funds and put an attorney to work on an appeal of the Tó Ntsaa timber sale. Despite the fiasco of the previous summer, Leroy had not broken off the relationship with Forest Guardians. While most other members of Diné CARE had felt betrayed by Sam Hitt, Leroy maintained that he was still the best resource they had. Sam was, in fact, one of the handful of people whom Leroy regularly consulted over the phone.

There were factors that complicated the relationship. Forest Guardians had continued to raise money for the "Chuska Mountain Forest Campaign" throughout the preceding year. None of the money had found its way to Leroy, Diné CARE, or anyone else actually living in the Chuskas, however. It had been used to cover Forest Guardians' own legal and overhead expenses, a fact that had only added to the mistrust that Lori, Earl, and other members of Diné CARE felt for Hitt. At the same time, however, Hitt had hired a new attorney by the name of Steve Sugarman, a move that turned out to be good for relations with Diné CARE. Sugarman would ultimately prove himself to be reliable and responsive to the complex issues surrounding the representation of Navajo clients in matters that pit them against their own tribal governments. He also worked well with Bruce Baizel, who was (and still is) Diné CARE's most trusted legal counsel.

But there was still the nagging issue of the funding game to be worked out. Lori had sent Leroy to Santa Fe with explicit instructions to work out something equitable. "We can't have Sam raising money from the sweat off our backs," she told him. Leroy knew she was right, and of course he was no pushover, but he also knew that Diné CARE needed Sam and his experience and connections.

Sam was cagey. "I can probably come up with some funding to pay you," Sam told Leroy, "but we'll have to put your name on the masthead of our newsletter as a member of our staff."

Leroy told Sam he wanted to work with him, but he needed to talk to Lori first. Before long Lori was on the speaker phone in Sam's office. If Leroy was the good cop, Lori was definitely the bad cop.

"That's unacceptable," she told Sam. "Leroy will be paid as a consultant to your organization. His name is not to appear on your newsletter masthead. He is not an employee of Forest Guardians. And we will pursue funds to continue our organizing efforts on the Navajo Nation separately. If you don't want to work with us that way, we'll have to find another organization to work with."

Lori, the woman who by her own admission "couldn't say no to people selling magazines at my door," was fast becoming a tough and effective negotiator, mostly by virtue of her desire to protect the interests of her fellow members of Diné CARE.

"Sometimes I feel like I'm being a mother hen with the activists," Lori once confessed.

"The mother of all mothers," Earl once called her.

Sam reluctantly agreed to Lori's terms; Leroy did, eventually, get paid a few hundred dollars a month from funds raised by Forest Guardians. He would never wind up keeping any of it, however. He used the money to expand his efforts in the Chuskas beyond "defense" toward more proactive measures, including an attempt to start a forest-restoration effort (see chapter 12).

■|

When the boys returned home they were received with great rejoicing, and had a dance to celebrate the victory.

When their rejoicings were done, Monster Slayer said to his mother: "Where does Déélgééd dwell?" "Seek not to know," she answered. "You have done enough. Rest contented. The land of the Monsters is a dangerous place. The Nayéé' are hard to kill."

But Monster Slayer persisted, and in the morning, she found he was off to kill Déélgééd. He returned, successful as he had been before, once again to great rejoicing.

But he was not content to stay at home. The following day, he was off to battle the Monster Eagle.

In that battle, Monster Slayer was seized by Monster Eagle, who flung him on a broad level ledge on the side of Tsé Bit'á'í (now called Shiprock) where the monster reared its young. This was the way the Monster Eagle fed its young. The fall had killed all others who had dropped there, but Monster Slayer was preserved by the life-feather, the gift of Spider Woman, which he still kept. The two young of the monster approached to devour him, but he said "Sh!" at them. They stopped and cried up to their father: "This thing is not dead; it says 'Sh!' at us." "That is only air escaping from the body," said the father. Then he flew away, in search of other prey.

The warrior made the young birds tell him when their father and mother would return, and where they perched. When the monsters returned, he was ready for them. Monster Slayer shot his lightning arrows at them, and they tumbled to the foot of Winged Rock, dead.

The young ones began to cry, and they said to the warrior: "Will you slay us too?" "Cease your wailing," he said to them, "I shall now make of you something that will be of use in the days to come when men shall increase in the land."

He seized the elder and said to it," You shall furnish plumes for men to use in their rites, and bones for whistles." He swung it high in the air and let it go, and as he did it changed into an eagle, and flew away.

He seized the smaller bird and said: "In the days to come men will listen to your voice to know what will be their future: sometimes you will tell the truth; sometimes you will lie." He swung it back and forth, and as he did its head grew large and round; its eyes grew big; it began to say "Uwú, uwú, uwú, uwú" and it became an owl. Then he threw it into a hole in the side of the cliff and said: "This shall be your home."[12]

■/

Soon after he returned from his trip, Leroy found a fax, sent to him surreptitiously by someone in the office of Navajo BIA area director Wilson Barber. It was a copy of a letter sent by Barber and the BIA area directors for Phoenix and Albuquerque to the U.S. Fish and Wildlife Service. They were concerned with the case of the Mexican spotted owl, a species listed as threatened under the Endangered Species Act. Breeding pairs of the owls had been spotted in the Tó Ntsaa timber-sale area, so USFWS was required to review any timber-sale plans. The Tó Ntsaa contract was scheduled to pass through that office in the middle of summer 1993.

Like its cousin the northern spotted owl (although with considerably less national attention), the Mexican spotted owl became the focus of intense debates on symbolic and cultural values.

In the Diné tradition (as in many other North American Indian traditions) the owl is a messenger of warning. The sighting of an owl, especially on repeated occasions or near one's home, can bring a sense of foreboding. People who encounter the owl know they need to have prayers said or take other corrective action. The owl thus carries with it a certain "negative" connotation in Diné belief.

> In the Protection Way ceremony, there are feathers from birds that are associated with negative, associated with evil, that are used. And these are the owl, the whippoorwill . . . then some animals like the coyote. And also, owl feathers are used in war caps, hunting caps. They're also used in Yé'ii Bicheii ceremonies.[13]

It has become a well-recognized fact in anthropology that symbolic meanings are always "up for grabs." Where money and politics are at stake, the grabbing can be vicious. In their letter to U.S. Fish and Wildlife the BIA area directors played on this "negative" symbolism of the owl, using it as a justification for their request for exemption from the Endangered Species Act.

> Not only are issues of sovereignty and economic development involved, but also cultural issues as well, since the owl is traditionally held in low esteem by Navajo, Apache and Pueblo Indians of the Southwest.[14]

The BIA area directors went on to claim that, as the "original environmentalists," the tribes in their jurisdictions were better suited than the federal government to implement conservation efforts.

This letter provoked quite a response from Diné CARE, whose members almost couldn't believe the audacity of the BIA. "These guys can't even live up to what the bilagáanas put in place to protect the land," Leroy said. "But those federal regulations are all we've got. This 'original environmentalist' stuff is a bunch of gobbledygook." (He was not one for harsh profanities.)

The whole incident sparked a lively discussion among them about the importance of owls. As Lucy Charlie put it, "there's a good side of it and a bad side of it. If [the BIA] are going to think the owl is all bad then, they're just promoting themselves. If it were to be lost, that would take a portion of our beliefs with it."

Adella said much the same thing: "The way I understand, the owl is not bad. The way it was told, and I think a lot of when you go to school . . . somewhere along the way these things get misinterpreted for you. But the owl is not bad in itself, he's only a messenger. You know, when he does come, he's telling you a message to do something, it's a warning to have a prayer or something done."

Harry Walters, director of the Ned Hatathli museum at Diné College, told Leroy: "These animals [the owl, the whippoorwill, the coyote] are not 'evil' in themselves. They are necessary to be a part of the whole. If they are eliminated, there won't be a whole."

John Redhouse likewise pointed out that the owl is an "evil" that has been deemed necessary for the benefit of the People: "Like death, like old age, you know, these are the things that keep us in balance."

Thus bolstered, Leroy sent his own letter to USFWS, asking them to please disregard "this enraging distortion of our traditional beliefs."

■|

When Monster Slayer had finished destroying all the great monsters that plagued the world, he went after the last four Nayéé', old age, cold, hunger and poverty. Changing Woman, Monster Slayer's mother, had told him where to find all the other monsters, but she refused to help him with these. "Perhaps it is better for all of us in the long run that certain enemies remain," she told her son.

But Monster Slayer had to find out on his own. On each of four visits to Old Age, to Cold, to Hunger, and to Poverty, Monster Slayer went with the intention of wiping each enemy out. "Is it not better that people die at length and pass their wisdom and their responsibilities to those who are younger?" argued Sá, the old woman called "Old Age." "Once I am dead it will always be hot on earth . . . the land will eventually dry up from exhaustion," said Hak'az asdzą́ą́ the Cold Woman. "If we were to be slain," said the old man and old woman Poverty Creatures, "[people] would have no reason to replace anything, no cause to improve upon the tools they are accustomed to using." "If you kill us," said the twelve ravenous creatures of Hunger, "people will lose their taste for food. . . . But if we live, they will continue to plant seeds and harvest crops. They will care about livestock . . . and remain skilled hunters." Thus, each convinced Monster Slayer that people would be better off if some "evil" were left in the world.[15]

■|

It was becoming depressingly clear to all of them. They were going to have to mount another timber-sale appeal, possibly even a lawsuit.

Leroy knew this meant it was time to start beating the bushes for money and legal assistance. He was hoping that this time around, they might be able to get a little weight behind them, perhaps one of the major environmental organizations. He traveled to Denver to meet with the Land and Water Fund and the Sierra Club Legal Defense Fund. He was hopeful that with this kind of weight behind them, the people of the mountains might make their voices heard.

It soon became evident, however, that the mainstream national organizations simply were not willing to stick their necks out for a small group of Indian people, especially when it meant taking a stand against a tribal government—a high-risk proposition from a PR perspective that would look too much like meddling with tribal sovereignty. While staff members at Land and Water Fund expressed an interest in Leroy's cause, they were prevented from getting involved by their board of directors. For their part, representatives of the Sierra Club Legal Defense Fund gave him no hope at all.

"They told me they just don't understand this sovereignty business," Leroy said with considerable discouragement when he returned. "They don't want to get involved with a bunch of Indios fighting each other."

In the middle of this increasingly grim situation, new opportunities dawned unexpectedly. Sometimes fault lines shift almost overnight. In July of 1993, Leroy was cautiously approached by a small group of contractors to NFPI, including loggers and log haulers, as well as some members of NFPI's own payroll, workers from the mill. They, too, had had enough of the mill's board and management.

The workers invited Leroy to an evening meeting in Crystal, New Mexico, in the heart of the Chuskas, the place where many loggers and mill workers happened to live. Crystal was the only chapter in the area that had not passed a resolution supporting the efforts of Diné CARE. It was also the chapter where the effigy of Leroy had been hung and set afire only a year before.

Leroy was eager to hear the loggers and mill workers out. Adella was suspicious.

"You can't go up there," she told him. "How do you know they don't want to ambush you?" She was only half joking.

"Sheeuh," he told her with a grin. "Those big old loggers couldn't get the drop on me."

"I'm going with you."

"Great. My wife has to come along to protect me from a bunch of loggers."

So, on a warm July evening after Adella got off work and fed the kids, they made the thirty-mile drive up to Crystal. They pulled in at the chapter house to find that most of the loggers and mill workers had already arrived—their beefy pickups were parked out front.

There was no ambush that evening. They did, however, encounter a litany of complaints against mill policies and management that ran well into the night. Mill employees complained of poor safety conditions at the plants, no drinking water, toilets that didn't work, and long shifts with no breaks. Loggers—contractors to NFPI—reported being stiff-armed by the mill over credit and charged extortion-like prices for equipment. One logger showed Diné CARE a paycheck which, for over one hundred hours of work, after deductions for his saw and fuel (both purchased from company stores) amounted to net pay of less than three dollars.

"What do you want from us?" Leroy asked the workers. "We're here to protect the forest."

"We want to get rid of NFPI's management," the workers told him. "You can help us." With Leroy and Adella's assistance, the forestry workers drafted a resolution calling on the Navajo Nation Council to resolve once and for all the problems facing the Navajo forests. The resolution asked that NFPI be subjected to a thorough historical audit, and that management be carefully reviewed. It also requested that the tribe extend a greater effort to identify alternative industries for employing displaced timber-industry workers, and requested retraining programs based on the model of what had happened with displaced timber workers in the Pacific Northwest. All of these ideas, of course, were Leroy's. The loggers needed his coaching, but they were fully in favor. The resolution was drafted and submitted to the council the following week.

Leroy and Adella returned from that meeting encouraged that more people were beginning to realize the depths of the problems at NFPI. At the same time, they remained guarded about the possibilities of really working with loggers and mill workers. Beneath all the complaints and rhetoric, these people continued to echo one simple sentiment. Keith Little, a logging contractor for NFPI, put it the most directly: "We just want to get back to work." None of them seemed to grasp what Leroy and Adella already knew: things had to change—logging as NFPI had known it had no future on the Rez.

With no outside funding and a vague sense of growing support on the ground, Diné CARE decided to schedule another Spiritual Gathering in the mountains, this time at Adella's summer campsite.

ten

When the alien monsters had all been destroyed, when Changing Woman had gone to her home out on the shimmering waters far to the West, White Shell Woman returned to the waters near the place of emergence, where she stayed for five days. She was very lonely. On the morning of the fifth day, in the early dawn, she heard the voice of Haasch'ééłti'í, Talking God, calling in his usual way: "Wu'hu'hu'hú."

White Shell Woman related to Talking God the story of her survival amidst the alien monsters, and told him of her current lonely condition.

Talking God took pity on her. "Remain where you are for four more days," he told her, "and I shall return with your sister, Changing Woman, the divine ones of all the great mountains, and other gods with me." When he left, she built for herself a good hut with a storm door. She swept the floor clean, and made a comfortable bed of soft grass and leaves.

At dawn on the fourth day the gods returned as promised. There were many of them. Talking God laid the sacred blankets on the ground, and spread on top of these one of the sacred buckskins with its head to the west. Talking God took two ears of corn, and did not immediately place them on the buckskin with their heads to the east, but rather nearly placed them four times, with their heads facing to the south, the west and the north, as well as the east—each time alternating his own call with the call of Haasch'éé' ooghaan, the Growling God. So the ears were turned in every direction, and this is the reason the Diné never abide in one home like the Pueblos, but wander ever from place to place. Over the ears of corn he laid the other sacred buckskin with its head to the east, and then Wind entered between the buckskins.

Four times, at intervals, Talking God raised the buckskins a little and peeked in. When he looked the fourth time, he saw that the white ear of corn was changed to a man, and the yellow ear to a woman. It was Wind who gave them the breath *of life. He entered at the heads and came out at the ends of the fingers and toes, and to this day we see his trail in the tip of every human finger.*

The Rock Crystal Boy furnished them with mind, and the Grasshopper Girl gave them voices. When Talking God at last threw off the buckskin, a dark cloud descended and covered like a blanket the forms of the new pair. White Shell Woman led them into her hogan, and the assembled gods dispersed.

No songs were sung and no prayers uttered during their rites, and the work was done in one day. The hogan near which all these things happened still stands; but since that time it has been transformed into a little hill. Seven times old age has killed since this pair was made by the holy ones from the ears of corn.

From these people are descended the clan of the House of the Dark Cliffs, so named because the gods who created the first pair came from the cliff houses of Tségíhi, and brought from there the ears of corn from which this first pair was made.

—Adapted from Matthews, *Navaho Legends*

∎/

Directly down from the summer site of Adella's family, in a little depression just across the highway, a cold water spring comes from deep beneath the Chuskas. These waters have been used by locals for generations both for human needs and to water livestock. Several years ago the spring was enclosed by a well and is now serviced by a heavy iron pump.

Adella's brother James and the anthropologist had arrived at the spring with several large blue plastic barrels, which they intended to fill with water and haul back up the mountain in preparation for the following day's Spiritual Gathering. It was a hot day, and they had already spent much of it doing the kind of manual work that is inevitably required for a large outdoor gathering, including digging large pits for the latrines, peeling logs for the ramada and lashing them together, gathering firewood, and a host of other chores.

James took off his big cowboy hat. He grabbed the pump handle and leaned into the flow of water. He released the handle and cupped his hands as the water continued to flow. The water made a gentle splashing noise on the pebbles beneath the tap. He lifted his hands to his face and drank.

"I like this water," he said. "The tap water at Adella's house [the house by the clinic] has too many chemicals. You can taste the chlorine. But this water, it's real pure. It tastes sweet."

The anthropologist took his turn, leaning into the flowing water. It was cool on his scalp and sunburned neck. He cupped his hands and filled them with water, closed his eyes and drank. For just one moment, everything was suddenly still. No birds sang. No trees swayed in the summer breeze. There was only the cool water.

He opened his eyes again. James was smiling at him—a huge, broad smile. His whole face was smiling in the bright sunlight.

"Now you're drinkin' like a Navajo," James said.

Leroy, the Bambina, and Eli soon arrived. As they all bounced back up the logging roads to the homesite, Adella's big truck—her *chidí*—pitched and skidded wildly. A summer rainstorm had passed through the night before, leaving the logging roads in several inches of mud. Leroy wasn't a reckless driver, but he had to keep his momentum going or risk getting stuck in the mud and the "sugar sand" that had washed down the mountain slopes in increasing amounts since the logging roads were cut.

They reached an intersection with another abandoned dirt road. Passing pickups had carved a couple deep channels in the mud. Leroy gunned the engine, and they slid and bounced through. The struts on Adella's pickup were very stout. Eli and the Bambina squealed with delight as they were knocked off their jump seats in the back of the cab.

"Go faster!" the Bambina squealed with delight.

"Cowabunga, dude!" Eli said in an imitation of the Teenage Mutant Ninja Turtles (they were at the age where they had become quite fond of reciting long stretches of dialogue from their favorite cartoons and movies. Eli in particular seemed to have an uncanny knack for it).

They passed great splintered stumps and towering piles of slash that had been left by the loggers two years earlier. This was the same view that had first inspired Leroy and Adella to begin their opposition to commercial forestry back in the summer of 1991.

Leroy laughed as he reminisced, "You know, when I first got started in this whole forestry thing, I thought I would set aside one month, maybe two or three at the most, to do it. I figured then everything would be straightened out and I could get back to my trading business." He had no idea even how to begin, let alone what it would entail. By this time, it had been two years since he and Adella first saw the damage and decided to do something about it, and no end seemed in sight.

In a journal Leroy had kept during his time as a forestry activist, amidst the detailed notes about meetings with politicians from Window Rock or lawyers from Santa Fe, he had interspersed personal reflections on any number of topics—the work, his own state of mind, the forests. Amidst the daily details, the notes about meetings, the privately aired complaints (meant for no one else's eyes), and the various other jottings, was a stark declaration that seemed to both explain Leroy's stamina and put every other journal entry into context. Near the bottom of one page he simply wrote: "I know now that I was born for this."

■/

When they returned to the camp, most of the other preparations had already been completed. Members of the Core Group had begun to arrive, as usual with their children in tow. Bruce Baizel, who had left his job with Forest Trust so he could work with Diné CARE more directly, had traveled down to help them plan their legal strategies.

He stood near the edge of a ramada they had just repaired. It was covered with two large, blue tarps that provided some shade and (partial) shelter from the rain. Next to him was a blackboard Lori had hauled from Colorado, covered with diagrams and acronyms. "I think our prospects look a little better this time," Bruce said, referring to the possibility of an appeal. The new undersecretary of the Interior for Indian Affairs (head of BIA), Ada Deer, seemed to show a little more empathy with community-based groups than her predecessors.

John Redhouse next rose and stood in front of the group. The clarity of his vision of this struggle was always impressive. "One thing we have to face," he said, "is the possibility of the mill's closing. The people of the mill want to frame this thing as trees versus jobs. This is not about trees versus jobs. Don't let the mill people impose this way of thinking about it. The real issue here is defending our sacred mountain."

They all sat in silence as John talked about tribal politics, allies and enemies, contingencies and possible outcomes. A summer storm began to gather—a few large rain drops pelted the tarp above their heads with crisp little puffs. Gusts of wind kicked up. The patter of rain and the rustling of the plastic in the wind began to make it difficult to hear. John raised his voice to compensate.

"We need to think about what all this is going to mean for Leroy in the coming weeks and months," John said, almost shouting. Suddenly the sky opened up with a vengeance. A thunderbolt struck the ground no more than two hundred yards away with a deafening crack. A powerful gust shook one corner of their makeshift roof free and the rains started to pour. They all scrambled, laughing and rapidly getting soaked, for the safety of the hogan. They would have to wait to learn about Leroy's fate.

■|

Many years passed. The people of the House of Dark Cliffs clan saw no other living people in all this time. Then, one night, they spotted the distant sparkle of a firelight. The following day, they explored the place where they thought the firelight came from, but they could find no one. Four nights the people saw this distant fire, but each day, when they searched for its source, they found no other people. Finally, the Wind whispered to one of the searchers, telling him the desert terrain was deceiving their eyes. Wind directed them to a cleft in the mountains. "And before they had gone far over the ridge he spoke about, they spied the footprints of adult men." Then they found footprints of women, then of children. "Then, at last, to the surprise of none of them by that time, they came to a small encampment of five-fingered Earth Surface People like themselves.

"One party rejoiced as much as the other. They embraced each other and hurled greetings back and forth."

And so it went. The original group of people was joined by bands from many places. They were joined by the people of the Grey Streak clan, the people of the

Dark Streak of Wood clan, the people of the Water's Edge clan, the people of the Traveler's Circle Mountain clan, and many others.

"Earlier the Navajo had been a small and a weak people. But now they found themselves numerous and strong. Some among them, especially the younger men, began to observe their increased numbers and their added strength. And now and then they talked of making war."[1]

■/

The morning of the second Spiritual Gathering dawned cool, and moisture still hung in the air from the previous night's storm. They sat huddled near the fire, still trying to emerge from a short night's sleep. Small pools of water had accumulated in the depressions of the tarp that covered the shelter. Anyone unlucky enough to be sitting near the edge of it when a breeze blew by risked being doused. Lori's boys, along with Eli and the Bambina, found this very amusing and did their best to arrange people accordingly.

"Sit here," they said to anyone foolish enough to listen (for example, an anthropologist). "It's the best seat."

Adella, Leroy, and Ray sat quietly near the fire nursing cups of dangerously strong black coffee. Ray was unhappy with the early turnout. "I don't know why more of the medicine people don't come to this. They should be here." He thought about calling his son, who worked for the roads commission and knew how to operate a grader.

Adella looked very tired. The previous night, she had sat with Leroy back down at the house by the clinic in the dim light of the kitchen, until well after the kids were asleep. "I think I need to step back from this forestry stuff for a while," she said.

They found themselves called away from home more and more to attend chapter meetings, to visit elders, to meet with the rest of the Core Group or to solicit outsiders for necessary resources. Leroy was always on the road. Adella was working full time at the clinic and doing all the activist work in the evenings.

Leroy had once said, "My kids are my power. I guess a white person would say my hope. Bilagáanas want to leave their kids money. I want to leave my kids that forest and those mountains." The irony of it was, the work they did for their children was taking them away from their children.

Adella had risen early the next morning, long before she needed to, to get ready for the day's event. "Really," she joked later with Lori, "I just wanted to sneak out into the living room to see what John Redhouse looked like without his sunglasses on." John had spent the night on their couch. No one in Diné CARE's Core Group had ever seen him out from behind his shades.

Adella was not to be the first. "He was already awake when I came out," she complained.

Meanwhile, people were gradually beginning to arrive. The atmosphere was far different from that of the year before. The crowd was not limited to elders and herbalists from the mountains. Loggers and mill workers were also showing up. At first there were only a few; they kept their distance, drinking coffee and hanging around their trucks parked at a safe distance.

Then there were a few odd and unexpected attendees. An Italian film crew had managed to find their way, although no one could figure out exactly how. Without a lot of fuss Adella's sisters fixed up the Italians with breakfast, along with that strong coffee that they probably appreciated, being from the land of espresso themselves. The first person the Italians spotted was Earl, who had risen early and sat facing the morning sun on a tiny stool. He was not an unusually tall man, but he had a large and sturdy frame. His arms were folded across his chest. On one wrist was a thick silver and turquoise bracelet. A red bandanna was tied around his head. Within minutes he was talking to the camera.

Another early arrival that day was Leroy's old friend Rudy. He and Leroy had been friends since their childhood days—a couple of young jokers who were always giving each other a bad time. Rudy was just about the most talkative guy around these parts, and a bit of a schemer. He had, in fact, talked a couple young Germans into giving him a ride.

The German couple were both clad in the standard accoutrement of the tragically hip—black denim and T-shirts. Their skin tone was blanched. The young man, whose name was Thorsten, was tall and astonishingly thin. He came from the Ruhr Valley, a dense extended metropolis of industrialization in the heart of Germany. His girlfriend, Jäquie, likewise tall but not nearly so emaciated, had auburn hair and pretty green eyes that were perpetually arched in an expression of sadness.

They were touring around Indian Country looking for a medicine man. They didn't know one personally. They had never actually seen one. But they were convinced that they needed to find one to help them "get their lives straightened out." Rudy had persuaded them to bring him up here with the vague promise that a medicine man might be at the gathering to help them.

There was, of course, no medicine man there to help them—this wasn't Taos or Sedona, after all. Still, Diné CARE welcomed the young couple with the same casual grace they had shown the Italians, fed them, and invited them to sit with everyone else around the fire. While they sat and ate, Thorsten spoke only a little (one time to remind the anthropologist of the "American people's" reprehensible record of relations with Indians). Jäquie did not speak at all.

At the time, they seemed odd, a little pathetic—even mildly amusing. It was only later that it became apparent that the problem from which they were hoping to "straighten out" was not so funny. His complexion and build might have given it away sooner. A chance glimpse of his arm finally made it obvious: he was a junky. He had pinned all his hopes for escape from his demons on the romantic belief that somewhere out there was a medicine man who could help him break the bonds of a heroin addiction. It is astounding what desperate dreams the vastness of the American West can still harbor.

After nibbling a few bites and sitting with the group for a few hours, they wandered off and pitched their tent some distance away in the same meadow beneath the silent visage of Tsaile Peak. They hardly came out of that tent for the rest of the weekend. Then they left, looking as sad and dejected as when they arrived, and no one in Diné CARE ever saw or heard from them again. It is to be hoped they found their medicine man.

■|

The sun was fully up. Earl convened the Gathering with a prayer.

The first person to stand and speak at length was Louise Benally. She came from Big Mountain, a place from which she and other Navajo families have been ordered evicted pursuant to a long and rather complicated legislative and judicial history that has ruled that these lands belong to the Hopi people. Many readers may be somewhat familiar with the so called "Navajo-Hopi land dispute," which has been painted as a "longstanding" issue between the two tribes. In fact, the conflict can more accurately be traced to demand for the region's rich deposits of low-sulfur coal.[2]

Louise was a resister. She refused to be relocated. Living in a crumbling shack that has been legally barred from capital improvements, prohibited by law to raise stock or even to gather firewood, Louise remained on the land because of a promise she made to her father and grandfather (both since deceased) when she was only thirteen years old.

Oddly, because of her stand, she had become something of a celebrity. An odd assortment of people from around the country—college kids, mostly—routinely gathered in tents, old campers, and buses around Louise's home in Big Mountain. Some of them actually provided assistance—writing letters, transporting clothing or food to local families, or even just hauling safe drinking water. Others show up just to be part of something hip and politically correct and to participate in drum circles.

The effects of all this political tourism on the locals, who must remain to pick up the mess, have not always been positive or productive. Outsiders sometimes provoke resentment on both sides of the issue, and other times are simply a distraction. One poor old woman, Louise once reported, had been scared half to death one afternoon by the horrifying specter of a young white man—one of the "volunteers"—chasing after a herd of sheep without a single stitch of clothing on his body. As a rule, the Diné are a modest people. There is probably nothing in that poor old woman's life that could have prepared her for such an awful vision.

Louise was accompanied to the Gathering that day by a group of young activists from Flagstaff. "This place is a paradise," she said to the gathered audience that morning, looking out from under the dripping tarp in wonderment at the mountains that surrounded her. "I just imagine if I lived here. I'd have peach trees, and lots of fat sheep. Where I live it's dry and hard. We could never think of having those things.

"Shame on you people for wanting to cut all this down."

Meanwhile, the bashful first few mill workers and loggers had now become a critical mass, and they wandered into the ramada to officially join the gathering. At first they took their seats and listened quietly to the talks.

Soon the first of them took the floor. They stood up one by one and once again aired their long list of grievances—working conditions at the mill, logging contracts, their inability to make a living under current circumstances. As they had done in their earlier meeting with Leroy and Adella, the loggers and mill workers seemed to have two contradictory messages: they wanted Diné CARE to push for reform, while they simultaneously asked Diné CARE to help them "get back to work."

In every talk, this mixed message came through with such consistency that at one point, in a very uncharacteristic fashion, Leroy could contain himself no longer. He interjected, rather testily, that he couldn't help them if they didn't even understand their situation clearly. He challenged them to think more creatively, to press the tribe for alternative forms of employment and retraining, and to help him explore economic alternatives in the forest. By this time, Leroy had been actively exploring the possibility of securing federal funds for forest-regeneration work. "There are millions of dollars out there from U.S. Soil and Conservation," he told the loggers. "Millions that could come to the Navajo Nation if we just show a little initiative and get together to reclaim this land."

In the afternoon, as the talks by the disgruntled loggers and mill workers wore on, Robert Billie, the acting head of Navajo Forestry, took Leroy aside. "You've won." He said. "We've answered your demands. There is now a Navajo running Navajo Forestry. We're going to do things right. You just have to give us some time to get there."

■/

Later that night, back down at the house in the clinic neighborhood, Leroy was troubled. He hadn't expected Robert Billie to approach him that way, and the loggers and mill workers had also affected him. For the first time since he started, he seemed at a loss.

On the counter in front of him sat a large, brown paper bag filled with mountain tobacco. "Adella's mom gathered this for me," he said. He creased a cigarette paper, deftly sprinkled some tobacco into it, and rolled himself a smoke. He offered the bag to the anthropologist and went over to the stove to get a light.

"I don't know," he said. "Maybe we should just give them time."

"Huh?" the anthropologist said. He was trying to roll his own cigarette. He fumbled with the paper and spilled some leaves into his lap.

"Maybe we should let them ease into it like Robert said . . ."

The anthropologist had by this time managed to produce a fat little wad in a cigarette paper that looked like a tiny, white, cherry bomb. Trying to emulate Leroy's example, he went to the stove. The bizarre shape of his cigarette made lighting it impossible. The empty paper sticking beyond the over-fattened wad quickly shriveled to a charred nothingness while the full burden of the tobacco refused to ignite. Then, in literally a flash, the anthropologist felt a sharp piercing in his nostril and right eyebrow. He jumped backwards as his brow was singed and smoking.

Leroy was deep in thought and didn't seem to notice. He was still thinking out loud. "But how long are they going to take? By the time they get it right, the forest will be gone."

The anthropologist, rubbing his face in pain, tried to follow Leroy's monologue. Pretty soon Adella came in with the kids and another load from the campsite. "What is that horrible smell?" she asked with a sour look on her face.

"It's your mom's tobacco," Leroy told her.

"It smells like burning hair," the Bambina said with her nose crinkled up.

■/

Two nights later, Diné CARE held their first conference call. It had not been long since all of the Core Group members had finally gotten telephones in their homes—a costly proposition but to them well worth it. Phone conferences, over the course of time, would become a key way for them to reach decisions on critical matters.

"OK. I guess are we all on now?" Lori asked after the operator had connected everyone.[3]

"Ao'"," Earl said in a way that was the Navajo equivalent of "yup," then he added, "ya bunch of high-tech Navajos."

Leroy got right to the point. "What caused me to really take a better look at this thing was Robert Billie," Leroy told the group. "During the Gathering Robert and I had a discussion on the appeal. He said they have gone to great lengths to, to appease all of Diné CARE's concerns. So, his thinking was, they did everything the way it should be done in the EA [environmental assessment], and, at that point, what are we going to appeal. That became a concern to me, because I could not respond in a technical manner, not legally or in biological forestry terms." But, he added, Bruce Baizel and Steve Sugarman had informed him that the USFWS found lots of problems with the way the environmental assessment had been prepared. "So that partially answered some of my concerns," Leroy concluded.

Anna Frazier was the next to speak. She started by explaining what she knew to be happening in Window Rock, which involved some detailed explanation. That was when the group had their first mishap with the technology.

After speaking for about five minutes, sometimes with fairly lengthy pauses in the middle, Anna suddenly stopped. "Is anyone on the line?" she asked, with a slight waver in her voice. They had all been listening so quietly, and with none of the visual cues of face-to-face interaction, Anna was suddenly struck with the horrible feeling that she might have been talking all that time to nothing but a dead phone line—a monologue to the emptiness of uninhabited cyberspace. It's happened to many of us, no doubt, but it's tempting to wonder, because they typically listen so quietly and are far less likely to interrupt one another, whether phone conferences among Navajo people might be more subject to this.

"We're here," the others all said finally, as they started laughing.

Anna was working at the time as a "special assistant" to Navajo Nation President Peterson Zah. The job had been offered to her completely out of the blue, a largely transparent attempt perhaps to follow the dictum of the Godfather: "keep your friends close but keep your enemies closer." She was clearly professionally qualified, but understandably suspicious, and only took the position when her fellow Diné CARE members urged her to do it and be an "ear to the ground" for the group.

Anna explained that NFPI had projected they would need over thirty-three million board feet from the Tó Ntsaa timber sale to address their debts and break even on the sale. That much timber would have constituted one of the single largest timber sales ever conducted in the Southwest. Navajo Forestry had publicly suggested the harvest would be roughly half of that. The tribe was not only trying to push a timber sale ahead, but they seemed to be lying about the actual amount, a figure that had purposely been left vague in the contract.

Meanwhile, Anna and Lori had both heard that the tribe was considering simply forgiving NFPI's debt—an amount that was now calculated at over six million dollars. They thought that that issue had been put to rest months before with the hearing on the stumpage fee payments.

Earl Tulley, who likewise had a constant ear to the ground in Window Rock, pointed out that Ed Richards, NFPI's general manager "doesn't really believe that we're going to do it. He doesn't think we're capable of doing it. And that's what he's playing Russian roulette with, he's trying to manufacture the thought that, you know, 'these guys are only talking big.'"

John Redhouse reminded the Core Group members of the fact that over a dozen people had come forth from the Tó Ntsaa area wanting to have their names listed as appellants: "The negotiations, the meetings, all this other stuff that we've done for the past two years, has resulted in, really, in nothing. We have some responsibility to the people who live in the area and who are sticking their necks out as appellants."

With that, Leroy put it to the group: "So, my question, my concern right now is, do we take—do we go for the appeal and maybe cause these guys to collapse right here in the near future, or do we let them have their way, and just phase out?"

Earl was the first to respond. "I guess my heart is in a sense that, somewhere along the line, we have to say 'enough!'"

Lori Goodman agreed: "Another thing [I've been told] is that they're circulating a petition at NFPI, making their workers sign it, that an EA is not necessary. Then with this debt forgiveness, I think they're just laughing. They'll just go on and on. I think they need to be stopped."

Sylvia Clahchischilli likewise agreed: "I think just to wait on them to turn things around, I mean, we've been doing that. I personally, I just want to go ahead with the appeal. I think maybe there's some apprehension about blame . . . but eventually that all dies, it all settles. Some day people will say, 'Hey yeah. That was a good thing.'"

Lucy Charlie admitted she still felt some concern for the loggers who would be displaced. "For me I am always having a heart, you know, for the employees, one of my concerns is for the people that will lose their jobs." She continued, however, by adding that the reasons to appeal still outweighed that concern in her mind. "But, you know, there's not really any good points for not going through with the appeal. We have to have our own people out there being able to say what's best for everybody, not just a few people in Window Rock."

Finally, Adella, who had been listening with Leroy, took the phone. "For some reason, Robert (Billie) has always been up front with us, and when he said, you know, 'wait for us to get there,' I really thought about that, too. And, I guess for my part, I thought why should we take all the blame when they're going to die out anyway. Plus it's a lot of work going back up there into the mountains, with the notary public and all.[4] But, the other thing that I realize when I go up the mountains to those people that are going to be impacted is, they say, you know, 'go for it. Do it. We support you. You're there to help us and we want you to do something.'

"That's the thing that's in my mind and my heart when I feel like maybe it's time to give it up. I remember that there's fourteen chapters that want this to happen, and all those old people, and the way their lives are impacted, and their beliefs are impacted, that we should do something. There's a lot of people that don't understand exactly what's happening, that don't understand the impact they're having on the traditional people, these people that still have their culture, still have their beliefs, that are still self-sufficient, they're really killing off these people just for a few remaining employees of the mill. I think we do owe these people, they want to go ahead with the appeal."

With that it was decided. They would go ahead with the appeal and the possible consequences it might have, both on NFPI and on their own organization.

eleven

Lori Goodman sat comfortably behind the wheel of a great hulking Chevy Suburban and traced a familiar path from her home in southern Colorado through Shiprock, New Mexico, past the northern ridge of the Carrizo Mountains, the communities of Teec Nos Pos and Mexican Water, past the turnoff to Blanding, Utah.

"Mom, tell Seth to stop looking at me." It was Mike, the third of her four boys.

"Sethie, are you pestering your brother?"

"I'm not doing anything."

"Yes you are. Mom, he's looking at me with puppy dog eyes."

"Where are we going, anyway?" asked Seth, the youngest.

"To your grandparents' for a ceremony."

"It's not for the trees?" asked Mike.

Lori laughed. "No, not something for the trees this time."

Lori's youngest three sons were in grades seven, six, and four at the time and routinely made trips with her to the Rez. These many hours on the road made for frequent backseat battles, but Lori had a strategy: hitchhikers. "They're a lot quieter with a stranger in the car," she commented with a laugh. Although hitchhiking is still more common and far safer on the Rez than most other places in the United States, there's no telling how many local hitchhikers have been scared out of their wits by Lori's driving—which, quite frankly, is like a bat out of hell. Most of the smart ones have probably learned to keep walking when they see that big Suburban coming their way.

Lori's extra passenger that day was not a hitchhiker, however, but an intern from the local college, a young woman who would eventually become (in quite typical fashion) Lori's adopted daughter. "People may have one-night stands with other organizations," Earl Tulley had once joked with the intern, "but Diné CARE is a long-term relationship." He wasn't kidding, although at that point no one could have guessed that in a couple years she would wind up married into Diné CARE . . . in a manner of speaking.

Lori, her boys, and the intern were on their way to gather the extended family for an Enemy Way ceremony that was scheduled to be performed for Lori's dad. The Enemy Way is a major undertaking. Lasting multiple days and nights, it is both a complicated healing ceremony and a major social gathering, including an event that, not unlike weddings in Anglo-American culture, provides a widely recognized way to meet members of the opposite sex. Owing to this social element, the events have become known as "Squaw Dances." During summer months one will often see the hand-painted signs for SQUAW DANCE at any number of places around the Rez.

Apart from all the socializing is the more sequestered healing ceremony itself, a rite held to exorcise Diné warriors of the ghosts of those they've killed in battle and to restore them to health and harmony. The ceremony is offered, by extension, to cure any Diné who has come in contact with foreign elements that may have caused sickness.

It was not long after they arrived at the grounds of the ceremony that Lori was scolded by her mother. "Don't ask them if they're hungry," she said to her daughter, "just give them the food." Guests had arrived from all over the area—they were not only relatives or close friends. Chastened, Lori turned and piled the plate of each guest with roasted mutton, potatoes, corn, beans, salad, and fry bread. She didn't ask anyone if he or she were hungry.

An elderly Navajo woman leaned over toward the intern, who was peeling potatoes, and said something in Navajo. The intern looked at the woman, blushing a little, not knowing how to communicate the fact that she didn't speak any Navajo.

Lori laughed. "She's not Navajo, she's Eskimo."

"And Filipino and Irish," the intern added.

The women all laughed at the mistake, and continued to laugh as they looked more closely at the dark-skinned intern.

"She really looks Navajo," they said to each other, and giggled some more.

Robert Joe was suffering from liver cancer. At the time no one suspected a possible relationship between this cancer and the extensive mining of uranium on the Navajo Nation. It was only a year or so later, at his funeral, that Lori found out that the cancer that claimed his life had claimed the lives of ten of his relatives, all of whom had grown up herding sheep near uranium mines. "I only found this out because it was a funeral," she explained. "Navajos don't talk about the dead, except for four days following a death. That taboo has kept us from finding out that a lot of our people are dying of the same things."

Large-scale uranium mining on the Navajo Nation is as old as the atomic energy program in the United States. In the early 1940s deposits of carnotite (a mineral containing both vanadium and uranium) were found in Monument Valley and the Carrizo Mountains, attracting the attention of the U.S. government. From 1942 to 1945, over eleven thousand tons of uranium-bearing ore were mined at Monument Valley. Diné men were already supporting the American war effort as soldiers and Code Talkers; they now extended their war contribution as uranium miners. The ore was trucked to Durango, Colorado, where it was milled into yellowcake, then transported to Los Alamos, New Mexico, where the Defense Department used it to make the first three atomic bombs.[1]

From 1946 to 1968, over thirteen million tons of uranium ore were mined on the Navajo Reservation by such companies as the Vanadium Corporation of America, Kerr-McGee, AMEX, and Climax, all under contract with the Department of Defense and the Department of Energy.[2] Areas on and near Navajo lands, including the Grants Mineral Belt and the San Juan Basin of New Mexico were the sites of "the heaviest uranium exploration, mining and milling activity" in the entire United States.[3]

Miners were exposed to small but steady doses of radiation, which have been found to be a higher risk than single large doses. The primary dangers of such exposure were "radon daughters"—unstable isotopes resulting from the decay of radon gas—and radioactive dust from the mined rocks. Such exposure has been shown to cause a variety of respiratory diseases in miners. Other risks associated with exposure to uranium and radon included cancers of the kidneys, liver, pancreas, bile ducts, pharynx, thyroid, stomach, and esophagus, as well as multiple myeloma, lymphomas, and leukemia.[4]

Miners spent shifts of up to thirteen hours underground. "In the worst cases, they were exceeding allowable weekly doses in less than one day, and were reaching total annual doses in just a week."[5] They took meal breaks in the mines, and even drank the water that dripped from the walls. Miners were rarely issued masks or other protective apparatus, especially in the early days. They were never informed of the dangers that radiation posed to their health, in spite of the fact that, by 1950, many of the hazards were already known—as evidenced by a Public Health Service engineer's report from that year that raised the concern that Navajo miners were exposed to dangerous levels of radiation.[6]

Mining continued on the Navajo Nation until well into the 1970s. Those miners who are still alive (hundreds have died) suffer not only from lung disease but from other forms of cancer and other diseases, open sores that will not heal, hair loss, and other skin conditions.

After a decade of advocacy and a handful of unsuccessful lawsuits, a few Navajo miners found some relief in the 1990 Radiation Exposure Compensation Act. RECA's original intent was to provide "compassionate payments" to ailing former miners, but as of 1992 (in fact, throughout the 1990s) only a small number of those harmed by radiation received any form of relief.

RECA claimants faced stringent requirements for documentation, put into place and enforced by the U.S. Department of Justice.[7] Only one particular type of lung disease was covered by the act, and standard chest X-rays, the only imaging technique accessible on the reservation, have been shown to be unreliable in diagnosing it. CAT scans, which have proven more reliable in identifying the disease, have not been available anywhere nearer than Albuquerque, and thus have been out of reach for most former miners.[8] Miners were also required to document that they spent two hundred "working months" in the mines between the years 1947 and 1971.[9] Those with fewer hours, or who performed any work in the mines outside this range of time, are considered ineligible for consideration (thus giving rise to a whole class of former miners known as the "Post-'71" miners). Providing the working months documentation proved difficult for a large number of miners, since records were poor in the early days of the mines. Smokers—any Navajos who admitted consuming tobacco even in

John W. Sherry

ceremonial uses were classified as "smokers"—have to prove minimum radiation-exposure levels of five hundred working months.

For those who did manage to meet the full burden of proof, there was still no guarantee of timely action. As recently as 1996, non-Indians were being certified for compensation an average of two to three times faster than Navajos.[10] By the end of the 1990s, about five hundred claims had been filed by Navajo miners, and only a fraction of those had resulted in settlements. Processing has taken up to four years in some cases. Many miners have died waiting for their settlement checks to arrive.[11] Widows of the miners who have died from the covered, radiation-caused lung disease are nominally eligible for payments under RECA. However, to qualify they are required to produce state marriage licenses—those married in traditional Navajo ceremonies are thus all but ineligible.[12]

Perhaps most importantly, the original act covered only miners. As later evidence would suggest, other Diné were at risk from other means of exposure. Uranium millers, those who processed the ore into yellowcake, were likewise exposed to harmful levels of radiation. Four major milling sites were operated on the Navajo Nation during the cold war years. The resulting debris from these sites, called "tailings," contained many harmful nuclides, including radium 226, which is especially toxic. Several million tons of radioactive tailings remain in place to this day.[13]

As of 1993, there were over six hundred radiologically contaminated dwellings on Navajo tribal lands.[14] Miners brought home work clothes covered with radioactive dust, hanging them inside their tiny hogans where all the family ate and slept. They shared wash basins in homes with no indoor plumbing. Many families living near mines or milling sites, never warned of the dangers, used easily accessible radioactive rocks to build dwellings. Their children played on the tailings. Water draining from these sites filled cisterns from which their livestock drank, or was even used by families for consumption and cooking.[15]

More recent years have seen Diné CARE's uranium efforts intensify. U.S.-government disclosures in the mid 1990s began to reveal the extent of America's cold war contamination. Between 1994 and 1996, a $22-million federal study revealed the U.S. government's culpability in cold war radiation experiments from Alaska to New England.[16]

In 1997, the National Cancer Institute concluded a fourteen-year study showing that the entire United States was exposed to radioactive Iodine 131 (linked to thyroid cancer) through the fallout of nuclear tests in Nevada. This latter study documented how, between 1951 and 1962, the U.S. government conducted some one hundred atmospheric (aboveground) tests of nuclear devices at the Nevada Test Site north of Las Vegas.[17] "Downwinders" of atmospheric tests were at risk primarily through the ingestion of dairy products. These new disclosures only added to the growing alarm over what was already known about unreclaimed mines, mill sites, and other dangers on the Navajo Nation.

Reproductive disorders similar to those reported among people of the Marshall Islands in the South Pacific, who were also subjected to massive radiation exposure from cold war atmospheric tests, have been documented on the Navajo Nation.[18] Cancers of the internal organs, leukemia, and a variety of other diseases that may be traceable to radiation exposure have occurred among Navajos in what some have called "pandemic" proportions. A rare kidney disease, Ig A nephropathy, which some have linked to environmental toxins, has been identified in unusually high rates among Diné populations in the Four Corners area, and Navajo teens have been noted to have an incidence of cancer of the reproductive organs seventeen times higher than the national average.[19]

But in 1992, Lori's education in the effects and politics of radiation were only just beginning. John Redhouse had been invited in the fall of that year to Salzburg, Austria, as part of a contingent of Navajo people attending the World Indigenous People's Uranium Forum, an event organized to allow a wide variety of native people from around the world to tell their stories (many of them horror stories of above-ground tests, mining, and the like) to a panel of "listeners" from the mainstream. John declined to attend, but sent Lori in his place. "It will be a good learning experience," he told her. ("He was right in ways I never imagined," she recalled later.)

It was on this trip that Lori first got to know Phil Harrison, who had begun a long career of advocacy on behalf of uranium miners after he lost his own father in the late 1970s to lung disease caused by work in uranium mines.

Beginning with that conference in 1992, Diné CARE embarked on what would become its most ambitious undertaking. Their goals were to change the Radiation Exposure Compensation Act (RECA) to broaden it to include a greater number of radiation victims, and to make it easier for claimants to actually collect on what Congress had originally deemed "compassionate payments" to cold war victims.

This effort would ultimately require close collaboration with non-Diné on a scale far greater than any of their other projects to date. Hopi, Acoma, and Laguna communities have also suffered from exposure to uranium mining, as have non-Indian miners from all over the American Southwest and beyond. Radiation has not only affected the Diné.

Among the more stirring moments at the Uranium Conference was the address given by Hopi elder Thomas Benyacya, in which he recounted teachings passed to him back in the 1940s by elders long since departed:

But when our white brothers make this gourd full of ashes, it's more like this there on Hiroshima and Nagasaki and burned over 200,000 families in a few seconds. Everything burned up. Many living things died from heat in the water. The Hopi people were talking about this, and I was amazed they described that without even reading books or can't even read, speak English, but there in the Hopi language they described exactly what happened at Hiroshima and Nagasaki, and they said that poison and ash will be floating there for many years. Many sickness will come out that medicine will not be able to cure them.[20]

Salzburg, the site of the forum and the picturesque setting for *The Sound of Music*, lies nestled in the foothills of the Alps, with history and architecture covering virtually every era from Roman occupation through the present. On an imposing hill that looms above the oldest part of the city stands a magnificent medieval fortress. It overlooks a walking district full of quaint shops, cafés, and restaurants; even the local McDonald's (which opened only after a prolonged and heated civic debate) was tastefully and discreetly tucked away.

Lori's reaction to the place was mildly shocking: "I hated it," she said flatly.

It was not exactly the town she hated. None of the Navajo contingent actually got to enjoy much of it. Every time they stepped out of their hotel, they were set upon by what Lori could only describe as "groupies"— a strange and slightly wretched mob of New Agers, "Wannabes," curiosity seekers, lost souls, and a variety of others who had descended upon Salzburg in the hopes of getting close to some exotic "Indigenous People."

"We literally had to run from the hotel to the conference. They would chase us and they're all saying 'Oh, Oh! I can feel the power emanating from you,' and they would try to touch us."

"'Leave me alone," I kept telling them. "I'm just a housewife." The Navajos' only choice was to hide out in their hotel room and wait for the conference to end.

Anthropologist Victor Turner called it "the spiritual power of the structurally inferior."[21] It is a surprisingly widespread phenomenon, this sense that the marginalized and the dispossessed, people living outside the normal structures of society, have access to spiritual resources and insight that the more economically and socially privileged do not.

The world's "wild people" have throughout much of history been on the receiving end of this curious act of attribution. For the Greeks living in Hellenic city-states, it was the Arcadians. Ibn Khaldun, the fourteenth-century Arab philosopher, writes of the superior moral character of the nomadic Bedouin compared to their sedentary relatives in the cities.[22] But without doubt none of them poured it on with the gusto that western Europeans have done to America's indigenous people. Blame Jean-Jacques Rousseau's "Noble Savage," or German author Karl May (who romanticized American Indians in countless popular paperbacks), or the whole juggernaut of New Age beliefs and merchandising. Whatever the causes, the market for "Native American Spirituality" seems insatiable.[23]

Salzburg was not the end of the problems. After the conference, the Navajo group went to Munich, to meet with members of an organization that had partly underwritten their trip. This organization, it turns out, was composed primarily of "Hobbyists," a surprisingly popular phenomenon in Germany wherein members get together to "play Indian." According to some reports, there are as many as sixty thousand Germans belonging to clubs whose members can live in teepees, participate in sweat-lodge ceremonies, or pursue other activities, including crafts such as the making of Indian-style jewelry or clothing.[24]

The Diné contingency was not long at the Hobbyists' camp before the situation began to turn a little strange. One of the hosts greeted them with a speech denouncing the atrocities of the U.S. government against Native Americans. The oration apparently met with great approval by the other Hobbyists, but did not elicit the desired response from the Navajo guests. Anna Rondon, at the time head of the Navajo Nation Environmental Protection Agency, chided them: "The time for this kind of finger-pointing is long past. First of all, who are these 'Americans' but transplanted Europeans? Second, this part of the world doesn't exactly have a sparkling human rights record. We are here so that today's problems can be solved, not so we can feel good about whose fault things are."

Her response apparently cast a wet blanket over the affair. It was bad enough the Navajo visitors wouldn't go along with the American-bashing, but the allusion to Germany's human rights record was particularly stinging.

After a meal and some awkward conversation, the Hobbyists pressed their guests to share their spiritual wisdom. Sensitized by the Salzburg experience, Lori had had enough. "Look," she told the group. "I am a housewife. I am not a medicine person. It's all inside you. You have your own traditions which tell you about this better than I could. I don't have any special spiritual wisdom to share with you people."

Once again, this response was entirely out of line with what the hosts were expecting. "Please, we ask you, as a favor to us in return for helping to bring you over here. Just share some of your spiritual knowledge with us."

This exchange apparently continued for more than a few minutes, much to the exasperation of both sides, when a self-proclaimed Tai Chi master (also a guest at the camp) intervened. Taking the Navajo contingency aside, he counseled them privately: "This can be very lucrative for you, if you just give these people what they want."

"At that point," Lori said, "we were out of there."

Their Diné heritage has become a stumbling block for all kinds of outside groups. At another uranium-related conference, one of the organizers, a prominent American physicist, put Lori on the spot: "The first thing he did was come up to me and start crying. 'Oh I am so sorry for what my people have done to your people.'" She laughed as she talked about it. "I had to tell him just to get over it. 'Please. I don't hold you personally responsible for what happened to my ancestors.'"

On numerous occasions, people with whom Diné CARE members would have liked to collaborate first had to be "educated" (as Lori put it) that, just because they were Indian people, they were neither necessarily victims nor somehow "dysfunctional." Lori recalled another bizarre conversation, this time with a staff member of a grant-making foundation.

> *Staff member:* Do you have a step program?
> *Lori:* Sometimes.
> *Staff:* Only "sometimes"? I don't understand.
> *Lori:* Well, sometimes I'll do aerobics, or sometimes I just go jogging, or take my boys to the park.
> *Staff:* No, not a "step aerobics program." A step program. Like AA.
> *Lori (now more confused):* "AA?" Well . . . we are on the road quite a bit, so we've tried to provide all our members with some sort of coverage. The roads of the Navajo Nation are mostly unpaved and isolated though, so we . . .
> *Staff:* Not "triple A." AA. Alcoholics Anonymous. You know, their twelve-step recovery program.
> *Lori (still confused, remains silent for a few moments):* Umm . . . what would we be recovering from?

"People want us to remain victims," Lori commented once. "So many of these outside groups want to 'help the poor Indians.' They want to 'do' something for us. We don't want anyone to 'do' anything for us. We can do for ourselves. We want to work *with* other groups, to cooperate as partners."

Thus it was with considerable trepidation that, some years later, Lori and the rest of Diné CARE became more deeply involved in the issue of radiation exposure and its inevitable pull toward all kinds of outside organizations and coalitions. "We are no longer interested in becoming a poster child for their funding efforts," Lori confided to Tom Goldtooth (her close friend and director of the Indigenous Environmental Network). "We are suspicious about people of color being recruited to help them solve their money problems. It could be a quagmire."

As they would all find out, it wasn't just people of color who were victimized either by silly misunderstandings or the inequities of the "funding game." In a battle no less vicious and more far flung than the conflict over the forests, Diné CARE would eventually join a coalition involving community people from around the Navajo Nation, from the Pueblos and many rural non-Indian people as well, as they attempted to wrestle control over the fate of reform of the Radiation Exposure Compensation Act from a few lawyers, well-placed government staffers, and others who had long "ridden herd" (in the words of one activist) on radiation survivors.

All of that, however, happened years after the gathering in Piñon, where her father's ceremony moved from early nights' purification to the restorative later nights, and the socializing and dancing were about to begin. Lori, protective mother that she was, packed up the intern and her boys and returned to Colorado.

When she got home, she heard from Adella that Leroy was missing.

twelve

"You're being witched," the medicine man said.

Leroy was dubious. He wouldn't even have come if their oldest daughter Michelle, a high school student at the time, didn't make him. "Don't be so negative," she had told him, "maybe he can help your headaches."

By the end of summer 1993, Leroy had been experiencing migraines with increasing frequency, sometimes several in a week. Migraine is a distinct type of affliction. A number of sufferers experience the onset in the form of "flashing lights" or an "aura" caused by the constriction of blood vessels in the brain. Soon, the blood vessels swell, causing intense localized pain, sensitivity to light and noise, dizziness, disorientation, and sometimes nausea. Researchers have linked migraine variously with diet, hormones, and stress. Migraine sufferers usually report wanting only to lie down in a dark, quiet place to sleep during an attack.

Leroy found little relief from his migraines. He had even subjected himself to brain imaging at an Albuquerque hospital, which was inconclusive. With no causative factors to control, he had been prescribed a potent concoction of Tylenol III and Valium, which made him feel, in his own words, "a little dopey," but which helped him control the pain so he could keep working even during an attack.[1]

It was a sunny weekend morning in September as Leroy and Adella, along with their kids and the anthropologist, made their way down from the hills into Chinle in Adella's big, white pickup, its diesel engine rumbling powerfully as they idled their way through town, past the Canyon de Chelly park entrance. They pulled into a spacious gravel parking lot in front of the medicine man's hogan. A sign posted on the outside wall had been hand-printed in large block letters: CUSTOMER PARKING—a rather unusual sign to see outside a hogan.

A group of European tourists chatted outside with great animation, waiting to pile into their tour bus. One of them, who had been "treated," pointed to what looked like a small hickey on his neck and smiled through his sunburn while the others looked on and joked excitedly.

The bus pulled away, heading no doubt for the nearest trading post, while Adella and Leroy peered hesitantly in through the doorway of the hogan. It was cool inside, and more spacious and brightly lit than most hogans. It featured eight sides instead of the traditional six. Sunlight came in through the doorway and the roof, which had two skylights, one just west of the entrance, bubble shaped, the other, a raised octagon at the center, composed of eight stained-glass panels. Above the entryway door hung a large U.S. flag. Near the back, against one of the walls, a small shrine had been erected, a card table on which stood a large plastic statue of Jesus, adorned with votive candles, artificial flowers, and other decorations, like something one might see a few hundred miles to the south, across the border to Mexico.

To one side of the shrine hung a large blue and gold banner: United States Marines. Indeed, the medicine man, now that their eyes had adjusted to the darkness, looked like an ex-Marine who had not entirely left the corps behind. His hair was cut "high and tight" and, despite a little bit of a paunch in the midsection, his physique was muscular. He was maybe fifty years old.

He immediately directed Leroy, Adella, and Michelle to bring three chairs to a point near the center of the hogan, just slightly closer to the doorway than to the back wall. They sat facing the door, Adella in the center, Leroy on the right, Michelle to the left, as he stood in front of them, pacing back and forth briefly, inspecting each one carefully. The Bambina, Eli, and the anthropologist found chairs off to the side.

He was not, needless to say, a traditional Navajo hataałii. Navajo ceremonies comprise a formal and highly elaborated corpus, consisting of scores of particular rites; a hataałii must specialize in one or at most a few particular ceremonies. The training is rigorous, and the actual ceremonial performance must be according to the strictest discipline. Anthropologists have noted great consistency across time and space among different practitioners of particular Navajo ceremonies, in terms of both the sand paintings they produce from memory for many ceremonies, and the songs and prayers they recite.

Whereas a Navajo hataałii is usually a healer, there are others whose function is diagnosis. These tend to display a bit more idiosyncrasy in practice. Such diagnosticians include crystal- or stargazers, as well as practitioners known as "hand tremblers" (so named for their use of a quivering hand in the practice of diagnosis). If a hataałii can be called a "priest," diagnosticians are closer to what most outsiders might call "shamans." It is more of a natural gift, a less formalized talent. This is not to say the callings are necessarily mutually exclusive. Some individuals may be skilled at both forms of treatment.

This eclectic medicine man seemed to fit more in the informal "diagnostician" class. He told his patients he was half Hopi, and many of his practices involved elements from Hopi healing ceremonies, including extractions (achieved by sucking foreign bodies out through the patient's skin) and manipulations of the limbs, joints, and back.

He took out an ordinary plastic cup, small and clear, and filled it halfway with water. Then, standing in front of Leroy, looking at him through the water, he said "move your head" and gently wagged his own head from side to side as an example. Leroy imitated him, in slow motion, with a dubious expression on his face. The medicine man watched him continue this wagging for about thirty seconds, then suddenly asked, "You get a sore back, too, huh?" Leroy nodded, the look of skepticism still clearly in evidence.

The medicine man moved to his right and stood in front of Adella. He told her to uncross her legs, and take off her glasses. Same routine: "move your head from side to side." While he gazed at her through the cup, he said something that sounded like "you like to be lazy," followed by some Navajo that no one quite caught. Adella looked puzzled and started to giggle.

Next, he moved on to Michelle. He looked at her for about fifteen seconds and said, "You have a short temper, eh? You get mad easy." Leroy and Adella both laughed.

He took the glass of water outside, turned toward the morning sun and raised the glass so that the light shone through it. He adjusted the position and squinted into the illuminated water. After about two minutes of this he called everyone outside. He held up the glass and pointed at a place on

John W. Sherry

its side. "There. It's the deer—his antler." They all looked without saying a word. "And there. A bear."

The antler, the medicine man said, was a sign that someone had put the deer spirit into one of them (probably Leroy): It was the spirit of flight, of skittishness, to split them up, make Leroy want to wander. The bear spirit is one of protectiveness, irritability, territoriality. These were the two spirits that had been put into them. The medicine man claimed to see the image of a woman in the glass of water. "This has been done by a woman," he said. He also told them that it had been done at the request of a tall man.

They filed back into the hogan, where the medicine man sat them down again. He told Michelle to stand up. He pointed to two places on her body, on her chest just below the neck, and the right side of her abdomen. He told her to pull her shirt down a few inches off her neck. He then sucked something from the base of her neck and spit it onto a blue Kleenex. He did the same on her abdomen.

Leroy was next. On the medicine man's orders Leroy stood up, took off his sweatshirt and sunglasses, and handed them to Michelle. The medicine man's apprentice, who had come into the hogan shortly after the diagnosis began, came forward and stood just in front of Leroy with his back turned so that Leroy could place his hands on the young man's shoulders. The medicine man went around behind Leroy and pulled his shirt up in back. He bent over and drove the top of his head into Leroy's lumbar curve, rocking back and forth slightly. Continuing this rocking motion he rolled the top of his head up Leroy's spine. He then stepped away and made a regurgitating sound. He spit something out onto the blue Kleenex and showed it to Leroy: it was a small whitish object that looked like a shell.

He then proceeded to Adella. He took her hands and placed them on Michelle's shoulders, just as Leroy had done with the apprentice. The medicine man told Michelle: "Don't let her fall down or I'll spank you." He first extracted something from the back of Adella's neck, which he again spit into the blue hanky. Then he performed the same rolling of the head on her spine that he did for Leroy.

Once the extractions were complete, he instructed them to share a cup full of water—the same clear plastic cup, in fact, he had used to envision their diagnosis. Adella, as skeptical as Leroy, looked at it closely to see if the side had patterns (of deer, bear, etc.) cut into it.

Once they finished the water, he dismissed them with one simple injunction: no salt for twenty-four hours.

They dropped Michelle at a friend's and turned for home. "I didn't see any bear or deer in that cup of water," Leroy said as they headed back up along the rim of Canyon del Muerto. He was behind the wheel with a smile on his face. Far in the distance were the gleaming cliffs of the Lukachukai Mountains.

"It wasn't a deer," Adella corrected him. "It was an antler. I could see that. I couldn't see the bear, though."

"And what's so bad about the bear? Maybe it's good to be a little irritable," Leroy hunched his shoulders and growled, "a little grumpy. Keep those guys out of the forest."

He turned around and growled at the Bambina. She was unimpressed. "That's not very scary."

"The only guy that's really been able to do anything for these headaches," Leroy told the anthropologist, "is this Hopi medicine man I know up at Second Mesa. He's really good. Maybe we can go up to the Tuba City Fair [it was coming up in a few weeks], they have a road run there. Then we can go see that medicine man."

After a short silence Leroy continued: "You know, a lot of people need to lean on something, I used to see that a lot when I was working with people with addictions. They need to lean on something, if it's religion or support groups or whatever." He paused for a long time while he watched the road. "And that's OK, if that's what gets them by, if that's what gives them their strength." He fell silent again. They were miles from the mountains and the shade of the trees. Brightness surrounded the truck.

"Me, I rely on myself."

Adella was sitting between Leroy and the anthropologist in the front seat. The anthropologist thought he noticed her wince and shake her head ever so slightly. In a few months, in the midst of her pain and confusion, she would remember Leroy saying this with great dismay.

Playing on the car's tape deck was the recording of a more traditional Navajo hataałii's chant. "I taped this a long time ago," she said with a conspiratorial, impish grin (taping Navajo ceremonies is generally forbidden). "It's such a beautiful song. It's for expectant mothers. Some day, when she's ready, I'm going to give this to Michelle."

> I am White Shell Woman,
> I have this beautiful object in my hand;
> My shoes are made of white shell,
> I have this beautiful object in my hand;
> My legs are made of white shell,
> I have this beautiful object in my hand . . .

■/

It had been only weeks since Diné CARE's second Spiritual Gathering and the effects were clearly being played out in Window Rock. Vice President Marshall Plummer invited Diné CARE to participate in a newly formed Presidential Select Task Force on Forestry. Its charter was to "resolve the crisis currently facing the Navajo Nation's forests" to the satisfaction of all interested parties. It was to include the BIA area forester, representatives of NFPI, loggers, members of the ten-year forest plan interdisciplinary team (including archaeologists, biologists, planning department representatives, and other professionals from tribal government offices) and finally, "local people," which really meant Leroy Jackson and no one else.

With guarded optimism Leroy attended the first task force meeting, only to find the agenda dominated by two concerns: (1) How to expedite the next timber sale; and (2) How to pay the $500,000 it would cost for an Environmental Impact Statement on the next ten-year plan.

One logger (who, incidentally, had been one of the people who had first approached Leroy asking for his help in ousting mill management) complained of the fact that he had trailer payments to make and a business to run, and he suggested that Diné CARE should be made responsible for paying the cost of preparing the Environmental Impact Statement. Mill general manager Eddie Richards seemed to love this idea, and pointed out that some states had passed laws making environmental organizations post large bonds before they could delay economic development with legal challenges.

Leroy felt as if he'd been set up, and in his anger turned on the other attendees. He questioned aloud whether this was another of the tribe's many attempts to stall him with meaningless gestures. He argued that his sole seat on the task force did not amount to sufficient representation of a large number of people in the mountains who were concerned about the forests. Most of all, he resented the use of his time to pursue goals (specifically, expediting the timber sale) to which he was directly opposed.

He singled out BIA area forester Jim Carter, an "old-school" forester who had always promoted an aggressive timber-harvest schedule on the Navajo Nation. Leroy asked Carter directly: "How come the BIA can't afford $500,000 for the EIS? Maybe we should conduct an audit of the BIA area office." (In fact, the BIA has been called "the worst federal bureaucracy." A 1994 GAO report charged the BIA with "gross mismanagement"—the bureau was at the time unable to account for over $2 billion in lost funds.[2] Many have suspected worse than mismanagement.

Leroy's thinly veiled charge apparently hit a nerve.

Carter retaliated with a threat of his own. "Where do you get your money to do this?" he asked Leroy. "Who's paying you off?" Carter informed Leroy that he had friends at the IRS. It wouldn't take much to get them interested in Leroy's income over the past few years.

Later that week Leroy went into the back bedroom where he kept his buckskins, jewelry, and blankets and pulled out all his records from the previous years' trades. This seemed a little strange: his trading business had been considerably less active over the previous months, and he had always been a diligent recordkeeper. "These guys are paper tigers," he used to say about NFPI, the tribe and the BIA. "They talk big, but behind it, they don't know what the heck they're doing." Still, he wasn't going to take any chances.

No question, the strain was taking its toll. Leroy's hair had been all black when he started. In two short years it was mostly gray. He looked tired more often. He joked a little less.

But it would be wrong to say that it was beating him. He was as energetic as ever. He was looking into alternative, value-added industries, the kind that Hispanic minimill owners in New Mexico were pursuing. He had also begun to hunt down federal funds from U.S. Soil Conservation Service.

Supposedly there was money for community-based forest-restoration projects. He hoped that by bringing in such funding, he could spur more creative thinking about the economic opportunities in the forest. With the few hundred dollars Sam paid him, Leroy hired a local man named Gibson Montano, his cousin with whom he had just become reacquainted after years of separation. It would be Gibson's job to guide local permit holders through the endless red tape to actually get their hands on the federal funds.

Leroy was well aware that none of the alternative economics would fly until the mill was shut down. As summer ended in 1993, it began to look as if open conflict was inevitable. Everyone dug in for what was coming. Leroy, Adella, the Redhouses, and other members of Diné CARE gathered in the mountains for prayers and a blessing. Virtually all of Diné CARE's major undertakings were preceded by such blessings. At a previous ceremony, they had seen an eagle, a sure sign of the good will of the Holy People. The day of this ceremony, however, the air seemed to be a little different. After some prayers inside a hogan, they came outside. Leroy suddenly became light-headed. He bent over and grabbed his knees for balance. Adella looked at him. "Are you alright?" she whispered. He waved her off. When he straightened up, he had blood coming from his nose—a sign which Ervin Redhouse felt was a clear indication that someone was indeed using witchcraft on Leroy and the group.

Leroy's favorite uncle Alex had a farm near Shiprock. "Come up and get some of these watermelons," Alex had told Leroy. "There's more here than we can handle."

They piled into Adella's big pickup. Up in the higher slopes of the Chuskas, the aspens and the oak trees had already started to change to their deep autumn golds. Down in Shiprock, the cottonwoods were still in the fullness of their summer. The warm breeze flowed through their higher branches; their leaves fluttered light and dark green: Níłch'i, Holy Wind, whispering as it had since the worlds below.

They cut down some old corn stalks and used them to line the bed of the pickup. They backed the truck to the edge of a field that looked rather picked over, but which on closer inspection still had a large number of melons left. They were big ones, too. Some were too big for the Bambina or Eli to lift—though they continued to try with great frustration. After about a half hour of hauling melons across the field, Leroy said to the anthropologist, "Let's go jogging."

■|

Not long after Monster Slayer and Born-for-Water were born, they were challenged to a race by Talking God and Rain God. The gods won easily. The Twins jumped to an early lead but Rain God and Talking God caught them before even the halfway point. They teased the boys mercilessly, and whipped them with switches made of mountain mahogany.

They promised to return in four days to try again.

After the race Nítch'i, the Wind, came to the boys before they fell asleep, giving them encouragement, telling them to practice, that they were growing stronger.

When they raced a second time, the results were the same, although on this second occasion, Monster Slayer and Born-for-Water managed to finish a little closer. On a third such race, Talking God and Rain God once again outran the boys, but they had to push themselves to do so.

After each race, the Wind came to the boys before they fell asleep, each time encouraging them to practice and persevere. After the third race, when they had managed to at least finish close, Talking God and Rain God promised they would return in four days to race once again.

The fourth time they raced, the Twins started quickly. But this time, they never gave up the lead. When they finished, Talking God and Rain God were far behind. When these Gods finally finished, they laughed and slapped the boys on the back.

"Well done, grandsons!" they told them.[3]

■|

Running has a long and fairly prominent tradition in these parts. Pueblo feasts dating well before the arrival of Columbus frequently featured running competitions. During the Pueblo revolt of 1680, runners played an important role in the communication networks of the indigenous people of the Southwest. In the spring and summer of 1680 runners spread both instructions and timing for the revolt from the Rio Grande all the way to the Hopi pueblos three hundred miles away. The ensuing revolt chased the Spanish colonists from the Southwest for a dozen years before Don Diego de Vargas led a reconquest in 1692. One of the most important outcomes of this was a thorough crippling of Spanish control and the restoration of the kivas, the religious centers of the Pueblo villages. "The church and the kiva have coexisted to this day. The revolt remains a victory."[4] The runners who spread the message are still commemorated with annual races.

Adella once reminisced about the way her grandfather used to wake her brother and cousins in the mornings before the sun came up. It seems to be a familiar scenario, or at least it was once. Every Navajo man over the age of forty seems to have stories of being awakened in the morning and told to go out and run, to roll in the snow, to jump into icy streams.

"My grandfather would roust those boys: 'Get up, grandchildren. Get out there and go run. Make your body strong and have endurance. Get tougher. How do you want them to find you when you die? Do you want them to find you with twelve arrows in your chest? Or do you want to be a wimp? Do you want them to find you in the ditch with just one arrow in your back? Get out there and go run.'"

It's not clear that Leroy was subjected to this as a kid, but as a grown man he definitely liked to run. It was also one of the only ways he controlled his migraines. He said that, on the days when he might be likely to suffer a migraine, even before he saw the telltale "aura," he just had an indescribable feeling that one might be coming on. "If I can go for a run, sometimes I can catch it before it hits."

Leroy and the anthropologist left Adella with the kids to fend for the melons, crossed a small arroyo that was thick with undergrowth, then ducked through a tunnel of reeds. They climbed up a steep bank to the top of a low mesa. It was dry and barren. They ran along a truck trail that followed the edge of the bluff and talked about some of the things that were going on: an upcoming trip Leroy was planning, the health of the new churros, the house he was planning to build at the top of the meadow below Saddle Butte, at the family's summer grazing site.

"I have a buddy in Phoenix who's an architect. He's going to design me a house that can take advantage of the sun up there. I don't want nothing big and fancy, though." He wanted to make it a model of sustainability and self-sufficiency.

They slowed down, and Leroy bent over to trace the house plan in the dust. His excitement was obvious. It was shaped like a curved hallway that opened into larger living spaces at each end. Each of these ends would be the shape of most of a hogan (four out of six sides), while the hallway itself would be convex facing south, with large windows to catch the sun at different parts of the day. This open plan and the use of solar panels would provide all the energy its inhabitants would need. "One problem is that the meadow slopes from east to west. I don't know if I want to spend a bunch of money on a foundation or just lay cinder block."

To run a power line to the house would have cost about forty thousand dollars. "We might be able to use wind power. The Hopis have been doing a lot with solar at their places."

They had traveled along the bluff until it came to the power lines from the San Juan power station. They turned to the east along a dusty road into the wind for a few more miles. As they turned around to head for home, Leroy grew quiet. Neither of them said a word the rest of the way. Maybe Leroy's mind was already on what he would be facing in the coming week or two. He had another task force meeting to attend, he was on his way to Taos Pueblo after that, for the feast of San Geronimo, and then he would be going to Washington, D.C.

They reached a badly eroded wash that led down from the mesa, dropped down into the arroyo, came up through the brush and passed between a couple towering cottonwoods. They were confronted by the image of the big, white pickup piled high with watermelons. There must have been over a hundred of them. Adella had probably covered as much distance going back and forth across that field—carrying melons, no less—as Leroy and the anthropologist had on their run.

"How did you do this?" they asked her as they stood around the truck drinking water; they were all covered in sweat and dust.

"While you boys were off playing I just kept picking up melons," she said.

■∣

On the way back home they stopped at the post office. Leroy came out with a large manila envelope that had no return address, just a Missouri post-mark. In it, along with news clippings of Diné CARE and other materials, was a copy of Dylan Thomas's poem "Do not go gentle into that good night." This seemed like a very strange thing to send anonymously through the mail. Leroy did not seem overly disturbed by it, although both he and Adella thought it was a little strange. It was only after the fact that the whole packet seemed so ominous.

> Do not go gentle into that good night,
> Old age should burn and rave at close of day;
> Rage, rage against the dying of the light.
> Though wise men at their end know dark is right,
> Because their words had forked no lightning they
> Do not go gentle into that good night.
> Good men, the last wave by, crying how bright
> Their frail deeds might have danced in a green bay,
> Rage, rage against the dying of the light . . . [5]

Leroy read through the poem a couple of times in silence. He said it reminded him of when he was younger, shortly after his father (from whom he had been separated at a young age) had died.

"I wrote a poem to my dad, too. This reminds me a lot of those times." He began to laugh. "I remember being in a park in Salt Lake. I had this poem I had written. I was so proud of it. I was reading it to a buddy of mine. Can you imagine a couple of young drunk Indios in the park reading poetry to each other?" He laughed, still looking at the poem, and shook his head. "It's probably a good thing I can't remember it now."

■∣

The dispute in the forests had developed a new twist. U.S. Fish and Wild-life had delayed the Tó Ntsaa sale because of the spotted owl decision. That was the good news.

The bad news was: NFPI, tribal Forestry, and the BIA had come up with a response. Since they couldn't convince USFWS, they were going for the bigger play: they were going to join foresters from other timber-producing tribes in a petition to the federal government for exemption from the Endangered Species Act. Playing on the popular notion of Indian people as "the original environmentalists," the tribes (or at least certain factions from within a variety of them) were looking for a broader defini-tion of sovereignty.

The members of Diné CARE all knew what was at stake. They agreed that, regardless of the importance of tribal sovereignty issues, to exempt tribes from federal environmental regulations would once again leave Indian lands vulnerable to all kinds of exploitation. This had major impli-cations, not only for timber, but for the development of coal, oil, gas, or any other natural resource in the Chuskas.

"There's nothing bad about what we're doing here," Leroy once told Ervin Redhouse about this issue. "We've got to use what we can to pro-tect our land. What we're doing here is good. It's right."

The Core Group agreed that Leroy should take a public stand against this, and decided to send him to Washington. Lori tapped into her newly developed network of contacts to arrange a meeting between Leroy and the BIA's solicitor general, a close assistant to Ada Deer, to persuade him not to override the USFWS. Leroy would also ask the BIA to identify funds so Navajo Forestry could conduct an Environmental Impact Statement and get on with the new long-term forest-management plan.

A few days before he was slated to leave, Leroy, Adella, and Leroy's mother, Jane, were making some last-minute preparations. Like Leroy, Jane traded and sold at powwows and other events. Also like her son, she loved the life of movement and travel. She often came up to Leroy and Adella's place from her home in Phoenix. As Jane measured and pinned the hems on a pair of new pants Leroy had gotten just for the trip, Leroy tried on a necktie he had kept in his closet for years. He was joking and teasing Adella. "I should have gotten me a nice silk tie."

"A tie?" Adella blurted out, laughing. "You'd look ridiculous dressed up in a bilagáana businessman's uniform."

"Sheeuh," Leroy laughed with his familiar mixture of amusement and mock disgust. "You don't know nothin' about what I been known to wear. Besides, then you'd have something nice to bury me in."

"Stop that squawking and quit moving around," Jane scolded him, "or I'll stick your leg with a pin."

■|

Late that night, Leroy was still in his kitchen office, sitting at the counter, rereading the Dylan Thomas poem.

> Wild men who caught and sang the sun in flight,
> And learn, too late, they grieved it on its way,
> Do not go gentle into that good night.
> Grave men, near death, who see with blinding sight
> Blind eyes could blaze like meteors and be gay,
> Rage, rage against the dying of the light.
> And you, my father, there on the sad height,
> Curse, bless, me now with your fierce tears, I pray.
> Do not go gentle into that good night.
> Rage, rage against the dying of the light.

The anthropologist saw Leroy sitting there. This was not particularly odd—Leroy often worked late into the night when everyone else was in bed—so he didn't say anything. What was going through Leroy's mind at that time one can only guess and wonder.

Two days later, Leroy was on his way to another Forestry Task Force meeting in Window Rock, and from there he was heading to Taos Pueblo. It was the fiesta season in the Pueblos. The feast of San Geronimo was coming up at Taos, and every year Leroy made the trip to do some trading.

Before he hit the road, he made a few last calls. He got Earl on the phone at 5:45 A.M. "This is your wake-up call," he told him.

Earl later reflected that he initially thought Leroy was just referring to the early hour. But then Leroy said "It's time for us to get serious here." They discussed the upcoming task force meeting, and what Diné CARE should do if the task force was still being used for NFPI's agenda. They decided, on the basis of conversations with other Diné CARE members, that they would probably have to withdraw from the task force. Diné CARE could not afford the time, expense, or frustration, and could certainly not endorse the task force's attempt to propose expediting the unauthorized timber sale.

Leroy arrived in Window Rock for the task force meeting on the morning of September 28. Forest Guardians lawyer Steve Sugarman was also there. It was another exercise in futility. After telling the rest of the attendees that he could no longer allow Diné CARE's time to be wasted, nor could he allow himself to be party to any attempts to use the task force as an excuse to restart the forestry program, Leroy left the meeting early.

He arrived in Albuquerque late that afternoon, and met with John Redhouse. He spoke to Lori Goodman that night, updating her on the task force situation. He was, as she recalls, in good spirits despite the task force fiasco. The two of them discussed some logistics: Leroy was to leave for Washington the following Tuesday, October 5. In the meantime, he would conduct some trading business in Taos, then drive back across northern New Mexico to meet his family at the Shiprock Navajo Fair on the weekend.

■/

During his trading trip to Taos, Leroy stayed at the home of an acquaintance named Mark Marcos, who lived just south of Taos, a man he described as a "burnt-out, ex-hippie kind of guy." Some of Leroy's trading partners and other acquaintances he had made through the business were people on the fringes, and this one was just about the nearest to the edge. He was a recovering heroin addict who, Leroy once said, "has been sent up a time or two."

Leroy laughed when he told the story of Marcos's girlfriend. "She got caught in St. Louis driving his car with a trunk full of marijuana. He was mad as hell. He's still on parole. Now he's worried what's gonna happen to him." Leroy shook his head, then laughed again. "He's pretty hip, though. He's got some good things to say when it comes to knowing how to deal with guys like Dexter."

On the night of September 30, Leroy called home. He was upset, as Adella recalled later, because one of his trading partners—who owed Leroy money—had missed a Thursday appointment, so he was going to have to wait around Taos again on Friday, October 1. He and Adella finalized their plans to meet at Shiprock in the morning of Saturday, October 2. With all the burdens they had carried as a family, Leroy wanted them all to be together. "Make sure all the kids come with you," he told her. "We're a family. We got to hang tough together."

■/

On Saturday, Adella made the trip to Shiprock with Eli and the Bambina in tow. They waited for Leroy at the arranged spot. He didn't show. They watched the parade, spent the afternoon looking at the booths, and went on a couple carnival rides. Leroy's van wasn't around, but the Navajo fairs are huge events, and she thought she might have just missed it. By late afternoon, however, Adella was convinced Leroy had gotten hung up in Taos again.

She and the kids spent the night attending a ceremony that was held in conjunction with the fair. All the while, she kept an eye out for Leroy, but he never showed.

On Sunday morning, when there was still no sign of him, she returned back home. At this point, she was somewhat concerned, but by no means alarmed. Leroy had been detained before, after all. As any Diné will tell you, plans are always tentative, subject to forces beyond human control.

Sunday night came and went, and still there was no word from Leroy.

Adella spent Monday on the phone, tracking down Leroy's trading partners, trying to find out where her husband was. By evening she was sure that something was wrong. Leroy's flight to Washington was set for Tuesday, and his tickets and clothes for the trip were at home. He was on the brink of missing this much-anticipated trip.

On Tuesday Adella spent half an anxious day at work, then went to Chinle, to file a missing persons report. The sinking feeling of desperation and disbelief began to settle in. On her way back from Chinle she went to see a singer to have prayers said for Leroy, to help him stay safe, to guide him home.

That night, Adella had a terrible dream. She was visiting a hand trembler. He pressed in on her sternum—a pressure that created a feeling of panic. In her dream, she tried to pray but could not; instead of words coming out, she was foaming at the mouth. She woke up gasping, feeling as if someone were in the room with her.

■/

On Friday night, October 1, Gibson, the cousin whom Leroy had hired to oversee the local forest-regeneration project, lay in his hogan with a high fever. He jumped out of bed calling Leroy's name. His wife calmed him down, then put him back to bed. As he lay there delirious, he saw Leroy come into the hogan. "Get up," Leroy told his cousin.

"Let me get dressed," he said from the bed. "I have to find my shoes."

"No. I need you right now. Come on."

He sprang out of bed a second time. He was on the floor in the middle of the hogan, fumbling around in the dark, sobbing and calling Leroy's name. His kids were so scared they started crying, and his wife was unable to calm him down. The next morning, in spite of a continuing fever, he hurried over to Adella's house to make sure nothing was wrong, but Adella had already left for Shiprock to meet Leroy.

"I went to ask a grandpa about it." Gibson said some time later. "He told me that Leroy was asking for my help in his time of need. I don't know what I could have done," he said, unable to fight back the emotion.

The experience left him shattered for months.

■/

On the afternoon of Friday, October 1, Ervin Redhouse was cutting wood outside his hogan. He watched the weather come in over the mountains. A brief rainstorm let loose on the slopes above him. As it began to clear he could see the mist rising from the washes up high in the hills. A rainbow formed in the mist. Ervin recalled a discussion he had had recently with Leroy, a discussion about rainbows being Father Sky's sheltering arms, nestling his children under his wings like the eagle. Leroy had been moved, Ervin said, during that discussion. Seeing the rainbow again made him think about Leroy, his clan father.

He thought about what Leroy had said to him: "Nothing about what we're doing here is wrong."

Ervin rose early the following Tuesday morning—he and McQueen would join the others looking for Leroy. He went outside into the morning darkness to say his prayers before setting out for New Mexico. There, sitting on his woodpile outside his hogan, was an owl. He tried to shoo it away but it wouldn't leave. While he was praying, his nose began to bleed. "I started to feel a little sick," he said later, "the owl and the nosebleed, I think deep down I knew something was wrong, but you never want to believe it."

■/

While Adella was at the singer's, one of Leroy's trading partners called the house and talked to Michelle. "Is there any news on Leroy?" he asked.

Michelle told him there wasn't any. They were still trying to find him, or find out what happened to him.

"It's really a shame," he told her. "He was a good man."

Only later did Michelle reflect on that call. They hadn't even found her dad yet. Why was this man talking about him as if he were already dead?

■/

"We've got to hang tough together," he had said in that last message. They had been through so much. They seemed poised to make it through the hardest times. And now, somewhere between Taos Pueblo and the Navajo town of Shiprock he was out there. He could be as far south as Santa Fe, or as far north as Colorado, maybe somewhere on the Jicarilla Apache Reservation, maybe hidden behind an old building along the back street of one of the many small towns that dot the expanse of northern New Mexico, maybe broken down far up some forgotten logging road.

On Wednesday, October 6, they set out from the reservation and its surrounding areas. They traveled alone or in pairs, across the state. Lori and Bruce traveled from southern Colorado via Wolf Creek Pass to Pagosa Springs and down through the mountains into New Mexico; Ervin and McQueen explored the routes through the areas south of Shiprock, through the Jicarilla Apache Reservation, Adella and Michelle traversed the road from Shiprock to Chama; Dave Lange, father of Eli and the Bambina's best friends Ben and Tom, also took to the roads, including the very highway that Leroy was most likely to follow, Highway 64 between Taos and Chama, the first stop on the way to Shiprock. They scoured the countryside grimly in a desperate search, looking for the white van, looking for a sign of Leroy.

It seemed almost futile in that vast area. But what else could be done? Pickup trucks with gun racks were parked in every pullout and scenic viewpoint. It was hunting season. The lingering summer had abruptly given way to fall in some of the higher elevations, making for a day that was incongruously beautiful: leaves on the cottonwoods and oaks shimmered gold. The aspens at the highest elevations were already bare. The air was cold. In the open spaces, the rains could be seen in the distance reaching the ground in gray streaks that slanted at graceful angles in the force of the wind.

The white van was nowhere to be found.

■/

On Saturday, October 9, the Civil Air Patrol, responding to an APB, spotted a white 1990 Dodge van in a scenic overlook near Brazos Bluff on U.S. Highway 64 between Taos and Chama. They notified the state patrol in Chama, who drove up to the busy parking lot to investigate. The van was locked, and curtains were drawn around the windows. They called a local wrecker driver up to the scene. He finally gained entry by breaking the driver's side wing window. Inside the darkened van, they found the decaying body of Leroy, laid out on its side in the semiflexed position on the back seat, covered entirely (even the head) in a heavy blanket. The body was removed from the van and sent to the New Mexico State Medical

John W. Sherry

Examiner's office in Albuquerque. The van was towed to a wrecking yard in Chama under the supervision of officers from the New Mexico State Highway Patrol.

No photos were taken at the site where the van was found. No one dusted for prints. No one bothered to try to determine how long the van had been at that spot.

■/

On Friday, October 15, at the request of a police investigation unit from the State of New Mexico, Adella traveled to Chama to identify Leroy's belongings. There at the wrecking yard, even from across the property, perhaps one hundred feet or more away from the van, a horrible unmistakable smell drifted out from it—six days since the body had been removed.

The van was isolated with yellow police tape, but other than that, it was not protected. The door had a new, large dent in it. The junk yard owner came out of his house a few minutes later. He had towed the van down from Brazos Bluff. The damaged door, he explained, had resulted from the fact that the door had not been secured during towing, and swung open and hit a construction barricade.

He then launched into a detailed description of the state of Leroy's body when he found it. As he did, Adella began to shake and her legs became weak. With a little assistance she made her way back to her truck and climbed in and sat waiting for the police.

When the New Mexico state cops arrived a half hour later, they did not let Adella or anyone else near the van. A police photographer pulled on a surgical mask, climbed in through the driver's-side door, and began shooting busily.

The officer in charge seemed nervous. He probably hadn't realized, the prior weekend, that this was going to be a high-profile case. After getting a positive identification from Adella that the van was indeed Leroy's, the police asked her to follow them back to the station for questioning. At the station, the local officer was joined by a detective from Farmington. He was neatly groomed, tan, and put together like a bodybuilder. He also appeared thoroughly bored.

As they entered the small offices, another state trooper arrived. Like the detective, he was built like a man who enjoyed working out. It was a cold day. The short sleeves of his uniform were stretched taut by his biceps. He made a great show of opening his trunk and removing a large automatic rifle.

Inside the station, the detective began running his tape:

"October 15, 1993, Chama, statement of Ms. Odelia Johnson . . ."

"That's Adella Begaye," Adella said softly.

"Weren't you his wife?"

"Yes. But I kept my last name."

"OK. The statement of Odelia Begaye, wife of Leroy Johnson . . ."

"My husband's last name was 'Jackson,' not 'Johnson.'"

"Okay, statement of Ms. Odelia Jackson . . ."

"Adella Begaye . . ."

Maybe this routine was intentional, a way of testing the consistency of a testimony, or maybe it was just simply inconsiderate. Throughout forty minutes of questions, during which time his sense of inattention seemed almost studied, he was never able to get Adella's name right. Nor was he able to ever get the details of her statement right—such as what day was Leroy first reported missing, when she saw him last, what was their last conversation. Adella was so numb, or maybe she was just so used to it, that she apparently did not care. She went on patiently and grimly correcting his mistakes.

In the adjoining room, where they could hear the interview, the muscular trooper sat facing the anthropologist in silence with his feet up on the desk. His hands lay folded on his chest. He wore a pair of wraparound "shields," so it was impossible to tell what he was looking at, or if he was asleep.

Suddenly, he spoke up. "I don't know what you people are looking for."

"Excuse me?"

"You people are trying to politicize this thing, when there's nothing to politicize. You got a media circus going here." (No one had showed up besides Adella, Bruce Baizel, and the anthropologist—although Bruce's friend, Howard Burkis of National Public Radio, had been with them earlier.) "You're trying to make this guy a cause or something. But I was

John W. Sherry

there when they opened the van. I used to be in the narcotics squad in Albuquerque. I can tell you, there's no foul play here. I've seen a lot of these situations, where people who've been engaged in the use of alcohol or controlled substances just . . ."

"Leroy didn't do that kind of thing," the anthropologist interrupted.

"I'm not saying he did. All I'm saying is, there were no signs of foul play. I say, wait for the examiner's report, see what they have to say about substances in the blood, and go from there. You people are trying to make something out of this before you even know what happened."

Suddenly it became clear why there had been no investigation when they found the van, and why a number of other elements in the police account simply never added up. To them, all the signs pointed to just another Indio who drank himself to death in the back of a van.

The drive from Chama back to Adella's home took about five hours. She didn't say a word the entire trip.

Leroy used to tease Adella: "You're smilin' brown face don't mean nuthin.'"

■|

Leroy's body had been so badly decomposed that Adella was never allowed to view it.

Patricia McFeeley, the New Mexico state medical examiner, eventually ruled that the cause of death was accidental overdose of methadone, the drug used to wean heroin users away from addiction. Given the circumstances, she really had no basis to rule otherwise. There was simply no evidence collected where Leroy's body was found. "It was a small amount," she said. "A seasoned heroin user probably would have been able to handle it. But it could have been enough to have a toxic effect on someone who had never taken it before."

Even after the medical examiner's report, no one who is close to Leroy really feels satisfied that the full truth is known regarding what happened to him. As of this writing, the case was officially still open, although it is doubtful that any of the questions that Leroy's friends and family have raised will ever be answered. During the week when he was missing, on

Wednesday, October 6, Dr. Dave Lange had explicitly checked the parking lot where Leroy's van was eventually found; it hadn't been there. A wrecker driver, cruising the same route, looking for business at the peak of hunting season, likewise reported that he saw nothing in that parking lot on October 5, noting that he would have been sure to spot it if it had been there.

According to the state police in Chama, one unidentified source did eventually come forward, claiming to have spotted the van on Saturday, October 2. However, if it really had been there all week, it seems unlikely that no one would have reported it sooner. This was a popular parking lot during hunting season. It was also the middle of an extremely impoverished and rough part of New Mexico. Even the state police admitted that it is unlikely that the van could sit there for a week without being stripped, or at least vandalized.

When the police did finally check, they found no fingerprints—Leroy's or anyone else's—anywhere on the van, including the door, the steering wheel, or the empty pill bottle containing traces of methadone (hidden in a panel beneath the dash) from which Leroy was supposed to have died. The pills that originally occupied the bottle, some antihistamines, were scattered in the folds of a heavy blanket in the back, as if they'd been dumped out hastily. Those pills had not been found by the police. They were found much later by a private investigator.

According to *Denver Post* reporter Kit Miniclier,[6] the gas tank of Leroy's van was empty. Some have suggested that this is evidence that he was parked at the spot with the engine running to keep warm. However, there was no key in the ignition—in fact, the police were unable to find the key.

Finally, and perhaps most importantly, the members of Diné CARE question the circumstances of Leroy's death from the perspective of bitter experience. Death has always stalked Indian activists. There are many Native American activists who have died in the last twenty years under unexplained and rather suspicious circumstances. Within a year of Leroy's death, Fred Walking Badger, from the Gila River Reservation south of Phoenix, had gone out on a simple errand with a young assistant one afternoon and never returned. His car was found burned to the shell on a deserted road miles away, and his body was never recovered.[7]

On the morning of October 13, the day before Leroy's funeral, in a move one can only assume was calculated to take advantage of the situation, NFPI management approached the Navajo Nation Council with two requests: one was to call on the BIA area director to expedite the Tó Ntsaa timber sale; the other was to reconsider (basically, forgive) NFPI's six-million-dollar debt. It was a bold, if unoriginal, request, justified with the same arguments as before: the tribe owed NFPI this consideration, the mill had built the town of Navajo, New Mexico, with its high school and shopping mall, et cetera, et cetera.

This time, the council wasn't buying it. Daniel Tso, a delegate from Torreon, directly questioned NFPI's timing. Tso had become an outspoken advocate for Diné CARE in the council, and pressed the speaker to give the organization the chance to respond.

At Tso's request, the council speaker adjourned the session until other voices in the forestry issue—most notably, Diné CARE—could be heard from. Diné CARE had exactly two hours (the duration of a council lunch break) to prepare a response.

Tso contacted Anna Frazier, who at the time was still under the employ of President Zah in Window Rock. Anna contacted Lori, and Lori called Adella.

They knew there was no way to make an appearance in front of the council—neither Lori nor Adella lived anywhere near enough to go to Window Rock themselves. Anna was unable to speak on the group's behalf by virtue of her position with Zah's office. Normally, Earl would have been able to slip out of his office long enough to make a council appearance, but he was on a site inspection somewhere and out of reach.

So they settled on the solution that had served them well in Huerfano. Adella hand-composed a statement, faxed it to Lori, who edited and typed it up, then faxed it to Anna Frazier in the office of the president. Anna then hand-delivered the half-page statement to the council where Speaker Nelson Gorman read it into the record. In their statement, Diné CARE proposed that the council schedule a session devoted to hearing a wider range of citizens' concerns about the forests. The council liked the idea. NFPI's requests were tabled and November 17 was set aside for a special session on the Navajo forests.

■|

Leroy was buried in an unobtrusive grave, a final resting place beneath the trees, high in the mountains near the family homesite. His aunt complained to Adella that, as a veteran, he should have been given a military burial at a proper cemetery. Leroy's mother Jane, and his uncle Alex, both reassured Adella that this was the setting and the ceremony that Leroy would have wanted.

After a few of the family members had spoken, John Redhouse stepped to the front. The October sun was still low and it shone in his face. He gave a stirring eulogy to the small group that had gathered to pay their respects. "Like our great chief Manuelito, like Fred Johnson and Don Noble,[8] Leroy sacrificed everything for his people. It is up to us to honor his memory by carrying on the struggle that he gave his life for."

Michelle then stood up. She read aloud a short poem, one that Leroy had read to her when she was a little girl. The morning had been still, but as she spoke a sudden breeze made the trees shudder. A single oak leaf separated from its branch above her and floated gracefully toward the ground. In a moment that no one who was there will forget, the leaf floated directly toward Michelle, lightly brushed her hair and shoulder as it passed by, then settled directly on the page from which she was reading.

Afterward they all climbed silently into their vehicles; a somber line of pickups slowly descended the mountain in clouds of dust. They turned toward Adella's house, where the reporters had already begun to gather.

thirteen

They seemed to materialize at the front door as if by magic. They came from Los Angeles, or New York, or Denver, or Boston—a combination of freelance writers and journalists on assignment, a weeks-long procession fed by the AP wire, professional competitiveness, or some other vast distributed network of gossip and opportunity that was mostly invisible from that neighborhood by the small IHS clinic at the foot of the Chuska Mountains.

Adella didn't seem to know or care how they all managed to find their way. She had begun to slip into a state of numbness. The parade of reporters gave those months a sense of surrealism, and, together with the fact that nothing had been resolved in the forest, certainly contributed to the toll that seemed to be slowly tearing her apart.

Not all of them were strangers. Leroy had known a few of them personally. Earl or Lori called them, at first while Leroy was still only missing, in the hope he might be found alive.

A few of them were respectful, many were not. Adella said later that ABC's Barry Serafin struck her as "a very nice man." Mark Marcos, the man with whom Leroy last stayed, claimed to have fired shots at Serafin and his camera crew a few days later when they came to interview him.[1]

The most memorable were the crew from the TV tabloid *A Current Affair*. They arrived on a sunny but cool Sunday morning in November. The reporter was a tall woman with a dour mouth and deep red hair. Her sound engineer and cameraman were young guys sporting two days' worth of beard growth and their ball caps on backwards. They had prominently stashed a twelve-pack in the back window of their rental car, and were surprised to learn the Rez was "dry." Adella obligingly brought them up to the homesite in the mountains, and showed them where the trees had been cut.

The sound man was a Florida resident who had apparently not spent a lot of time out West. He looked up at Tsaile Peak and declared in no uncertain terms: "That's the mountain from *Close Encounters*."

"Uh . . . I don't think so," said the anthropologist (the mountain is actually Devil's Tower in Wyoming).

"No, no. That's it," said the sound man. "That's the mountain."

As she combed her auburn locks and got her makeup ready, the reporter turned casually to the anthropologist: "How do you know the family?" she asked.

He had managed to mumble about a half-dozen words when she brought him up short. "Anthropology!" she cooed. "That's soooo innnnteresting." She immediately turned to her sound man, "Is that microphone going to work in this breeze?"

They sat Adella on the massive stump of a recently cut grandfather tree, facing the reporter in the middle of what was once a heavy stand of yellow pines but was now an open space featuring stumps and slash. As she began to explain how the pines take hundreds of years to mature, the reporter asked her to identify Leroy's killers. Adella, caught off guard, declined to speculate.

The reporter prodded her: "What people wanted Leroy out of the way?"

Adella didn't answer. The reporter grew a bit more intense. She wanted names and accusations. She had come a long way to get this story, she told Adella, and endured a lot of inconveniences.

"What people? Don't you want to find out what happened to your husband?"

"I'm really not comfortable talking about this," Adella said, and ended the interview. The reporter, clearly agitated, remained silent, looking as though she were plotting her next move. They followed Adella back to her house by the clinic where she fed them all lunch.

Lori and her three youngest boys stopped by not much later, returning from yet another trip to Dilkon, where her father slowly wasted away from cancer. When she agreed to an interview, the cameraman immediately set about rearranging the house to get a good background shot, while the reporter told Lori she'd look better without her glasses. Meanwhile, the kids parked in front of the TV. The original cartoon version of *101 Dalmatians* was playing on the VCR.

Lori told the anthropologist, "Don't let me say anything I'm not supposed to."

Five minutes into the interview, the reporter posed Lori the same question: "Who do *you* think killed Leroy?"

Perhaps a bit overzealous, the anthropologist found himself interven-
ing. Like George the bashful Dalmatian owner, he managed to stutter
something like: "Y-you can't ask her th . . . that!"

"OK, Cut!" the reporter shouted. She turned on the blushing anthropologist, her face as crimson as her hair.

"Son-of-a-bitch!" she glowered. "You pa-ter-nal-ist-ic . . . These people
don't need you to protect them!" She had, she pointed out once again, traveled a long way, was very tired, and had endured a lot of inconveniences
to get this story. She was not about to be foiled by some meddling anthropologist who, one had to admit, was as much of an oddity in this picture
as she was.

"L-l-look," he stammered, "they don't need you asking them that . . ."
As he looked from face to face he noticed that the camera and sound guys
appeared surprisingly . . . bored.

"Do you have any more of those sandwiches?" they asked Adella.

Lori just laughed. Like Leroy, she had her own laugh, one she always
seemed to come out with in the oddest situations.

Before they packed up their equipment and left that evening, the
reporter attempted to give everyone a hug, including the anthropologist,
who almost fell over his chair.

The next day she went to Window Rock where she interviewed Earl
Tulley, then Brenda Norrell. Brenda was a local newspaper reporter and
acquaintance of Leroy's who wound up being featured more heavily than
anyone when the story ran on television some weeks later.

■/

The autumn sun had settled behind the neighbor's house as Adella stood
at the kitchen sink, preparing dinner. Her back was to the windows that
looked from Leroy's little office into the front yard. She couldn't say, later,
why she turned just when she did. Whatever the reason, she turned to see,

in the fading light, an old man coming down the walk to the front door. She saw him clearly, she said later, clearly enough to see him taking a few strides. It was still light enough for her to make out a few details from a singular momentary glance: he wore a red baseball cap and a tan windbreaker; he seemed old, thin, and feeble; he walked with a bit of a stoop. He was clearly approaching the front door.

"See who's there," she yelled to the Bambina, "but don't open it." Since Leroy's death, the doors remained locked at all times.

Bambina ran to the front door. "There's no one there," she called back.

"Are you sure?"

"I don't see anybody."

Adella left the sink and came to the door to look out. "Maybe it's the meter man," she mumbled. The clinic houses, mostly occupied by nonlocal doctors and other health-care workers, enjoyed such urban amenities as natural gas and electricity. "Get the dog out of the backyard so he can go back there."

Bambina looked out the back windows. "There's no one back there, either," she said. Winner, the dog, lay curled up in a corner of the yard, dozing in oblivion.

"Eli," she yelled to the back bedroom. "Look outside and see if somebody's out there."

"What in the world are you talking about?" Eli yelled back. At age five he was already beginning to develop a flair for the use of adult expressions.

Adella opened the front door. There was no pickup in front. Had someone showed up on foot? Perhaps he was taking a shortcut from the highway over to the college? That seemed highly unlikely, as he would have had to pass the dog and climb a fence to get out of the backyard.

"I swear I'm not just seeing things . . ." she said, half out loud, half to herself.

It was not the last of the strange things that happened at that house during this time.

■|

A freelance writer from Los Angeles arrived one afternoon while Adella was out, and promptly made her way back to the bedroom, where she proceeded to gather photographs of Leroy and Adella and the kids from a dresser drawer. (This was after Adella had told her on the telephone that she wanted no photographs of the children to appear in print). "Can't I just borrow these for a little while?" she asked. "I'll send them back as soon as I get copies made."

Another reporter gripped the wheel of his rental car with a visibly mounting sense of excitement as he sped down the highway from the clinic toward the homesite in the mountains. Finally he could contain his excitement no longer. "This is better than a fucking Tony Hillerman book!" he blurted to his photographer.

With the variety of reporters came the inevitable variety of angles, and thus all the darkest speculations played out in public, before Adella's already horrified eyes: It was a suicide; it was a murder; it was a mystery; it was, according to Dexter Gill, Diné CARE's doing, because they wanted a martyr or because Leroy was too "soft" on the logging interests;[2] or it was witchcraft.

"Tell me about witchcraft," at least half of them demanded. There had to be a Hillerman angle on this one.

■/

Adella sat on the passenger side of her big pickup, silent, with her eyes closed, unconsciously balancing and adjusting as the truck jolted and skidded through the ruts of the muddy logging roads. The anthropologist was at the wheel, glancing over at her occasionally, trying to determine if she was asleep or awake.

The sun still shone but the days seemed darker anyway, and the house never could seem to get enough light or air. As Leroy's story unfolded in the local papers, other little horror stories clustered around it: In Crystal, a family put out a desperate plea for help finding their grandfather, who had last been seen climbing into a pickup in Chinle with two unidentified young men and subsequently disappeared without a trace; in Grants, three teenage boys took a fourteen-year-old girl up Mount Taylor—Tsoodził, the sacred mountain of the south—where they raped her, cut her with knives, tried to set her on fire, and eventually drowned her in a puddle; in Mogadishu, the dead and stripped bodies of United States military personnel being triumphantly dragged through the streets . . .

It woke Adella at night and prevented her from sleeping. Night after night she lay awake, wondering what had happened, her heart pounding, partially paralyzed with an obscure sense of fear. To combat her insomnia she had hit on the dubious strategy of staying up as late as possible and going to bed exhausted, but this didn't work. She had even experimented, for a short time, with the practice of having a couple drinks before bed. This didn't work either, and she knew that she couldn't let herself slide into drinking with her children depending on her. She thus made her way through the days in a kind of numb trance. This seemed to be precisely her condition as the pickup lurched along the mountain roads.

They passed a fork in the road on the shady side of the mountains and took the high route. It was colder up here, and the ground was still frozen. Tiny speckles of sparkling, white ice glistened along the ridges of tire ruts cut so deep into the road that the bottoms were all but hidden in shadows of the low morning sun. Tsaile Peak appeared in and out of the trees, silent and constant, its jagged level peak shining with a light dusting of snow.

They reached the top of a large rise behind Saddle Butte. From up there, the entire western portion of the reservation seemed to stretch away before their eyes. Beneath them, not far in the distance, smoke curled tranquilly upward from a hogan hidden somewhere in the shadow of the trees. Wheatfields Lake lay past it. Its edges were already beginning to freeze. Its water disappeared underneath the roadway, then plunged into the shadows of a deep ravine. The waters made their way invisibly from there down to the mouth of Canyon de Chelly.

The elders know that all things are in motion, all things change. Everything has its time, then fades away. Even the language of the People. Even their ceremonies and their knowledge. There is increase, abundance and diversity, but there is also decrease, diminishment, loss of diversity.

In the beginning . . . it was as if there was a perfectly still body of water. And then a stone was thrown into the middle of this pool and ripples started to move out from the center. At a certain point (now past) the ripples started to turn back around and move back toward this center. Time has turned back around. Soon it will be still again.[3]

The creek fed by Wheatfields Lake was slowly clogging up with silt that ran off the logging roads in rapidly growing arroyos on the hillside above.

Adella sat shrouded in silence. "The thing I can't understand," she said after a long time, "was how the Holy People could have let Leroy die that way. He was a good man. How could the Holy People have let his body be desecrated and remain outside the ground like that?" She looked as though she were about to cry, but she never did. Maybe that was part of the problem.

"I keep thinking back to when he said 'I only rely on myself,'" she said after some silence. "I wish he would have never said that."

The anthropologist sat by her, awkward and mute. What can a middle-class Anglo-American raised on a steady diet of happy endings possibly say to someone in this woman's position? What words of consolation could possibly be offered with any ring of truth or understanding? Who in the world could promise her that everything would be all right, that things happen for the best?

They sat together in silence with the morning sun cold and pale at their backs. After a few moments she stood up. "Well, we better get to work."

They returned to the truck and took out the camera. The special session that the council had granted at Diné CARE's request was coming up, and they would need photos—pictures of damage, of erosion and newly carved washes, of stumps on slopes that were, by law, too steep to be logged, of piles of slash left on grazing lands.

■/

About a month later, Ervin Redhouse, who had taken Leroy's death as hard as anyone, leaned back against a wall in the foyer of an Albuquerque auditorium and looked at the ground. He was not overcome with grief, as one might have suspected at first glance. He was trying not to laugh. He reached out and poked the anthropologist in the ribs. He pursed his lips in the direction of a young couple. It was not hard to see what he was looking at: a tall, thin young man with long, blond dreadlocks and a huge flowing beard. He wore knee-high moccasins, leopardskin tights, and a buckskin jacket. Underneath the jacket he wore no shirt, even though the night was well below freezing. His date, over whom he towered, wore a skintight, white, leather miniskirt with matching coat and spiked heels.

They weren't on the Rez anymore.

"Man, where's *your* leopardskin tights?" Ervin teased the anthropologist. "You've gotta start dressing right if you're going to hang out with us Indios." *Indios.* That was the word Leroy always used.

It was the weekend before the special council session. They were gathered in Albuquerque, all of the Core Group, for a memorial event in Leroy's honor. It had been organized by the students' association at UNM and well publicized by an Albuquerque-based environmental-justice organization. All the arrangements were already in place when the organization's director finally got around to asking Adella's permission. Adella didn't have the energy to argue. If nothing else it gave them an excuse to get together and plan their presentations to the council.

People came from all over Albuquerque and around the state—from Santa Fe, Taos, even a few from Colorado. Women in furs sat next to aging hippies in their bandanna headbands and leather vests. They were joined by their concern, their curiosity, or at least their common love for all things turquoise and silver.

The event took on a surprisingly conciliatory tone, given the circumstances. John Trudell, the AIM activist, poet, and recording artist, provided the keynote talk. "We are all tribal people," Trudell told the audience, "for some of us it's just been a little longer."

A world of tribal people trying to master the monsters they've bred.

From Earl, Diné CARE's spokesman, came similar words. "We are all members of the five-fingered clan," he told the audience, as he counted off his fingers. "We are earth, we are air, we are fire, and we are water." He paused, then he raised his thumb, "And lastly we are hope. This is the hope of our children, and our children's children, from whom we are borrowing this earth."

At the end of the talk, almost the entire crowd came forward toward the stage of the auditorium; light-skinned and dark, some wealthy, some not so wealthy, some old and some young. They filed past a blanket that the organizers had set out, and dropped donations in Leroy's memory.

■/

Three days later, the members of the Core Group all descended on Window Rock for the special council session on the forests. The huge, hogan-shaped council chambers were packed. People who could not get inside spilled outside into the cold, clear morning.

The group had decided that Adella, Lori, and McQueen would speak that day. Just as they arrived at the council chambers, however, Lena Nakai, an elder from Sanostee Chapter (which was another designated timber-sale region) told the women that she wanted to speak as well. They didn't know her well, but they agreed instantly nonetheless, and shuffled their talks to fit her in.

The session opened inauspiciously. While NFPI's management, Navajo Forestry staff, and even the Navajo Nation's controller's office made their presentations, the chambers echoed the usual buzz and murmurs of semi-interested delegates. Councilmen wandered to the back, shifted distract-edly in their seats, and talked quietly with one another.

When the women from Diné CARE took the microphones, however, the place grew suddenly still. There was not a soul in the place who hadn't heard about Leroy. One by one, first Lori, then McQueen, then Adella presented Diné CARE's case: the mill was no longer profitable or viable, the forests had paid too high a price, a price that took much from the Diné as a people. Finally, by the time Lena Nakai took the floor, the council floor was reduced to complete silence. Maybe it was the fact that this conflict had gone on for so long, or Leroy's death, or the fact that it had suddenly become high profile. Whatever the cause, at least for that day the voice of an elder still carried a sense of authority that had not been completely eradicated by more "rationalized" political structures.

"You children should be ashamed of yourselves," Lena told the delegates, speaking in Navajo:

Have we lost our values, the values that make us strong as a people?

Our pine trees and our aspen trees are being cut down. It has been happening for many years now. They have cut down all the good pine trees and desecrated the sacred places. The pine trees that have been hit by lightning are used for ceremonial purposes and are given offerings to. These they do not see as sacred and have cut them down. That is why I do not like what is going on up there. There is trash everywhere, they only clear up what is by the roads and where it is visible . . .

The lumber, the wood they make in Navajo [at the mill] they do not give back to the people. They ship it off somewhere to the white man's land . . .

We Navajo people were put here some time ago and we were told that these places were sacred and holy. Navajo people have our laws. Some other people think that these places are not holy, these places are not important, but to me these places are sacred. This is why I'm concerned.[4]

Lena then described how she had supported her six children by herself with wages she earned at the Fairchild semiconductor plant in Shiprock. She was put out of work, however, when the plant was shut down in the 1970s, after local people attempted to organize a union, and after others had protested the plant's use of precious water from the San Juan River. Instead of negotiating a relationship with the community, Fairchild simply packed up and left in the dead of night.

"We never went on welfare. We got by, because we always trusted the Holy People would provide for us," she told the members of the council.

The people of the mountains scored a minor victory that day. The council declined NFPI's requests for an expedited timber sale and the new payment method. In addition—and this seemed very significant at the time—the council ordered the Navajo Nation controller's office to conduct a detailed audit of the mill's operations.[5] Still, there was little time for celebration. NFPI was not about to roll over and die, and despite all the chapter resolutions stating their support, Adella was left without anyone to help her locally in the daily work of organizing the communities of the Chuskas in opposition.

Not long after the special session, Adella was sitting in the house watching the rain turn to snow when the others arrived. Anna and Sylvia showed up first. They brought food for dinner. Then Lori came over with more food. Then Earl arrived. They had all come from miles away, hours or more of driving. It was not at all clear how they had all orchestrated this; it was as if they had been silently summoned.

Lucy Charlie arrived not long afterward. From her home outside Aztec, it was three hours by car at least. She sat with Adella while the others prepared the food. Death seemed to stalk human beings a little more closely or visibly on the Rez. They had all seen family members die young—brothers, sisters, nieces and nephews, sons and daughters—to accidents, disease, alcohol. But Lucy knew exactly what Adella was going through right then. She had gone through the same thing not even a year earlier, as she was in the middle of her struggle to protect *Dził Ná'oodiłii*. Just at that time her brother had been killed by a hit-and-run driver in Aztec, and shortly after, her husband was found beaten to death.

Lucy sat in silence on the sofa next to Adella. Their knees almost touched. She just sat with her, not saying a word, as the gloom of the afternoon faded into the darkness of night. "It's the hardest for the first year," Lucy said quietly. "After that, it starts to get a little better." If there was ever any doubt they had become something of a family, it was obvious by now that their bonds were far more than a matter of environmental concerns.

■|

In December, Sam Hitt approached Adella with a proposal. An anonymous donor had given Forest Guardians five thousand dollars to hire a private investigator. All Sam needed was Adella's permission. After consulting with the other members of the Core Group, Adella agreed, but with conditions that John Redhouse helped her spell out. First, she wanted no publicity about this. She had grown tired of the swarm of reporters, and felt that the PI could work better if he did so discreetly. Sam agreed: no newspapers, no publicity. Second, the PI would be working for her, not for Sam. All of his findings would go to Adella and Diné CARE first.

One month later, the *Santa Fe New Mexican* featured a story and photograph of Sam Hitt. He had prepared a press release announcing that Forest Guardians had hired a private investigator to look into the murder of his good friend and associate, Leroy Jackson.

■/

One afternoon, months later, a call came from California. This time it wasn't a reporter. He was a movie producer—actually a lawyer who was also a movie producer. "I'd like to buy the rights to the story," he told Adella. She wasn't interested. "It can really help your people's cause," he said.

Not long after that proposition, Adella received a dinnertime call from an acquaintance in Michigan. At a meeting of the local chapter of a major environmental organization, an unidentified man stood up and made an announcement: "I am here as a representative of the family of the recently murdered activist Leroy Jackson. As you may know, Mr. Jackson was found dead last October amidst suspicious circumstances. I will be passing a hat during this meeting. If you can, please donate whatever you can spare to help his wife and children, and to help the continuation of his work."

Adella had never met the man, and knew nothing of any fundraising efforts. And, of course, neither she nor anyone else in Diné CARE ever saw the money he collected that night in Michigan.

■/

Weeks had gone by and there was no word from the PI or from Sam. In the meantime, the New Mexico medical examiner, Patricia McFeeley, had released her findings. Lacking other evidence, she ruled Leroy's death an "accidental overdose" of methadone, the drug used to wean heroin addicts.

Adella decided to call Santa Fe. By this time, Sam and the PI had already begun to piece together a scenario of their own, without ever consulting those who knew Leroy best.

It was not a pretty picture. They based their theory of Leroy's demise largely on interviews with some of the traders with whom Leroy was in contact during the last days of his life. Some of the traders dealt in more than just Indian art. The New Age astral centers and desert utopias of the leisure class such as Sedona and Taos attracted other types of business. Despite the Disneyesque façade, Taos has a dark side. On its fringes are drugs, violence, and predation of all sorts. The people of the local Pueblo mix uneasily with the incoming developers and hucksters. Class and ethnic conflict are always just beneath the surface.

The PI placed a surprisingly heavy emphasis on the account of Mark Marcos, the "burnt-out hippie type" (to use Leroy's words) with whom Leroy had stayed the last few nights of his life. Marcos lived in a long, narrow, and squalid building on a spacious back lot in Rinconada, just south of Taos. The building had doors every fifteen or twenty feet, as if it was originally designed to be a row of very small apartments, or even a tiny motel. Most of the doors remained permanently locked, maybe even nailed shut. Marcos had rented it from the elderly Hispanic couple who still lived in the big, old house in front of it.

This was the man who had been wrestling with a longtime heroin addiction, and whose girlfriend had been busted in St. Louis in his car with a trunk full of marijuana (Leroy had really laughed when he told the story). He made a living as a silversmith, though from local accounts he was unreliable. "He made me some beautiful concha belts once," a local dealer once told the anthropologist, "but he just didn't seem that interested in working."

The PI may have been swayed by other evidence, including the fact that trace amounts of marijuana were found in Leroy's blood. (The coroner's report had put these amounts within the range attributable to passive inhalation.) From this the PI began to piece together a picture that Leroy somehow led a "secret" life, of which Adella knew little or nothing.

Even Sam began to buy in to this theory. "I still love [Leroy]," Sam told one of the writers who came to cover the story, "and I miss him desperately . . . but he had a dark side."[6]

It wasn't enough that Leroy had physically been taken from her, Adella was now left with the horrible feeling that her time with the man she thought she knew was only a delusion.

The investigator, still convinced Leroy led a double life, had found Leroy's journal and decided that he wanted to write his biography. He pitched the idea to Adella, proposing to split the royalties with her fifty-fifty. She declined.

In one of her darker moments, she confessed that she sometimes felt "all white people are basically greedy and crazy for money."

■/

At one point in the dead of winter, it threatened to envelop her completely. She had once said that, even if no one else in the world had supported her, she would have continued her fight for the trees. Now, she told a friend on the phone one night, she felt as if she couldn't go on. She hung up the phone and lay face down on her bed and buried her face in the pillow so her kids wouldn't be able to hear her crying. She was motionless except for the convulsions brought on by the sobbing. Later, she admitted that was as close as she came to completely giving up.

Her crying was interrupted by the sharp and unmistakable sound of shattering glass. Adella sprang from the bed. Her first thought was for the kids. She ran to doorway of the bathroom, where she thought the crashing sound had come from. It was dark. She flipped on the light and peered inside.

Eli and the Bambina came running from the opposite direction. They looked around their mom from behind. "What did you do?" asked the Bambina, as they all gazed on a spray of shattered glass. "Did you throw the mirror at the wall?" Eli asked innocently. Tiny reflections sparkled everywhere—on the floor, the rug, even in the tub.

"I wasn't even in here," Adella said, studying the scene. Her eyes were a little red and swollen from crying, but they had suddenly become alert and tense as well.

It was inexplicable, and more than a little frightening. A small hand-mirror that had been perched against the wall on top of the toilet tank seemed to have just flung itself across the small bathroom and shattered against the opposite wall. It clearly didn't just slide off. It had clearly broken against the opposite wall, not the floor. Even stranger, it had taken nothing in its wake; a shampoo bottle that had stood in front of it remained standing exactly as before, undisturbed.

"Don't walk in there," she blurted suddenly and instinctively as Eli took a step into the bathroom. She shivered as she examined the damage. She was almost beginning to expect these kinds of events.

■/

They were all getting one sickness after another, especially the kids. First it was the stomach flu, then the measles, then strep and a series of persistent ear infections. The kids were at home as much as they were at school from Thanksgiving through January. Adella returned to work, making her way through the days like a zombie, still waking at around three o'clock every morning in silence and darkness, waiting for the time to get up.

The work couldn't wait for them to grieve and recover. Earl took on many of Leroy's activities in Window Rock—he was in constant contact with Jacques Serronde of the Navajo Division of Natural Resources, with A. K. Arbab of Navajo Forestry, with Boyd Nystedt at Navajo EPA, and a handful of other Window Rock contacts whom Leroy had called on regularly. Earl was about fifteen years younger than Leroy, but he was levelheaded, and had the same ease in the "two worlds" on and off the reservation. His Navajo was better than Leroy's, and he was a natural for public appearances.

Lori, already busy managing the overall affairs of the young organization, took a greater role in mediating contact with such outsiders as Sam Hitt and Leroy's legal resources. She was also busier than ever with the funding game. It was the funding game, in fact, that kept her from attending Leroy's funeral, as much as she wanted to be there. Instead, she found herself far from the Rez, surrounded by golf courses and swimming pools at a luxury resort in Tucson, where a coalition of wealthy grant makers from back East had gathered for an annual conference. Lori later said she never felt so lonely in her life.

She let the grant makers have it with both barrels. "Leroy would still be with us," she told the foundation representatives, "if the people who are supposed to be our allies were really helping us. The money is not making it into the hands of the people who need it the most, the people you want to fund the most."

■/

It was early February. The sun was shining. A medicine woman wearing a heavy, velvet blouse colored a deep cobalt blue sat next to a small fire she had built in the center of the corral down at the winter hogan. This was the same corral the churros had occupied since their arrival the previous summer.

The churros had been dying. For their first few months on the reservation, they had been fine. Then, after Leroy's death, they started to succumb, one by one, to an unknown disease. Three of them had already died by the time Adella could get a veterinarian, who was unable to diagnose them. Two more were gone by the time she got a hold of the medicine woman.

She was very old. Her voice cracked and wavered as she sang her prayers for the sheep. Adella sat across the fire from her, bundled in a big, red ski jacket, clutching Eli tightly with one arm and the Bambina with the other.

The medicine woman crumbled some herbs in a tightly woven shallow basket, then poured in a small amount of water. She stood up and walked toward the sheep. She was stooped with age but she seemed steady on her feet. The skittish and active churros were strangely docile. She waded through them with the holy water and a swag of sage and juniper. She dipped the swag in the water and raised it above her shoulder, blessing the sheep in a motion that looked somehow uncannily universal, a motion no different than a priest sprinkling holy water on the congregation at High Mass.

She then directed all the people—Adella, her kids, her sisters—into the hogan. She took out some tobacco, said more prayers, and filled a small horn. She passed it to Adella, instructing her to smoke and to share with the others. Hesitating just a little, Adella handed the horn to the Bambina, who inhaled a tiny amount and began to cough. She grinned, embarrassed and slightly elated by the novelty of it. Adella then gave the pipe to Eli, who, to everyone's astonishment, tasted it, puffed on it, then inhaled deftly and without a cough, like a little man who had done this all his life. Where he had learned this was a complete mystery. It was too much. Even the medicine woman couldn't help but laugh.

"I think this one's going to be a medicine man when he grows up," she said.

After that blessing they never lost another churro.

fourteen

The Lukachukai cliffs smoldered in the twilight sky. Snow clung to a few ledges and crags, and covered the trees that grew on the slopes above. Adella stood motionless and silent at the door of McQueen and Ervin's hogan, gazing at this scene in the gathering chill as the sun's last light disappeared.

She seemed beyond emotion. Lori once commented that her anger over the loss of Leroy helped motivate her to keep going, keep pushing, but Adella didn't even seem angry. She just carried on with a kind of frozen resolve.

She entered the hogan and turned immediately to her left inside the door, carving the customary sun-wise path one makes upon entry, especially before a ceremony. The smell of coffee, fry bread, and beef stew filled the room, along with stray smoke from a wood-burning stove that, as in many hogans, occupied the center of the room. Earl was already present, along with Anna, Sylvia, and Lori, who had brought the intern, her adopted daughter. Members of Diné CARE were already beginning to tease the anthropologist and the intern every time they exchanged small talk.

The medicine man—Ray Redhouse's brother, who was a specialist in Protection Way—had long since arrived as well. He looked up as Adella came in the door with her family in tow.

"Who's the bilagáana?" he asked in Navajo. It was one of the few questions the anthropologist recognized easily by this time. Lori and McQueen both laughed. "He's my son," Adella said. Satisfied, the medicine man set about the task of preparing himself, gathering his powers, resting with his eyes closed on a pad against the western wall.

"This is a Protection Way," Earl explained to the anthropologist and intern. "We're holding this ceremony so that we'll all be safe in our travels, to protect us as we head out in all directions." Adella would be leaving the next day for San Francisco, to a national meeting of forest activists. Earl was on his way to Washington, D.C., for a meeting of the National Environmental Justice Advisory Council. Lori would soon be heading to Boulder and Denver in search of funding. "But it's not just for that," Earl added. "It's for all the things we're setting out to do, for your studies, for all the projects and work we have still ahead of us."

Inside the dimly lit hogan, the singing did not start out well. Almost as soon as it had begun, the bottom section of the stovepipe burst apart violently in the center of the room, sending sparks everywhere. At any other time they might have all just laughed about it.

Things fortunately settled down again after Ervin was able to wrestle the chimney back in place. Earl sat as the "patient"—the one sung over. He took his place on a cushion on the floor against the west wall, next to the hataałii. Part of the role of the one sung over is to repeat each phrase—word for word and in rapid succession—uttered by the medicine man. The patient thus takes on an intensely active role in the process of the ceremony and must maintain tremendous concentration for hours at a time. It is very demanding. While Earl participated this way, Lori, Adella, McQueen, and the others quietly attended, sitting in a rough circle around the perimeter of the room, some of them repeating the prayers silently to themselves.

There are many layers to these prayers and ceremonies—they reference stories about the past, about the Holy People from whom the ceremonies come, reenactments that make them alive again; they are situating stories that invoke the power of the land, engaging the imagination and promoting powerful acts of identification; they are sacred words invoking the powers of the Holy People. It is probably impossible for an outsider to ever comprehend all these different layers and their complex interactions—in fact, even medicine men themselves may reach an advanced age and state in their vocation before they gain access to all the corpus of stories and other esoteric knowledge underlying a repertoire of ceremonies.[1]

Still, it is not impossible to appreciate these prayers and ceremonies. More than one observer has noted the interesting use of language that assists the patient in achieving a sense of efficacy. "The sequence of verbs in Navajo prayers," writes Samuel Gill, "moves from plea for expected future actions to description of actions taking place to description of accomplished action."[2] The prayers move the patient (in a characteristic four-stage[3] transition) from the state of being a supplicant to the state of having received from the Holy People (and thanking them for) their blessings. Grammatical encoding helps bring about the shift in perspective in the patient that is necessary for the ceremony's effectiveness: by the end, the blessing has in a very perceptible sense already taken place.

The first portion of the ceremony lasted until well after midnight. Then, after a couple hours of sleep, everyone returned for its completion before dawn. Back in the warmth of Ervin and McQueen's hogan, while the darkness of night still surrounded them, they took arrowheads in their left hands as the medicine man prayed for their well-being. They each then took a pinch of white corn pollen and sprinkled it on their tongues, then on top of their heads, then out in front of them, as they said the short prayer *Hózhǫ́ nasháado*—"In beauty and harmony may I go about."

■/

Twelve hours later Adella had already arrived in San Francisco, where spring was starting to blossom. It was there she found the words for what would become her final position on the forest.

The event was convened by Pew Charitable Trusts, whose aim was to launch a widespread reform of national forestry policy "without leading the parade." Not far from the Presidio, in a spacious flat turned conference center, grassroots activists from around the country were mingled with representatives of a few of the larger and more established environmental organizations—professionals mostly from Washington, D.C.

In the opinion of the grassroots activists, the mainstream environmental groups had long since sold out to some of the country's most notorious corporate polluters.[4] This initial sense of mistrust was exacerbated by the fact that there was a considerable level of what can only be described as "testosterone" in the room. Of the sixty people present, all but a handful were white men, more than a couple of whom referred to themselves as "warlords." This mix of egos and sharp divisions didn't take long to erupt into open hostility. Within a couple hours of the start of the two-day event, there were interruptions, confrontations, and shouting matches. At one point, the hired facilitator was forced to resort to threats: "In the agreement we all signed, I warned you that I will throw people out of here. I'm big enough to do it, too."

It was, to put it mildly, a striking contrast to Diné CARE's meetings.

At the end of the first day of meetings, the "grassroots" groups were agitated and excited. They wanted to caucus. The purpose of the meetings was to establish a common position that all could agree on, and they would settle for nothing less than a major reform of America's national forest policy: no more commercial timber cutting in public forests. That evening they invited Adella to dinner with them. Everyone in the place knew Leroy's story. For all their aggressiveness and combativeness during the day, they were all thoroughly respectful of Adella and intensely interested in her take on the situation.

"It looks to me," she told them, "like nobody trusts each other. Until you get that, I don't see how things can work."

Despite the fact that she was one of only a few women in attendance, and the only minority, and despite the fact that Diné CARE's whole perspective and approach to the forests were different than those of these non-Indian groups, Adella nonetheless hit it off with the other grassroots activists. In fact, she found something in those meetings worth bringing back. She was no longer interested in bargaining "in good faith" with the tribe. She had sacrificed too much. Although the meetings themselves would ultimately fail to produce the nationally funded coalition that everyone had hoped for, at least Adella had found in the words of the other grassroots activists a position she could take on her own forest: "no more commercial cut."[5]

■/

As spring returned to the reservation NFPI was getting desperate. U.S. Fish and Wildlife had blocked all timber sales until a more thorough study of the Mexican spotted owl habitat was complete. Navajo Nation Forestry was no closer to producing a new ten-year plan—they had, in fact, yet to figure out how to fund an Environmental Impact Statement.

Sam Hitt claimed credit for much of this. "Thanks to the legal smart bombs Steve (Sugarman) and I have been lobbing," he told the group at a meeting in March 1994, "it looks like the mill won't be getting at Navajo timber anytime soon."[6] (The members of Diné CARE managed to tolerate this kind of self-congratulatory rhetoric more and more easily as time went on.)

NFPI had been able to secure a couple small, off-reservation timber sales, but this was not a viable long-term option. Without monopolized access and deep discounts on Navajo timber, the mill couldn't hope to stay afloat. It was at this time that NFPI launched a desperate last attempt to win a sympathetic audience on the Navajo Nation.

The stunt first caught the collective attention of Diné CARE's members one Saturday evening at Adella's. They had all come together that day in Tsaile to put on a 10K road race and fun run in memory of Leroy and in defense of the forests. Later that evening, as they munched on spaghetti, Lori pulled out copies of the *Gallup Independent* and the *Navajo Times*.

Everyone began to look over the lengthy and verbose ads that covered the entire back page of each of the papers. Gradually the room began to fill with laughter and expressions of disbelief.

The ads were formatted to look like standard news articles. One bore the title "Health of Forest Improved by Industry." It contained a detailed discussion of how technical management was necessary for the health of the forest—both for the trees, that is, and for those who live in it, as dead and dying pine trees posed severe threats by falling and crushing hogans, corrals, sheep, and people (a claim those present found particularly funny). The ad denounced the "misguided" efforts of "special interest and environmental groups" whose only concern was to "preserve the forest as a museum relic, regardless of the cost to jobs or lives." It implied that such groups intended to limit other activities on the mountain, including more traditionally recognizable ones such as wood gathering for fires, wood cutting for fence posts, and most importantly, grazing.

They all fell silent as they considered the best way to respond.

"I think we need to do a radio spot or something to respond to this," Lori said.

"We do, definitely," McQueen agreed, "but the radio doesn't seem right. We need to make sure the same people who saw the ads see our response."

Adella agreed. "We need to put something in the paper."

"I just don't think we should do an ad like this," Earl said, shaking the newspaper. "We can't afford a full-page ad and nobody reads all that garbage anyway."

Lori then started giggling. She proposed an idea to the rest of the group. Pretty soon, everyone was giggling. It was decided. Within two days, thanks to Ervin's skilled drawing, and a flurry of activity on the fax machine, they had submitted the following to both the *Gallup Independent* and the *Navajo Times:*

"Health of Forest Improved by Industry," by Diné CARE. (Headline in NFPI's back page ad in *Gallup Independent*, April 13, 1994.)

It was a subtle and inspired bit of cultural innovation, really, fitting Coyote into an editorial cartoon. On second thought, maybe it's not too surprising. Coyote—*Mą'ii*—is famous for crossing all sorts of boundaries. He is "sneaking, skulking, wary, shrewd, tricky, mischievous, provoking, exasperating, contrary, undependable, amusing, disarming, persuasive, flattering, smug, undisciplined, cowardly, foolhardy, obstinate, disloyal, dishonest, licentious, lascivious, amoral, deceptive, sacrilegious, and, in a sense, persistent."[7] But he is more than that. He is, in fact, "too much for academic systems, too lively and too restless to submit to analytic scalpels."[8]

Folklorist Barry Toelken points out that "[t]he stories about Coyote are themselves considered so powerful . . . that elliptical reference to them in a ritual can invoke all the powers inherent in their original dramatic constellations."[9] Yet, at the same time, Coyote is a buffoon, a clown at whom people routinely laugh "for doing the things which would earn them derisive laughter if they were to do them."[10]

This aspect of Coyote served Diné CARE well. Their skillful use of him demonstrated a technique that the Navajo people themselves value highly: getting a moral message across without attacking the target too personally. Such teasing serves an important cultural function of teaching and correcting. Judging by the responses (a number of people around the Rez personally expressed their appreciation of the cartoon to Diné CARE members), they hit their mark.[11]

No doubt similar small, unheralded acts of genius probably go on all the time—that's what the cultural process is all about. From early historical encounters with Western systems of writing,[12] to the use of audiocassettes,[13] and now the use of video and the Internet,[14] people around the world are employing new technologies and new media in ways their designers might never expect.

Maybe the most noteworthy aspect of the cartoon was that it made Adella laugh for the first time in months.

■/

It is 7:30 A.M. on a Sunday morning. The day promises to be a hot one. John Redhouse had called it: "It's going to be a long, hot summer," he told the Core Group. "We may as well just accept that and be ready for it."

The house is filled with the smell of bacon and hazelnut coffee, the latter compliments of Lori, who brought a supply to Adella every time she passed this way. Adella brews up the coffee strong and dark. She fills a thermos, then pours herself a cup.

Eli and the Bambina come stumbling slowly out of their bedrooms in shorts and T-shirts. Their skin is dark from days spent out in the sun. "You want to go to your cousins' today?" Adella asks them as she puts hard boiled eggs, roasted green chilies, and a few strips of bacon into plastic bowls for them. They are still too sleepy to answer.

One hour later they turn off the highway along the gravel road to her folks' place. It is a hazardous washboard, and Adella has to slow down on the corner that passes over the creek without a guard rail. They pass Janet's place, then turn onto the dirt road that leads to the cabin near the top of the mountain. Leroy got his van stuck up here on this dirt road once. He tried to come up too early in the spring and got stuck on a nasty hairpin that immediately drops away blindly on the other side. He had to walk six miles back out to the highway and hitchhike back to the house at the clinic. Who would ever bring a van up here on this road in the early spring? Adella laughs as she talks about it.

She stops the pickup abruptly as Eli spots a tarantula in the middle of the road. It is a big one, bigger than their hands. Everyone is wide awake now. The sun is up well over the mountain. The kids are excited, they know they might get to ride their cousins' pony today.

When they arrive at the house they find Adella's mother hard at work on her loom. She owes money to one of the traders in Gallup; the rug will easily bring him double the amount he plans to pay her. It is huge, seven feet by five feet, a weave of yellow and black bands.

The kids find their cousins and disappear outside, up a steep sandy slope in the direction of the sheep.

By the time Adella returns to the highway it's already warm. She turns south, past Sonsela Butte toward Narbona Pass.

Not far from here, alongside a power line built in the 1970s is the path for another proposed high-voltage power line, set to cut through some of the holiest ground in the Chuskas. The Western Area Power Administration (a federal administration), in cooperation with the Diné Power Authority (a tribally run enterprise) had identified this as one of four alternative corridors to close a stretch of the power grid serving the Western United States. The proposed line would widen the swath already cut through Red Knife Summit and other key points along the route of Changing Woman's path to the west, the path she took to join her husband, the Sun, out beyond the ocean. Several Navajo medicine men, as well as numerous local residents, strenuously objected to the placement of the power lines there. By summer they approached Diné CARE to assist in that opposition.

Near the summit, Adella turns along a dirt road that winds through some of the most beautiful grazing lands in the mountains. There hasn't been any rain yet today, but yesterday's storm was big. The road is muddy and slick. Large ponderosa pines grow up here. Some of them are hundreds of years old. They were here since before the Long Walk. Some of them may have been here as long ago as the Pueblo Revolt. An early summer storm has left great pools of crystal clear water in the depressions of the green grass.

It is almost noon when Adella arrives at the hogan of Alice, one of the people who signed on to the appeal of the Tó Ntsaa timber sale. Alice's husband is outside, mending a rail on the *Dibé Baghan*—the corral (literally, the "sheep's house").

"What do you want her for?" he asks Adella. *What do you want her for?* This is always the question when she pulls up at someone's house looking for them. Adella explains that she is with Diné CARE and that Alice had expressed an interest in becoming an official appellant of the timber sale. "She's down in Naschitti," he replies. "She went to the chapter meeting."

She climbs back into the truck, thinking out loud. "The chapter meeting probably doesn't start until this afternoon." She decides to stay in the mountains and look for Robert and Rita, another couple who live in the immediate area, all of which is part of the slated Tó Ntsaa timber sale. Rita is an herbalist. Robert and Rita are indeed at home, but so is most of their extended family. A dozen or so pickups stand outside. In a green field beyond the house people are playing volleyball and barbecuing. Adella decides to come back later.

By 12:15 she has wound her way off the dirt roads and back onto the highway at Narbona Pass, heading down the eastern side of the mountains, into the arid lands, toward the Naschitti Chapter House. As she pulls into the parking lot, there is no pickup or car in site.

"No meeting today," says a young woman who happens to be inside, "the chapter meeting was canceled. Alice probably went back up the mountain."

It is hot down here below the mountains, and the wind is whipping the dust around. Adella thinks silently for a moment, then turns away from the mountains, farther up the road toward Shiprock. A nearby chapter, Sanostee, is also part of the timber-sale area, and two elders there, Jimmy Smith and Lena Nakai (who spoke at the November special session) have signed on as appellants. "Maybe they're having a chapter meeting," she says, "or maybe I can find one of them at home."

Twenty minutes later Adella pulls into the parking lot and steps from the blinding sunshine into the darkness of the Sanostee Chapter House, where she finds Jimmy Smith. He is sitting in a folding chair, his baseball hat pulled on tightly, his arms folded across his barrel chest. His hair is graying and his face is wrinkled, but he is sturdy and healthy-looking. His hands are big and thick, the hands of a working man. As she reaches her seat he leans slightly toward her, extending his right hand across his body to greet her. They sit together in silence for a few moments as the meeting trudges its way through the usual business. After ten minutes like this, Adella says something to Jimmy, quietly and in Navajo. Within moments they have stepped out into the bright summer sun.

"Can you record a message for the radio?" she asks him. "I can leave this with you and pick up the tape later."

"No, I can do it now," Jimmy tells her.

In the empty kitchen of the administrative offices next to the chapter house, Jimmy Smith stands silently for a few minutes, collecting his thoughts. Then, he turns on the tape recorder and raises the microphone. In one take, off-the-cuff, with scarcely any hesitation, repetition, or a stutter, he records his message (in the Navajo language) to his people:

> Hello my people, my relatives. I will speak to you who live near the mountains from the radio station . . .
>
> I don't know if you already know, but I will remind you. In the past, our elders, our grandfathers and grandmothers, used to talk to us about these things. You probably remember when you were young, the difference when you herd your livestock onto the mountain or when you moved onto the mountains. Those of you who spend your summers up there, those of you who herd your cows, sheep, and horses up on the mountain. Up there it is open, green with pine trees

everywhere. There are plants up there that our sheep can feed on, there are also numerous herbal, medicinal plants up there.

These people take chainsaws up there and are cutting down the trees. Our own people are doing this. They are doing this where our livestock roam and the trees are scattered all over the place . . .

Let's do the right thing and talk about it. My relations, my people, you probably notice this, especially the ones who make your summer camps up in the mountains . . . there have been many people who have spoken about this. The problem was worse but Diné CARE has put a standstill on the cutting. They told them to stop and wait because there are sacred places on that mountain. We would like things to be done right . . .

We all need money. Our children need money for their education. [But] We should think about this, talk about it and meet on it. Express our concerns and let others know how it disturbs us. Let's talk about this, think about how to do things right up in the mountains. It is possible! This is a reminder and thank you my people. Please remember this.[15]

With Jimmy Smith's tape in hand, Adella steps back out in the glare of the summer sun. She looks up at the mountains, where clouds had begun to gather. Maybe there would be a storm. She climbs behind the wheel and sits for a moment, indecisive. Then, she starts up the truck and turns south again, back to the pass and up to the mountains.

By 3:00 P.M. she has found the home of Marvin, yet another appellant. It is hidden behind a dense stand of trees and down a slope, but it opens onto a beautiful valley that drops away to the east over a huge panoramic view of the plains, far below to the east.

"What do you want him for?" a young man inquires as Adella pulls up outside the family house and asks for Marvin.

"He went to Shiprock," he tells Adella after getting a satisfactory answer. "He's herding sheep for his aunt today."

Another missed connection. For the first time today Adella lets out a sigh of frustration. It's been nearly four hours and she has made connections with only one appellant. City people have phone trees and E-mail.

Adella has her pickup. She decides to give Alice another try. "Maybe she has come home by now. I hope she didn't go to Farmington."

Finally, she is in luck. Alice is at home. They duck inside her small hogan just as the rain starts to fall. Thunder rumbles all around, and the rain pounds the roof. Alice offers homemade tortillas and strong coffee. They sit quietly for a few moments, then she begins to talk about her summers in the mountains as a girl, how things had changed since then. These elders have such a detailed knowledge of the land. Alice remembers exactly where individual trees once stood, and exactly where to find particular plants. Some herbs, she tells Adella, are "walking" herbs. They move through the forest from year to year. These are most susceptible to changes wrought by timber cutting.

It is now almost 5:00 P.M. The rain has stopped. In the humid air the cab of the truck smells vaguely like sour milk, possibly the remains of a spill by the kids. Adella still wants to talk to Robert and Rita. Since their place is roughly on the way back to the highway, she gives it another try.

The party has begun to break up. They invite Adella in to sit and talk. She pulls up a small stool around a fire that crackles under a shelter just outside the home. It is a large house, by Navajo standards, with multiple rooms. They still have a few hamburgers left, and some Kool-Aid, coffee, and cake. Adella tells them about the status of the appeal as aunts, uncles, children, grandchildren, and other interested parties look on, coming and going casually. They all shake her hand, silently and politely, as they enter the small porch area where she sits.

One very old woman approaches Adella and peers at her with great strain. "This woman is from Diné CARE," Rita says to her mother in a loud voice. "They're trying to stop the loggers."

The old woman takes Adella's hand in both of her own, patting it gently, smiling, speaking in comforting tones. Her eyes are clouded over and her teeth are gone, but she knows exactly what Adella is here for.

An hour later Adella is on her way home. It has been a fairly successful day: she has talked to four of the appellants. She would keep this up until she had met with all of them. It is a burden, not so much to the appellants, who never seem to mind the visits, but to Adella herself, who now has no one to help her with this time-consuming and arduous work. But whenever she meets them, her resolve is inevitably strengthened. "Keep it up," they all told her. "We're still with you."

By about eight she is back home with her kids. She puts in a load of laundry and starts dinner. Tomorrow she will be back to work at the clinic.

■|

The long, hot summer never quite materialized the way they had imagined. The loggers and mill workers held yet another rally, this time in Window Rock. They convened just prior to another special session on forestry in the Navajo Nation Council. They formed a convoy of pickups and logging rigs, and drove the main street through town, up to the doors of the council chambers. On their logging trucks they hung signs, this time not denouncing Diné CARE, but rather calling for the removal of NFPI's management and challenging President Zah to solve the forestry crisis.

Inside the council chambers, former mill workers recited their litany of complaints against mill management. NFPI made a feeble attempt to plead their side of the story. They seemed to sense their days were numbered. At the conclusion of the council hearing, BIA area director Wilson Barber told the council that, until U.S. Fish and Wildlife signed off on the spotted owl survey and environmental assessment, he was not about to sign off on the Tó Ntsaa timber sale.

No one from Diné CARE was able to attend the session. Their presence was felt there, nonetheless. "Diné CARE are the only people who have been concerned about our forests," one former mill employee told the delegates. "You should have been listening to them."

■|

One hazy afternoon near the end of summer, Gorman Yazzie, the newly appointed head of Navajo Forestry's interdisciplinary team for the next ten-year forest-management plan, came to visit Adella. He was joined by Anderson Morgan, head of Navajo Nation Department of Natural Resources. They were pleading with her. "Please, Auntie," they begged her. "People need to work. We'll get there. You're right about the forests.

Just give us this one timber sale. Things are changing in Navajo and in Window Rock."

They were too late. With the loss of Leroy, the long months of winter, and the subsequent visits to the elders in the mountains who told her time and again, "Don't give up," Adella's resolve had long since been hardened. She was no longer afraid of any "backlash" a mill closure might generate, and she no longer had any hope that the tribe could approach the forest with anything resembling good faith.

Realistically, there wasn't anything Adella could have done at that point anyway—nor could anyone else. The mill was sinking fast, U.S. Fish and Wildlife had still not received a satisfactory assessment of impacts on the spotted owl habitat, and the BIA was reluctant to approve another timber sale outside of the required ten-year plan.

After all the fighting in the forests, after the Spiritual Gatherings and Loggers Rallies, after the appeal, the threatened second appeal, and a host of counterthreats of various kinds, after Adella's loss of a husband, and all the rest, the mill went out with little more than a whimper and a short article in the *Navajo Times*.

On the day the mill closed, Adella called Sam Hitt to let him know.

"That's great!" he told her. "And you guys didn't have to do a thing."

■/

An old friend came to visit her one evening around that time, a former logger who had joined her and Leroy in the stand against timber cutting. He had brought with him a newspaper article—a follow-up story about the old man who had disappeared from Chinle right around the time Leroy died. Apparently his body had remained hidden until very recently, when it was discovered in a wash up in the mountains.

As she glanced at the story, Adella showed no sign of a reaction. It was something that occurred, after all, during the darkest days after her loss of Leroy. She admitted later that she at first wondered what the significance of it was.

Then she looked at the picture. Her mouth opened, but she said nothing. It looked exactly, she said later, like the man she saw through the front windows coming down the walk that late afternoon the previous autumn—the man who seemed to disappear right there at the front door.

"He was a medicine man," the logger told her. "Some people say he did ceremonies for the people of the mill . . ."

The implication was chilling. Such is the nature of witchcraft accusations. Probably no one will ever really know—but it should be noted that simply because the man's services may have been used by someone associated with the mill does not necessarily mean that he directed any harm toward Diné CARE.

What Adella really thought is impossible to say. "If it is true," she said didactically to the anthropologist later that evening, "it just goes to show that if you mess with that stuff it comes back on you." Beyond that, she offered nothing more, and never talked about it again.

∎/

A few days later, without any announcement, she got out the cleaning supplies. Angie arrived as if on cue with her daughter Brooke, who was Eli and the Bambina's favorite cousin and frequent babysitter. Together they all scrubbed the floors, the baseboards, and the walls. They cleared out the cupboards and washed the shelves. They emptied the refrigerator. They cleaned the rugs, took the mattresses outside and beat them, then the bedspreads and blankets, then the cushions from the furniture. They washed all the clothes, the sheets, and the towels. They hunted for cobwebs in the closets and corners of the ceilings. They washed the windows and the window screens. They scoured every exposed surface.

Adella went through Leroy's clothes. She took out the new shirt, shoes, and slacks that Leroy was going to wear to Washington, D.C. For a moment, she looked at them without saying a word. It was impossible to tell if she was thinking back to October, to what might have been, to what had been lost, or simply deciding what to do with these unused items of clothing. Finally, she folded them carefully and put them with a pile of other things to give away. The rest of his clothes she simply piled unceremoniously into garbage bags, which landed in the back of her pickup.

She went into the garage. The private investigator had managed to retrieve some of Leroy's things—clothes, some trade goods, a big bag of wool, all of which had sat in the garage for nearly a year by then. (Sam Hitt sold the van itself for salvage; no one would have been able to get the terrible smell out of it to drive it again.) She loaded everything into the back of the pickup, and drove up to the homesite.

She walked around the edge of the meadow, looking for fallen branches to get a fire going as the afternoon began to wane. She built a small fire, then fed it with more dry wood until it was large and hot enough to keep burning for a while.

Slowly, easily, she began to throw Leroy's things on the fire: pairs of pants, jackets, boots, shirts, a few papers, a big pillow that was in the van. The flames changed color and stinking black smoke occasionally came out of it as something plastic melted away. She burned it all.

That's the way the Diné say goodbye to those who have died.

fifteen

This resistance has been part of our lives since the Monster Slayers, since the time of Changing Woman. This is just the way things are and the way things are intended to be. It's maybe not good to question this too much. It's just what we were born of and born for. It's part of our role as Diné, as keepers and caretakers of the land.

—John Redhouse

■/

Long after this mill and the loggers are gone, after you've made your money and bought your big houses in Albuquerque, we'll still be here. We'll still be up there in the mountains with our sheep, taking care of the forest.

—Leroy Jackson

■/

It's been years since the mill closed. Some time ago it was declared a "Brownfield" site by the U.S. Environmental Protection Agency. Shortly after its demise former General Manager Ed Richards went to work for the Economic Development division of the Navajo Nation government, and at least through the end of 1998 remained a participant on the "interdisciplinary team" that was formed back in Leroy's time. He and a handful of others still insist that the mill is viable if they could just get enough timber from the tribe.

Dexter Gill, one-time head of Navajo Forestry whose bitter memo of resignation accused Diné CARE of being puppets of outside environmentalists, ran a bookstore in Gallup for a few years. The shop specialized in works on the Southwest, including a few titles on environmentalism and Native Americans.

In 1996 Sam Hitt ran unsuccessfully for the House of Representatives as a Green Party candidate. Since then, Forest Guardians experienced a protracted and often hostile confrontation with (mostly low-income, Hispanic) residents of the northern New Mexico forests that Hitt targeted for mill closures. After one rally in which an effigy of him was hung, he commented, "Now I know how Leroy Jackson felt."

The anthropologist and the intern both moved away in 1995, landing in the Pacific Northwest, far from the Diné Bikéyah. The anthropologist found himself in the employ of the world's largest software company, on a corporate campus of manicured lawns and gleaming architectural surfaces. There he joined some fifteen thousand others, mostly young engineers and M.B.A.'s, bound to each other and their work by the "golden handcuffs" of stock options, profit sharing, and employee stock purchase plans.

One shining summer afternoon the entire company convened in a local sporting arena for their annual meeting. Among the parade of high profiles that crossed the stage that afternoon was James Burke, author and host of the television shows "Connections" and "The Day the Universe Changed." He addressed the throng in an erudite British accent, waxing eloquent on the power of personal computing to undermine the authoritarian power structures that have plagued human history. He seemed strangely unconscious of any irony as he solemnly pronounced the ideological slogan that was projected in towering block letters on a massive screen behind him:

IDEOLOGY CAN'T STAND INFORMATION

"The things you people are creating," he told the rapt audience, "have the power to change the world forever!" The crowd applauded enthusiastically—but not nearly as wildly as they did scarcely a few minutes later, when the corporation's head of sales (now CEO) took to the stage, strutting back and forth like a great caged bull in pin-stripes and suspenders, pumping his fists in the air amidst a frenetic light show and blaring sound system. It was like the player introductions at an NBA game gone badly out of control. The crowd grew louder and chanted his name in unison. He stepped up to the podium. The place fell silent as he announced the year's revenues: "Eight ... billion ... dollars!" (a sum that has long since multiplied). The crowd lost all control. The stadium erupted in a raucous celebration.

There it was, so succinctly encapsulated in one ritual event, the seductive myth of material and technological progress:

> We're building a framework where all the world's civilizations can exist side by side and thrive. Where the best attributes of each can stand out and make their unique contributions. Where the peculiarities are cherished and allowed to live on. We're entering an age where diversity is truly valued—the more options the better. Our ecosystem works best that way. Our market economy works best that way. Our civilization, the realm of our ideas, works best that way, too.[1]

It was indeed seductive. All that wealth created by a bunch of young people in T-shirts and blue jeans whose work left no gaping holes in the earth or denuded landscapes behind them. It was almost possible to believe that centuries of brutal colonialism and industrialism might yet transcend themselves into something more universally humane and beneficial. It was almost possible to forget that the vast majority of the world's population may never have access to the Internet. It was almost possible to ignore the fact that, for all its benefits, high tech is still firmly harnessed to the old industrial economy of fossil fuels, hydroelectric dams, and toxic chemicals.[2]

But not quite. The anthropologist stumbled out of the darkened arena into the diffuse Seattle sunlight. An unbidden flood of memories suddenly overcame him, images from another world that, for all its difference from "linear time," seemed thoroughly irreconcilable with the New Economy buzz of Internet Time: the churros, Leroy's laugh, the hushed breeze through the corn, the simplicity of the hot August sun and the cold water flowing from the spring below the mountains, and James, Adella's brother, with his great big smile.

"Now you're drinkin' like a Navajo," he had said.

■/

And yet, computers have begun to play a bigger role in the work of Diné CARE, not just in the funding game but even in what Leroy called the "real work." Partly due to technology, for instance, there may yet be hope for Leroy's dream of bringing money in for forest restoration.

Several years ago, Diné CARE managed to scrape together a few thousand dollars to hire Ivan Joe, Lori Goodman's brother, who has both professional experience in land management and considerable technical knowledge useful for conducting a forest-inventory study. Ivan took the first steps in realizing Leroy's dream of a homegrown, forest-regeneration effort when he launched an innovative community-based forest-mapping project in the community of Sanostee (in the heart of the once-pending Tó Ntsaa timber-sale area). The project used state-of-the-art Geographic Information Systems (GIS) technology,[3] run entirely under the governance of chapter officials and local elders.

In pursuing this goal, Ivan accumulated better data on the forest than the tribe itself has managed to produce. In fact, Navajo Forestry has tried to hire him on two separate occasions.

The members of Diné CARE have now begun to lay plans for using GIS technology for an even more ambitious project—that of conducting a culturally based, thorough mapping of the incidence of health effects caused by uranium radiation on the Navajo Nation.

■/

Beyond GIS, of course, there's E-mail. Lori first gained access to it near the end of 1995. Before long she was dealing with dozens of messages per day. By the end of the decade, many of the members of the group were on-line as well.

In one of her earlier E-mail messages, Lori expressed an interest in "cutting back" her role in Diné CARE, something she has to this very day been unable to achieve:

> From: Lori Goodman
> To: John and Liling
> Sent: Wednesday, May 29, 1996 8:32 AM

Subject: Update

Congratulations! on your announcement.[4] We are very happy for the both of you. Boy, you sure had us holding our breaths.

Sorry I have been out of touch. There is too much going on with the family. Michael's team won their first baseball game.

I have cut back on my involvement with Diné CARE considerably. After all these years, I have bankrupted my standing and goodwill with my family (love, trust, faith, commitment). Not to mention my oldest's college funds. I am working to rebuild what I have lost.

My priority now is fundraising and that's all I want to concentrate on for this year. I will get out of book keeping when we can afford it. People that I will be making time for will be the board, potential funders and resource people such as the two of you.

It hasn't been easy telling people this. I still get requests that really should be going to [our new executive director][5], even after I tell people. I guess it just takes a while to make the transition. I am really looking forward to Adella and the kids making the trip with us to DC. We always have a good time being together.

Well, that's the update for now. Take care and congratulations. We'll see you in July!

Love,
Lori & boys

In her own words, Lori had once been naïve enough to believe she could "work herself out of a job"—to start the wheels of grassroots organizing in motion and step back out of the way. By 1996, she was ready to give this a try—as she pointed out in numerous E-mails at the time. It was not to be her fate. In fact, as Lori would come to find out, she couldn't even afford the relative luxury of focusing only on fundraising.

In 1996 Diné CARE had decided to hire an executive director, someone to formally and explicitly take on much of the burden that Lori had shouldered up to that point. It was a short-lived experiment that quickly depleted their funds and produced few desirable results. For a short while, it looked as though all they had fought to build was about to crumble—

not under the pressure of some external opponent but through the weight of their own efforts to formalize.

Meanwhile, the visibility they achieved in the early 1990s brought numerous new activists into their midst, moving Diné CARE, it sometimes seemed, from crisis to crisis:

- In Shiprock, Ray Benally, who had once worked at the Navajo coal mines, had finally grown so fed up with his company's failure to renovate lands affected by surface mining that he had quit and decided to form a citizens' oversight committee. He approached Lori in 1994. She spent much of their first year trying to help him identify reliable sources of financial and technical support (he was, in Lori's words, "being used" by such outside organizations as D.C.-based Citizens' Coal Council). Within about a year of starting their collaboration, Ray—a recovered alcoholic who had not been drinking for years—died suddenly and inexplicably of liver failure.
- From the Navajo community of Aneth (located in southern Utah), Lemuel Chee approached Diné CARE's board requesting administrative support. Two council delegates from Chee's area, Andrew Tso and Mark Maryboy, both supporters of Diné CARE, had been served with restraining orders after joining a community protest over public safety, potential water contamination, and hiring practices, issues that have concerned residents for over twenty years.[6] Chee became a member of Diné CARE's board in 1996.
- At Big Mountain, hundreds of residents still held out against forced relocation.[7] When, in 1997, a delegation from the United Nations made a historic trip to Black Mesa to investigate human rights violations, the elders from the area specifically requested Earl Tulley's presence as interpreter. After years of repeated exploitation and divisiveness caused largely by outside activists, many of the locals felt only Diné CARE—specifically, Earl and Anna—could be trusted. The UN human rights investigation was the first ever on U.S. soil; no major news services covered the event.
- In Blue Canyon, Cecilia Bedoni found herself in the bewildering position of leading a small community opposition to a streambed quarry

that even the Army Corps of Engineers had recommended against. Rebuffed by natural resource committee chairman Elmer Milford, she confronted the manager of the company doing the quarrying. "I'll stop you," she told him. As she got up to leave, the manager had just one last remark: "Remember what happened to Leroy Jackson," he told her.

At a meeting in the spring of '96, with their funds running out and their organization struggling under the burden of formalization, things looked grim. Board member Sylvia Clahchischilli expressed it most succinctly: "It seems like the more we do, the more we learn there is that needs to be done. It's like we're just digging a deeper and deeper hole for ourselves, and we haven't even scratched the surface yet. Our people, we're no longer living, we're just trying to survive. We don't have the energy to take back control of our land. We're just trying to get by from day to day."

After the meeting, in private, Earl put the question to Lori: "What's your biggest fear?"

"Not having the money to pay our people," Lori told him. "Why? What's your biggest fear?"

"That we might lose you."

She looked at him for a moment without saying a word, then laughed, as she always did in such situations. "Where would I go?" She said. "This was Leroy's life. This was what my father stood for. You're not going to lose me."

It was somewhere during this period that they found—perhaps rediscovered—the bedrock on which their organization was built. For Lori, who ultimately returned as de facto, unpaid executive director, it was simple: "We have to just admit it, we're a Navajo organization. We're not a bilagáana organization. We have to find a way that works for *us*." "The one thing I'll always get a charge out of," she added, "is if there's one of our people out there in one of the communities willing to do for themselves, then I'll keep doing this.

"It always comes back to *shik'éí*, to my relations."

As Earl said: "Maybe it's not our job to put a big *S* on our shirts and try to save the world. Maybe our job is just to pass the torch, to keep this struggle alive and to pass it on, to teach our children and let them take up the fight when their time comes. Maybe that's what the Holy People have in mind for us.

"If Geronimo or if Chief Manuelito were around today, maybe they wouldn't have the impact that they did. This is just our job, to keep this going for our children."

■/

Newly reenergized, the members of Diné CARE turned their attention to perhaps the most ambitious undertaking their organization will ever face: uranium radiation in the Diné Bikéyah. In the mid 1990s, amidst disclosures of the U.S. government's culpability in radiation experiments on its own citizens and an increasing awareness that the Radiation Exposure Compensation Act was not benefiting supposed recipients (see chapter 11), a handful of new activists came forward looking for Diné CARE's help. Melton Martinez, whose own grandfather, Paddy Martinez, had discovered uranium on Navajo lands in the 1950s, led an effort among Diné from the Eastern Navajo Agency. Hazel Merritt, from southern Utah, and Alexander Thorne, of Kayenta, led Navajo downwinders' groups for Utah and Arizona, respectively. Mr. Thorne became involved after his third trip to medical specialists in San Francisco, where his five-year-old daughter had been almost continuously in and out of treatment for childhood leukemia. "I look at my daughter suffering with this rare disease and I think to myself: I came from near the mines. Is this something that I passed down to her?"

Martinez and Thorne were soon named codirectors of a reservation-wide grassroots effort for the reform of RECA. This work quickly expanded beyond the borders of the Navajo Nation, to include a much larger coalition involving groups from throughout the Southwest.

Anna Frazier left her job with the Zah administration and became Diné CARE's only staff member. She spent much of her time engaged in public outreach. Before she came along, there had been precious little public education to alert families to the dangers of, for instance, using radioactive groundwater from near mill tailings to water their livestock, or using rocks from unreclaimed mining sites for building or repairing homes. She was also a leading advocate on the Navajo Nation for the reform of RECA. For most of the last half of the 1990s Anna worked full time traveling the Navajo Nation, attending meetings and providing education on radiation.

Anna proved to be a highly effective community organizer. After one chapter meeting, Alexander Thorne, who had only recently joined Diné CARE's ranks, called Lori Goodman from a pay phone: "Grandma's hot!" he told Lori. "She really knows how to do this job!"[8]

About this time, Diné CARE made the acquaintance of E. Cooper Brown, a lawyer and lobbyist in Washington, D.C., who had been working on RECA reform with Phil Harrison, head of the Uranium Radiation Victim's Committee and a friend of Lori's since 1992. Brown had a long history of involvement with radiation issues, including a ten-year stint as codirector of the National Committee for Radiation Victims (NCRV), and coordinator of the Task Force on Radiation and Human Rights. Together with partner Wally Cummins, Brown had also represented a variety of clients, including people living near nuclear production facilities outside of Cincinnati, Ohio, and a local development authority on Rongelap Atoll in the Marshall Islands, the site of truly horrendous U.S. nuclear-bomb testing that had caused massive dislocation and widespread health problems. Brown had also been connected with the original formulation of the 1990 Radiation Exposure Compensation Act.

Lori, Anna, and the other activists worked for a year to persuade the Navajo Nation Council to hire the firm of Cummins and Brown, along with Phil Harrison, as paid lobbyists for RECA reform. It was a move they would unfortunately come to regret.

Within two years, after a string of disagreements, broken engagements, and failed communications, Lori and Anna felt betrayed by the very people whom they had persuaded the tribe to hire. It looked to them like the all-too-familiar pattern from the "funding game." Cummins and Brown had been awarded over $300,000 by the tribe. They had declined to share any of this funding with any of the local activists (Mr. Thorne, Ms. Merritt, or Mr. Martinez), and, most importantly, by 1999 they were able to show little or no progress toward a reform of RECA.

Worst of all, the grassroots groups felt that the Washington lobbyists were trying to control them for their own benefit. After a confusing turn of scuttled backroom deals in Washington, public recriminations, and lots and lots of E-mail, the split between the grassroots groups and the lobbyists came to a head when the respective parties threw their support behind competing RECA reform bills.

A very public, very bitter conflict ensued. To the surprise of perhaps no one locally, Lori Goodman became the one most involved in the dispute with the lobbyists. Even some of her closest friends and colleagues privately voiced concern that this battle with the lobbyists might derail the RECA reform effort.

But to Lori's credit, she found the two issues inseparable. She had seen this pattern too many times before—she knew that when outsiders control the agenda, the work never seems to get done. When she took a strong public stance against Cummins and Brown and the National Committee for Radiation Victims, she was vilified in some quarters (most notably, those organizations and individuals local to NCRV), but cheered roundly in others. Those who supported her included many radiation exposure victims from all around the country, from Utah, Ohio, Alaska, and even some from the Rongelap Atoll, who were by this time in touch via E-mail.

One downwinder accused the NCRV "handlers" of "riding herd" on the victims from rural and isolated western communities, in order to secure themselves hefty legal fees and lifelong careers in the "radiation victims industry." Another personally thanked Lori "for your courage in speaking up and saying that there is a problem out there that needs remembering and needs some open discussion. . . . [W]e not only got screwed by our government but we also got screwed by many of our so-called best friends in the movement still there claiming to be our best advocates."

This time the grassroots activists, with Lori Goodman and the rest of Diné CARE in a leadership position, carried the day. In late 1999, a bill introduced by Utah Senator Orrin Hatch passed in the Senate, in no small part because of a lively education and support campaign by the grassroots groups from the Navajo Rez, the Pueblos, and elsewhere in the rural West. The bill passed the House by mid-2000 and was signed into law in August of that year.

As always, however, no victory is ever secure. At last report the federal government was issuing IOUs to RECA claimants, rather than actual payments.[9] Meanwhile, Alex Thorne's daughter finally succumbed to her leukemia in 1999. Leading non-Navajo activists from the Southwest, Carol Dewey and Paul Hicks, have both since died of cancer. And the number of aging Navajo miners who have managed to survive is dwindling.

■/

Even in the forest, no victory is ever secure. In the summer of 2000, Navajo Department of Forestry submitted a new ten-year forest-management plan. Despite the fact that the new plan fails to address most of the issues that killed the last long-term forest-management plan back in the early 1990s, no one in Diné CARE is taking it lightly. In August of 2000 the board gathered yet again to review their options, including a possible lawsuit.

■/

A year or so after Leroy's death, Adella lost her mother. No one even knew she was sick until she complained of difficulty breathing. The stunned doctors at Chinle's hospital found cancer that had spread throughout most of her body, including her lungs.

With little hope she was sent to a treatment center in Tucson, a nine-hour drive from Chinle, south through the White Mountain Apache Reservation, the Salt River Canyon, and the deserts of southern Arizona. When she returned she sat on the couch at Adella's with her legs curled up to her chest, tiny and emaciated, with an oxygen tube in her nose, and regaled her daughters with a lengthy, detailed description of the trip. She recounted every mountain range she had crossed (there were nine), different species of plants and trees, characteristics of the road, and a variety of other details about the land she had passed at highway speeds. It was an almost unbelievable display of alertness, observational powers and memory, all from an eighty-some-year-old woman, dying of cancer, who had never learned to read or write.

Adella has met someone new. One might even say she's happy again. Together they've been working on that home in the mountains that she and Leroy had always wanted. In fact, it's on the very spot that she and Leroy had always dreamed of building: at the top of the meadow beneath the silent cliffs of Saddle Butte, near the hogan where her dad, ancient and toothless, still spends his summers.

It's not quite the design that Leroy traced in the dust one September afternoon, but it looks just about as unusual. Adella laughed as she examined the steel-framed doorway and surrounding cinder block. "My family calls it 'the fortress.' This turkey will be here a long time after I'm gone."

Eli and the Bambina have grown tall and slender, physically fit from days spent herding the sheep, scrambling up and down the ridges and valleys that stretch out below the summits of Saddle Butte and Tsaile Peak, past piles of slash that stand slowly decaying amidst the sage and occasional prickly pears, beneath oaks, and pine trees, and cedars. As a flock, those sheep have become quite lively now that the churros are interbreeding with the rest. Adella sold off all the males a few years ago, but she kept the ewes, and now there are several new lambs with that highstrung churro blood. "You let them out of the corral," Adella's sister Angie once complained, "and they just want to take off running."

On a recent visit the kids lay on the ground with the anthropologist and the intern, next to a campfire, looking up at a sky filled with stars. The Milky Way rose with such brilliance that the two visitors at first thought it was a cloud moving in—illuminated from beneath by a city that wasn't there.

"Do you ever watch those science shows on TV," Eli asked, "about space and planets, that kind of stuff?" Their faces, sticking out of sleeping bags, glowed in the firelight. "Billions and billions of galaxies," said Eli, mimicking Carl Sagan, to giggles muffled by sleeping bags. "I wonder if there are people living in any of them."

The Bambina then spoke up. "In the old days, our grandparents said—well, they used to tell kind of a funny story about how the stars got that way. They said that the Holy People were putting the stars up in the sky very carefully, all in straight rows, in a straight line. First Man was taking the stars from a blanket one by one and placing them up in the sky. Then Coyote came along. He just wanted to get them all up there really fast so he grabbed the blanket and shook it and scattered them up there all over the place. That's how they got to be so messy up there."

■/

From time to time a letter will appear from the Rez, treasured connections from the house at the top of the meadow, which has no telephone and no E-mail:

Nov. 16, 1998

Dear John and Liling

Hi how are you doing? We wanted to say thanks for buying Eli the game and us the book . . .

Here in the mountains it rains a lot. It's been raining for over a week now and it snowed last Friday. I don't mind living here, it's OK, but I don't like getting up early in the morning. We have a hard time getting Eli up in the morning. Eli hates school but he gets good grades. I'm trying hard to get good grades but I guess I'm doing okay. I hope I am.

We have a lot of company, Angie and my grandpa live up here too, and those other guys [i.e., her cousins]. On weekends we usually watch TV over there at my grandpa's and we're sometimes on sheep patrol. Over the weekend we went to Albuquerque and saw Michelley and our little nieces and nephews. They are five months old, two years old and four. The oldest is a little conniver. She blames everything on me, and she got me in trouble a few times.

We have two roosters, one almost got eaten up by a mountain lion, but he outran the mountain lion. Ben and Tom camped out here about two weeks ago. We had a good time. We went pinion picking a few times, too. We have a cat named Kittsey, she's Eli's child. Oh, yeah, one of the roosters took over Winner's dog house so we had to borrow a dog house from Michelley.

Sincerely,

(The Bambina)

■/

Last summer the Bambina went through *Kinaaldá*—her puberty ceremony— her ritual reenactment of the transformation of Changing Woman. It's said of a young woman undergoing this transformation that she becomes holy. She is called upon, during the last day of the ceremony, to bless her family and neighbors—the children, to make them grow tall, and the adults, with their special requests for prayers and blessings. The ceremony ties the young woman to all those who went through the ceremony before her, and all of those who will go through it after her.

Among the other aspects during her four-day ceremony was an activity designed to remind her of her heritage as a Diné, a wanderer. Dressed in her finest jewelry and clothes, she was sent out in the morning, at noon, and in the evening to run as fast as she could for as long as she could. "She ran a long way up the mountain," Adella said with a laugh and a little pride. "Angie (her aunt) kept telling her, 'Don't run so far.' She didn't think she could make it back, but she did. She was a real strong runner!"

Her years of herding sheep have apparently paid off—or maybe she's just got a little of her dad in her.

■|

Changing Woman sat near the summit of Ch'óol'į'í on a rock. The Sun came, and sat beside her, and tried to embrace her; but she avoided him saying: "What do you mean by this? I want none of your embraces."

"It means I want you for my own," said the Sun. "I want you to come to the west, and make a home for me there."

"But I do not wish to do so," said she. "What right have you to ask me?"

"Did I not give your sons the weapons they needed to slay Nayéé', the Alien Monsters? Have I not done a great deal for you and your people, in truth? In truth, shouldn't you reward me for what I have done?"

Changing Woman was not moved.

"What you did you did of your own free will. I owe you no reward."

The Sun then urged her with another reason:

"When our son Nayéé' Neizghání the Monster Slayer last visited me, he promised you to me."

"What do I care for promises made by someone else. I am not bound by it. He has no right to speak for me."

Thus, four times she repulsed the Sun's advances.

The Sun pleaded with her a fifth time. "Come with me to the west and make a home for me."

"Let me hear first all you have to promise me. You have a beautiful house to the east. I have never seen it, but I have heard how beautiful it is. I want a

house just the same built for me in the west; I want to have it built floating on the water, away from the shore, so that in the future, when people increase, they will not annoy me with too many visits. I want all sorts of gems—white shell, turquoise, haliotis, jet, soapstone, agate, and redstone—planted around my house, so that they will grow and increase. I shall need animals to keep me company, because my sons and my sister will not go with me. Do this for me and I shall go with you to the west."

Ultimately the Sun promised her these things, and she agreed to accompany him.

From Dził Ná'ooditłii, she took leave of her sons, the Warriors, and her sister, White Shell Woman. With a retinue of Holy People and animals accompanying her, she began her journey west, past Red Knife Summit in the Chuska Mountains, through Chinle, where a ceremony was performed in honor of her betrothal.

Four days later, the group reached Dook'o'oosłííd, the mountains which the bilagáanas call the San Francisco peaks, on the far western boundary of the Navajo homeland. Changing Woman stretched out on top of the mountain, with her head facing the west. They manipulated her body and stretched out her limbs. She instructed the people to perform this same ceremony for all Navajo girls, when they turn from the ways of childhood to the ways of womanhood.

To this very day they seek to mould the body of a maiden into the perfect form of Asdząą nádleehé the Changing Woman, wife of Jóhonaa'éí the Sun.

What happened on the rest of the journey from Dook'o'oosłííd to the great ocean in the west is not known. But it is known that Changing Woman arrived at her floating house beyond the shore. There she lives to this very day. And there Jóhonaa'éí rejoins her each evening when his daily journey across the sky is completed. As he journeys towards the west, this is the song he sings:

In my thoughts I approach
The Sun God approaches
Earth's end he approaches,
Changing Woman's hearth he approaches,
In old age walking
The beautiful trail . . .[10]

notes

preface

1. John Farella, *The Main Stalk* (Tucson: University of Arizona Press, 1987).
2. The reader may notice the somewhat tortured construction of the author as "the anthropologist" in this book. As someone who was often present, perhaps even "in the way" of some of the events described in this book, I felt it fair to objectify my presence as I had done for the others.
3. See James Clifford and George Marcus, *Writing Culture: The Poetics and Politics of Ethnography* (Berkeley and Los Angeles: University of California Press, 1986).
4. See Bruno Latour, *We Have Never Been Modern* (Cambridge, Mass.: Harvard University Press, 1993). Also see discussion, chapter 6, following.

one

1. Some have pointed out, however, that sheep did not become an important part of the Navajo economy until much later, perhaps in the late eighteenth century–see Peter Iverson, *The Navajo Nation* (Albuquerque: University of New Mexico Press, 1981), 7.
2. Leroy was not the only Diné to be interested in reintroducing churros to the Navajo Nation. There were a couple organized projects at this time as well, one of which was a weaving co-op in the community of Ramah, and another sponsored in part by Utah State University.
3. *Bilagáana* is a Navajo term for *Anglo-American*, most widely believed to be a Navajo adaptation of the Spanish *Americano*. See Robert W. Young and William Morgan, Sr., *The Navajo language: A Grammar and Colloquial Dictionary* (Albuquerque: University of New Mexico Press, 1987).
4. Vine Deloria, *Custer Died for Your Sins: An Indian Manifesto* (Norman: University of Oklahoma Press, 1988).
5. Gladys Reichard, *Spider Woman: A Story of Navajo Weavers and Chanters* (1934; reprint, Albuquerque: University of New Mexico Press, 1997).
6. "People" here refers to the creatures of the fourth world, including many animal species.
7. Washington Matthews, *Navaho Legends* (Salt Lake City: University of Utah Press, 1994), 69.
8. Gladys Reichard, *Navaho Religion: A Study in Symbolism*, 2nd ed. (Princeton: Princeton University Press, 1963), 116.
9. *Diné* (roughly "The People") is the term Navajo people use to refer to themselves. "CARE" is an acronym for Citizens Against Ruining our Environment.
10. This quotation is from John Redhouse in a meeting with the Core Group in 1995. "[B]orn of" refers to the mother's clan into which one is born, "born for" refers to the father's clan. This is a characteristic Navajo way of reckoning kinship relations, and is a common part, for example, of personal introductions and greetings.

11. Thomas Hughes, *American Genesis: A Century of Invention and Technological Enthusiasm* (New York: Penguin Books, 1989).

12. J. Bradford De Long, "Slouching Towards Utopia?: The Economic History of the Twentieth Century," (1997) http://econ161.berkeley.edu/TCEH/Slouch_wealth2.html.

13. Sometimes, technologies have consequences that undermine their own intent. See Edward Tenner, *Why Things Bite Back, Technology and the Revenge of Unintended Consequences* (New York: Vintage Books, 1997). Tenner has called this phenomenon technological "revenge effects." Slow-to-emerge consequences are often direct replacements of more obvious catastrophic consequences: turn-of-the-century refrigeration systems, for example, whose unstable chemical compositions often resulted in explosions, were replaced with systems using chlorofluorocarbons (CFCs), revealed only much later to be causing depletion of ozone in Earth's upper atmosphere.

14. See Mark Dowie, *Losing Ground: American Environmentalism at the Close of the Twentieth Century* (Cambridge, Mass.: MIT Press, 1995).

15. Quoted in ibid., 125.

16. See David Western, R. Michael Wright, and Shirley Strum, eds., *Natural Connections: Perspectives on Community-Based Conservation* (New York: Island Press, 1995). Also see Barbara Rose Johnston, *Life and Death Matters* (Walnut Creek, Calif.: Altamira, 1997).

17. See Al Gedicks, *The New Resource Wars* (Boston: South End Press, 1993); Donald Grinde and Bruce E. Johansen, *Ecocide and Native Americans* (Santa Fe, N.Mex.: Clear Light Publishers, 1995).

18. Based on U.S. Census Bureau and Navajo Department of Economic Development data.

19. Earl Tulley recorded at a meeting of Diné CARE in November 1992.

two

1. Note that portions of this section and similar sections in this book are paraphrased rather than directly quoted from the original work. Also note that Matthews's original orthography for Navajo names has been replaced with the standardized orthography found in Young and Morgan, *The Navajo Language.*

2. Raymond F. Locke, *The Book of the Navajo* (Los Angeles: Mankind Publishing, 1992).

3. John Redhouse, *Holy Land: A Navajo Pilgrimage Back to Dinétah* (Albuquerque, N.Mex.: Redhouse-Wright Productions, 1985), 6. See also Klara Bonsack Kelley and Harris Francis, *Navajo Sacred Places* (Bloomington: Indiana University Press, 1994), 167.

4. Clyde Kluckhohn and Dorothea Leighton, *The Navaho* (New York: Doubleday, 1962), 40.

5. Douglas Preston, *Talking to the Ground* (New York: Simon and Schuster, 1995), 172–75.

6. Numerous sources contain various details about Kit Carson's siege of the Diné homeland and the subsequent years of exile. See, for example, Robert Young, *A Political History of the Navajo Tribe* (Tsaile, Ariz.: Navajo Community College Press, 1978); Ruth Underhill, *The Navajos* (Norman, Okla.: University of Oklahoma Press, 1956); See also Kelley and Francis, *Navajo Sacred Places.*

7. Iverson, *Navajo Nation*, 9.

8. Ibid., 16.

9. Young, *A Political History of the Navajo Tribe.*

10. Iverson, *Navajo Nation*, 17.

11. Ibid., 18.
12. Matthews, *Navaho Legends*, 2.
13. Iverson, *Navajo Nation*, 19.
14. Ibid., 20.
15. These included the Metalliferous Minerals Leasing Act of 1918, introduced by Arizona and New Mexico representatives in the U.S. House and Senate, and the General Leasing Act of 1920.
16. See Robert W. Young, "The Rise of the Navajo Tribe," in *Plural Society in the Southwest*, ed. Edward H. Spicer and Raymond H. Thompson (New York: Weatherhead Foundation, 1972), 187–88.
17. David F. Aberle, *The Peyote Religion among the Navajo* (Chicago: Aldine Press, 1966), 52–53.
18. Quote attributed to E. R. Fryer of the Navajo Service, in W. G. McGinnies, "Stock Reduction and Range Management," Navajo Service Land Management Conference. Quoted in Iverson, *Navajo Nation*, 27.
19. McGinnies, quoted in Iverson, *Navajo Nation*, 28.
20. Iverson, *Navajo Nation*, 33.
21. Ibid., 37.
22. Ibid., 21.
23. Arturo Escobar, *Encountering Development: The Making and Unmaking of the Third World* (Princeton, N.J.: Princeton University Press, 1995).
24. Russell Lawrence Barsh, "The Challenge of Indigenous Self-Determination," *University of Michigan Journal of Law Reform* 262 (winter, 1993): 277–312.
25. Escobar, *Encountering Development*, 83.
26. Barsh, "The Challenge of Indigenous Self-Determination," 295.
27. Matthews, *Navaho Legends*, 75–76.
28. Ibid., 77.
29. Young and Morgan, *The Navajo Language*, 296.
30. John Redhouse, *A Short History of Logging on the Navajo Reservation* (Albuquerque: Redhouse Wright Productions, 1992).
31. Ibid., 2.
32. Philip Reno, *Mother Earth, Father Sky, and Economic Development* (Albuquerque: University of New Mexico Press, 1981).
33. Navajo Forest Products Industries, Annual Report, 1978.
34. *Navajo Forest Products Industries: Twenty Years of Growth* (Shiprock, N.Mex.: NFPI, 1978).
35. Ibid., 2.
36. Both the Council delegate from Leroy and Adella's chapter, as well as the head of the Navajo Nation's Department of Natural Resources, were also on the board of NFPI.
37. Timber harvest rate as measured in board feet per acre.
38. Reno, *Mother Earth, Father Sky*, 91.
39. Based on the Navajo Nation Controller's report to the Navajo Nation Council, April 28, 1993.
40. Robert Billie, *Navajo Forest Timber Resources: A Condition Report*. Navajo Department of Forestry, 1981.
41. Normand Birtcher and Gorman Yazzie, *Navajo Forest Water Quality: A Condition Report*. Navajo Department of Forestry, 1981 (emphasis added).
42. A. K. Arbab, *Navajo Forest Regeneration: A Condition Report*. Navajo Department of Forestry, 1981.

three

1. Blessingway is one of the most central and most common of Navajo ceremonies.
2. Adella was no stranger to these kinds of experiences. On one occasion, while staying in a dormitory at a nurses' training seminar in Oklahoma, she had a vivid dream of someone in her room, at the foot of her bed, coughing furiously, gasping for air, trying to clear his lungs. "When I told the other ladies about it in the morning, they all kind of freaked out," she said. "They told me, 'This place used to be a TB sanitarium!'"
3. Navajo resistance to the capturing of words on paper or audiotape—particularly ceremonial utterances, can be found in Berard Haile, *Navajo Coyote Tales* (Lincoln: University of Nebraska Press, 1968); Reichard, *Navaho Religion: A Study in Symbolism;* Barry Toelken, "Life and Death in Navajo Coyote Tales," in *Recovering the Word,* ed. B. Swann and A. Krupat (Berkeley and Los Angeles: University of California Press, 1987); For a discussion of this resistance among Southwest tribes in general, see Elizabeth Brandt, "Native American Attitudes Towards Literacy and Recording in the Southwest," *Journal of the Linguistic Association of the Southwest* 4 (1981): 152–60.
4. John Farella, *The Wind in a Jar* (Albuquerque: University of New Mexico Press, 1993).
5. Personal communication between Harry Walters, director of the Navajo Culture Program at Navajo Community College, Tsaile, Arizona, and Leroy Jackson, August 1993, at which the author was present and which he asked to record.
6. See Trudy Griffin-Pierce, *Earth Is My Mother, Sky Is My Father* (Albuquerque: University of New Mexico Press, 1994).
7. Ibid., 24.
8. This too is changing in some places. Many architecturally "modern" homes may have hogans built nearby or adjoining as semispecialized ceremonial structures.
9. Kelley and Francis, *Navajo Sacred Places,* 156.
10. Walters and Jackson, personal communication, 1993.
11. Ibid.
12. Adapted from Berard Haile, *Upward Moving and Emergence Way* (Lincoln: University of Nebraska Press, 1981), 175–77.
13. Clyde Kluckhohn, *Navajo Witchcraft* (Boston: Beacon Press, 1967).
14. Louise Lamphere, *To Run after Them* (Tucson: University of Arizona Press, 1977).
15. James Berkhofer, *The White Man's Indian* (New York: Vintage Books, 1978).
16. Quote attributed to Thomas J. Morgan, Commissioner of Indian Affairs in 1889. In Francis Paul Prucha, ed., *Americanizing the American Indian* (Cambridge: Harvard University Press, 1973), 227.

four

1. Lamphere, *To Run after Them,* 38.
2. Sylvia Manygoats, elder from Navajo Mountain, quoted in Kelley and Francis, *Navajo Sacred Places,* 30.
3. Dowie, *Losing Ground,* 129.
4. Lori's father's clan—the Towering House People.
5. *A Strand in the Web,* Greenpeace Productions, 1989.
6. Matthews, *Navaho Legends,* 105.
7. For a more complete discussion of this topic, see Douglas Comer, *Ritual Ground* (Berkeley and Los Angeles: University of California Press, 1996).
8. Walter Howerton, Jr., "Indian Dollars Grease the Gallup Economy," *Gallup Independent,* March 27, 2000.
9. From the *Gallup Visitors Directory,* 1998. Emphasis added.

10. Ibid.

11. Howerton, "Indian Dollars Grease the Gallup Economy."

12. Jerold Levy and S. Kunitz, *Indian Drinking: Navajo Practices and Anglo-American Theories* (Tucson: University of Arizona Press, 1974).

13. The situation was so bad that, in 1973, nineteen-year-old Larry Casuse, along with fellow University of New Mexico student Robert Nakaidine, kidnapped and held hostage then-mayor Eddie Munoz (who owned one of the most notorious bars on the reservation border) to draw attention to the situation. After a short standoff, Casuse was killed by police gunfire.

14. Rob Tenequer, "Santa Fe Bound Marchers Draw Attention to Alcohol Problem," *Navajo Times*, February 23, 1989.

15. Patricia Guthrie, "No More 'Booze and Cruise,'" *Albuquerque Tribune*, March 6, 1992.

16. This and all subsequent quotes come from transcripts from audiotapes made by members themselves at early meetings of the "Core Group."

17. C. Dexter Gill, a non-Indian, was at that time head of the Navajo Department of Forestry.

18. Compare, for instance, with Kelley and Francis, *Navajo Sacred Places*, 148: The Diné "don't want 'historic preservation' efforts to preserve mementos of 'traditional' Navajo culture. They want those efforts to help keep the Navajo way of life itself alive. And the Navajo way can't survive unless its practitioners have some control over the whole landscape that they need to live."

19. See Klara Kelley, *Navajo Land Use* (New York: Academic Press, 1986).

20. Redhouse, *Holy Land*.

21. Reichard, *Navajo Religion*, 496.

22. Paul Zolbrod, *Diné Bahane': The Navajo Creation Story* (Albuquerque: University of New Mexico Press, 1984), 385.

23. Redhouse, *Holy Land*, 7.

24. "Medicine Man Tries to Stop Desecration of Sacred Mountain," *Navajo Times*, August 3, 1983. Cited in Redhouse, *Holy Land*, 8.

25. Kelley and Francis, *Navajo Sacred Places*, 180.

26. Klara Kelley, former Navajo Nation historic-preservation-department staff member, personal communication.

27. Cf. also Western, Wright, and Strum, *Natural Connections*.

28. Kelley and Francis, *Navajo Sacred Places*, 181.

29. "Indians Seek Protection for Religion," *Albuquerque Journal*, November 23, 1991. Zah was not successful at persuading the committee to include provisions for sacred sites lying outside reservation boundaries.

30. Lucille Charlie, personal communication.

five

1. Ten-year forest-management plans are required on Indian lands under the National Indian Forest Resources Management Act (NIFRMA). They specify each timber sale that will occur in a given ten-year period and provide details regarding what each sale will yield in terms of size of harvest, revenues, and environmental impacts.

2. An account of these murders and the aftermath, as well as John Redhouse's role in community organizing, is provided in Rodney Barker, *The Broken Circle: A True Story of Murder and Magic in Indian Country* (New York: Ivy Books, 1993).

3. Roughly adapted from Haile, OFM, *Upward Moving and Emergence Way*. See also Zolbrod, *Diné Bahane': The Navajo Creation Story*.

4. Reichard, *Navaho Religion*, xl.

six

1. Not too surprisingly, a lot of the new gadgets to hit the Diné Bikéyah over the last century have the word *béésh* in them. *Béésh* originally meant metal (as in the blade of a knife) but has now also come to represent machines and other things made of metal. A stove, for instance, is called *Béésh bii kǫʼí*, "metal with fire inside of it." The rest of the particles: *doo* = negative; *biyoochʼįįd* = "tells a lie"; *í* = "the one."

2. Keith Basso, *Wisdom Sits in Places: Landscape and Language among the Western Apache* (Albuquerque: University of New Mexico Press, 1996), 58–59.

3. Kelley and Francis, *Navajo Sacred Places*, 187.

4. Ibid.

5. Basso, *Wisdom Sits in Places*, 59.

6. Gary Witherspoon, *Language and Art in the Navajo Universe* (Ann Arbor: University of Michigan Press, 1977).

7. Griffin-Pierce, *Earth Is My Mother*, 73.

8. James McNeley, *Holy Wind in Navajo Philosophy* (Tucson: University of Arizona Press, 1981), 35.

9. Anna Frazier, personal communication, Gallup, N.Mex., 1997.

10. Cf. Ferdinand de Saussure, *Course in General Linguistics* (La Salle, Ill.: Open Court Publishing, 1992).

11. Wendell Berry, *Life is a Miracle* (Washington, D.C.: Counterpoint Press, 2000), 46.

12. Indian Forest Management Assessment Team for the Intertribal Timber Council, *An Assessment of Indian Forests and Forest Management in the United States* (Portland, Ore: 1993).

13. These scoping sessions were mandated under the National Environmental Policy Act.

14. This was the baldest statement of forestry's perspective on the nature of trees. At a different scoping session, Anderson Morgan, director of the Navajo Department of Natural Resources, formulated this perspective a little more subtly, gently co-opting traditional Navajo ways of looking at trees: "Our elderly, our medicine men have also said that within the four sacred mountains, within the rainbow of life, the Navajo Nation is blessed with various natural resources. We have been raised with that type of teachings. We also have spiritual, emotional, and religious ties to the land. Our Mother Earth provides different *resources* like grasses, plants and *timber*, rocks and sand is another *resource that is used to build roads and provide jobs*" (Shiprock, N.Mex., September 28, 1992; emphases added).

15. Carl Sagan, *The Demon Haunted World* (New York: Ballantine Books, 1996).

16. For a more thorough discussion of the role of expertise in the interpretation of visual representations, see Charles Goodwin, "Professional Vision," *American Anthropologist* 96, no. 3 (1994): 606–33. Goodwin demonstrates, for example, the role of "expert testimony" as a basis for interpreting visual representations in the now (in)famous 1992 criminal trial of members of the Los Angeles police force for the beating of Los Angeles motorist Rodney King. A key witness for the defense was Sergeant Charles Duke, an LAPD "expert" on the use of police force. In a detailed analysis, Goodwin has shown how Sergeant Duke carefully interpreted the widely publicized videotape of the beating, highlighting for the jury subtle motions of Mr. King as he lay prostrate, and interpreting these for the jury as examples of King's willful "escalation" of the encounter, to which the police officers, as "disciplined" academy graduates, were trained to respond in certain prescribed ways. With the aid of Sergeant Duke, what looked to "untrained" eyes like a savage beating of a helpless motorist, was thus reinterpreted as a disciplined response to a "'PCP-crazed giant' who was argued to be in control of the situation."

17. See John Seely Brown and Paul Duguid, *The Social Life of Information* (Boston: Harvard Business School Press, 2000).

18. Anna Alonso, "The Politics of Space, Time and Substance: State Formation, Nationalism and Ethnicity," *Annual Review of Anthropology* 23 (1994): 381. See also Timothy Mitchell, "Everyday Metaphors of Power," *Theory and Society* 19 (1990): 569.

19. Kelley and Francis, *Navajo Sacred Places*, 148.

20. Alonso's "Politics of Space, Time and Substance," and Mitchell's "Everyday Metaphors of Power" are two examples.

21. Leroy Jackson's reference to 1957 alludes to the year in which NFPI was founded.

22. Mr. Jackson's comments at each scoping session come from transcripts made available by the Navajo Nation Department of Forestry. In addition, the author had direct access to audiotapes of the Aneth scoping session made available by Diné CARE.

23. Leroy Jackson's words bear an interesting parallel to both feminist and radical constructivist critiques of science. Consider, for instance, the following quotation from see Latour, *We Have Never Been Modern*, 29. The separation between human and natural worlds underlies the "trick" by which science lays claim to its ultimate objectivity. In controlled experiments or elaborate models, "scientists declare that they themselves are not speaking; rather, facts speak for themselves. These mute entities are thus capable of speaking, writing, signifying within the artificial chamber of the laboratory."

24. Alex Shoumatoff, *Legends of the American Desert* (New York: Knopf, 1997), 439.

25. It is worth noting here that a few members of the original community group who formed to oppose timber cutting in the Chuskas likewise commented that they were a little uncomfortable with Leroy's interactional style. "He was too aggressive," one local once commented about Leroy in a personal communication with the author. "It's really not the Navajo way to be so confrontational." Although such individuals may not have associated closely with Leroy and Adella during this time, they did continue to support them in a variety of ways, demonstrating what various anthropologists have characterized as a Navajo tolerance for diversity.

26. Shoumatoff, *Legends of the American Desert*, 431.

seven

1. Brown's ruling was handed down on June 9, 1992. For a concise chronology of these events, see John Redhouse, "Navajos Oppose Logging" (Albuquerque: Redhouse-Wright Productions, 1992).

2. Crystal was the only chapter in the area of the mountains that did not pass a resolution supporting Diné CARE in 1992.

3. Not a direct relation to John Redhouse.

4. See Griffin-Pierce, *Earth is My Mother*, for a thorough discussion of Navajo astronomical knowledge in sand paintings.

5. See, for example, Aaron Cicourel, "The Integration of Distributed Knowledge in Collaborative Medical Diagnosis," in *Intellectual Teamwork: Social and Technological Foundations of Cooperative Work*, ed. J. Galegher, R. Kraut, and C. Egido (Hillsdale, N.J.: Erlbaum, 1990), 221–42. Cicourel points out that medical staff routinely consider the source in their appraisal of diagnostic information.

6. Adapted from Matthews, *Navaho Legends*, 112.

7. Nor is sweating an activity solely for men in Navajo society, although men and women do not sweat together.

8. Washington Matthews identifies "mountain tobacco" (which Ervin called this plant) with the species *nicotiana attenuata*.

9. Memorandum submitted to President Peterson Zah, October 20, 1992.

10. Redhouse, "Navajos Oppose Logging," 2.

eight

1. Quicken is a registered trademark of Intuit Corporation.

2. The funding organization's identity has been withheld here because, in fairness, this application was typical. It should be noted that Lori would never have even encountered this checklist if she had not previously submitted a preapplication form and passed the first qualifying round for the formal application process.

3. Edwin Hutchins, *Cognition in the Wild* (Cambridge, Mass.: MIT Press, 1995), 115.

4. See Wayne Senner, ed., *The Origins of Writing* (Lincoln: University of Nebraska Press, 1989).

5. Michel Foucault, *Discipline and Punish: The Birth of the Prison* (New York: Vintage Books, 1979), 170 (emphasis added).

6. Ibid., 170.

7. Ibid., 174.

8. Gary John Previts and Barbara Dubis Merino, *A History of Accountancy in the United States: The Cultural Significance of Accounting* (Columbus: Ohio State University Press, 1998).

9. Joanne Yates, *Control through Communication: The Rise of System in American Management* (Baltimore: Johns Hopkins University Press, 1993), 39.

10. Chief Johnny Jackson, a Yakima member of Indigenous Environmental Network, echoed this distinction in a talk at the Protecting Mother Earth conference in Stroud, Oklahoma, June 1993. Note also that a number of social scientists have shown that even in the most apparently "rationalized" environments, ad hoc interactions and a reliance on such "irrational" resources as interpersonal relationships not only persist but may also be responsible for the continued functioning of the organization. See, for instance, Cicourel, "Integration of Distributed Knowledge."

11. Hutchins, *Cognition in the Wild*, 115.

12. Lori Goodman, "Barriers to Effective Citizen Action on Native Lands," *The Workbook* (Albuquerque: Southwest Research and Information Center) 19, no. 2 (1994).

13. A very similar controversy, incidentally, currently surrounds managed health care in the United States.

14. Cf. Western, Wright, and Strum, *Natural Connections*.

15. Goodman, "Barriers to Effective Citizen Action," 63.

16. Ibid., 65.

17. Kevin Kelly, *Out of Control: The New Biology of Machines, Social Systems and the Economic World* (Reading, Mass.: Addison Wesley, 1994).

18. George Gilder, *Forbes ASAP*, March 1995, 63.

19. Quoted in Arthur Kaplan, "The Coming Anarchy," *Atlantic Monthly* (February 1994): 44–76.

nine

1. Specifically, The National Indian Forest Resources Management Act.

2. Letter dated February 9, 1993.

3. Letter dated February 25, 1993.

4. Navajo Department of Forestry memo, February 23, 1993.

5. Meeting of the Intertribal Timber Council, February 1993.

6. Leroy Jackson, statement to Navajo Nation Council Budget and Finance Committee, April 27, 1993.

7. Navajo Nation Controller's office, statement to Navajo Nation Council Budget and Finance Committee, April 27, 1993.
8. As mentioned above, the EA was actually prepared by the Navajo Forestry Department under contract for the BIA, who had ultimate authority to approve timber sales.
9. Letter from Bruce Baizel to Ed Sam of Navajo Department of Forestry, June 18, 1993.
10. Memorandum from C. Dexter Gill, director of Navajo Forestry Department, to Anderson Morgan, executive director of Navajo Nation Division of Natural Resources, June 24, 1993.
11. Adapted from Matthews, *Navaho Legends*, 110.
12. Matthews, *Navaho Legends*, 119–20.
13. Harry Walters, director of the Navajo Studies Program at Diné College (1993), personal communication with Leroy Jackson.
14. The strategy has since caught on. A number of tribes belonging to the Intertribal Timber Council (a coalition of sixty-five timber-producing tribes from the United States) have sought exemption from federal statutes governing timber cutting, especially such environmental statutes as the National Environmental Policy Act and the Endangered Species Act. Promoting themselves as "the original environmentalists," many ITC tribes petitioned the U.S. government for exemption from the ESA, claiming that their own native heritage left them better equipped to deal with wildlife and environmental issues than federal regulations ever could. The whole ideology is rather suspect. Adella points out that a tiny minority of ITC's member tribes actually have an Indian person directing tribal forestry programs. And, as I discussed in a previous chapter, BIA and tribal forestry personnel seldom represent the forest values of the people whose forests they manage.
15. Adapted from Matthews, *Navaho Legends*, and from Zolbrod, *Diné Bahane'*.

ten

1. Matthews, *Navaho Legends*, 138.
2. The history is a long and complicated one. The best sources to read to learn more about it include David Brugge, *The Navajo-Hopi Land Dispute* (Albuquerque: University of New Mexico Press, 1995); See also John Redhouse, *Geopolitics of the Navajo Hopi Land Dispute* (Albuquerque: Redhouse/Wright Productions, 1985).
3. Quotes from this conference call are taken from transcripts of an audiotape recording of the call made with the consent of Diné CARE members.
4. One of the activities incumbent on Leroy and Adella at this time was travel to the homesites of appellants to gather notarized statements from them for use in the appeal.

eleven

1. John Redhouse, "An Overview of Uranium and Nuclear Development on Indian Lands in the Southwest," *Southwest Indigenous Uranium Forum Newsletter*, September 1993, 6.
2. Peter Eichstaedt, *If You Poison Us: Uranium and Native Americans* (Santa Fe, N.Mex.: Red Crane Books, 1992).
3. Redhouse, "Overview of Uranium and Nuclear Development," 6.
4. U.S. Environmental Protection Agency. *Integrated Risk Information System (IRIS) on Radon 222*. (Cincinnati: Environmental Criteria and Assessment Office, Office of Health and Environmental Assessment, Office of Research and Development, 1993).
5. Eichstaedt, *If You Poison Us*, 49.

6. Henry N. Doyle, memorandum, "Survey of Uranium Mines on Navajo Reservation, November 14–17, 1949, January 11–12, 1950," U.S. Public Health Service, Salt Lake City, Utah, 1950 (cited in Eichstaedt).

7. Cate Gilles, "Navajo Miners Falling Victim to RECA Obstacles," *Navajo Times*, November 21, 1996.

8. Peter Eichstaedt, "Justice Delayed," *Albuquerque Journal*, September 15, 1996.

9. Working months are determined from a formula based on a worker's duration of employment in the mines and the given mines' richness of deposits.

10. Gilles, "Navajo Miners Falling Victim."

11. "Former Miners 'Frustrated,'" *Gallup Independent*, April 8, 1996.

12. John Redhouse, "Navajo Radiation Victims Still Denied Compensation," *Southwest Indigenous Uranium Forum Newsletter*, September 1993.

13. Eichstaedt, *If You Poison Us*, 148.

14. Redhouse, "Overview of Uranium and Nuclear Development," 5.

15. Testimony of former miner before Navajo Nation Council, reported by Cate Gilles, "Push on for Special Tribal Council Session," *Navajo Times*, November 7, 1996.

16. *Final Report of the Advisory Committee on Human Radiation Experiments* (Washington, D.C.: U.S. Government Printing Office, 1995).

17. Committee on Thyroid Screening Related to I-131 Exposure, Institute of Medicine, and Committee on Exposure of the American People to I-131 from the Nevada Atomic Bomb Tests, National Research Council, *Exposure of the American People to Iodine-131 from Nevada Nuclear Bomb Tests* (Washington, D.C.: National Academy Press, 1999).

18. Physicians for Social Responsibility, "Marshall Islands Stands at a New 'Crossroads,'" *PSR Health Research Bulletin* 3(1) (1996). See also Glenn Alcalay, Testimony before the United States of America Advisory Committee on Human Radiation Experiments, Washington, D.C., March 15, 1995. Local taboos also played a role in preventing researchers from understanding many of the effects on Marshall Islanders. Miscarriages and birth defects, for instance, went unreported for a long time because local women did not feel comfortable discussing them in the presence of other family members.

19. P. Mohai and B. Bryant, "Race, Poverty, and the Environment," *EPA Journal* 18 (1992): 6–8.

20. Sybill Nahr and Uwe Peters, eds., *Poison Fire, Sacred Earth: Testimonies, Lectures and Conclusions*. Proceedings of the World Indigenous Uranium Forum, Salzburg, 1992 (Munich: The World Uranium Hearing e.V., 1992). Also see: http://www.ratical.com/radiation/WorldUraniumHearing.

21. Victor Turner, *The Ritual Process: Structure and Anti-structure* (Ithaca, N.Y.: Cornell University Press, 1969).

22. Ibn Khaldun, *The Muqaddimah: An Introduction to History* (Princeton: Princeton University Press, 1981).

23. This fascination has led to some of the craziest acts of fraud, including the following, reported in the *High Country News*, November 15, 1993: "A man claiming to know secret Cherokee spiritual and sexual techniques has distressed Native American leaders. Harley 'Swift Deer' Reagan says he is a half-Cherokee reincarnation of Billy the Kid and an elder in the Twisted Hair Society, which takes parts of various religions and twists them into a new 'braid of knowledge,' reports the *Arizona Republic*. Reagan's center in Scottsdale, Ariz., holds $1,000 sexual training workshops which Reagan says are based on Cherokee techniques. Cherokee Nation spokeswoman Lynn Howard disagrees. 'His actions are culturally depraved,' she says. The nation denies his claim to ancestry and says he damages the Cherokee

reputation. 'Sacred traditions of all tribes were given to us by our creator,' adds Vernon Foster, of the American Indian Movement. 'We can't allow them to be desecrated by phony imitations.' Reagan's seminars, however, don't break the law. 'That's true,' concedes Howard. 'There is nothing illegal in being in atrociously bad taste.'"

24. "German Hobbyists a Tribe Apart," *San Jose Mercury News*, August 6, 2000.

twelve

1. This was before the more recent, more widespread availability of newer medications designed to treat the vascular activity underlying migraine.
2. Michael Satchell and David Bowermaster, "The Worst Federal Agency," *U.S. News and World Report*, November 28, 1994, 61–64. Accounting for these lost funds has been deemed "impossible." While Indian schools and medical care slump to standards that are the worst in the nation, worse, in fact, than many so-called third world countries, corruption, mismanagement, and waste have thrived at the BIA.
3. Adapted from Zolbrod, *Diné Bahane'*. Note that Zolbrod's choice of the term "Rain God" probably refers to the *Yé'ii*, whom the Diné refer to more commonly as "Water Sprinkler."
4. Peter Nabokov, *Indian Running* (Santa Fe, N.Mex.: Ancient City Press, 1981), 13.
5. Dylan Thomas, "Do not go gentle into that good night," in *The Poems of Dylan Thomas* (New York: New Directions, 1971).
6. Kit Miniclier, personal communication, December 1993.
7. Karin Schill, "Missing: Another Tribal Environmentalist," *High Country News*, October 17, 1994.
8. Fred Johnson and Don Noble were killed in a mysterious plane crash shortly after traveling to Washington, D.C., in the 1980s in an attempt to secure fairer royalties for Navajo resources.

thirteen

1. Shoumatoff, *Legends of the American Desert*, 450.
2. Ibid., 446.
3. John Farella, *The Main Stalk* (Tucson: University of Arizona Press, 1984), 18.
4. I would like to thank Alicia Keeswood for help with this translation of Lena Nakai's text.
5. The audit was ultimately conducted in the spring of 1994. Sadly, despite the requests of Diné CARE for a thorough historical, financial audit of the mill, the audit consisted of little more than a reiteration of mill management's position that "the mill remains a viable enterprise if given a timely supply of timber from the Navajo forest."
6. Shoumatoff, *Legends of the American Desert*, 442.

fourteen

1. James Faris and Harry Walters, "Navajo History: Some Implications of Contrasts of Navajo Ceremonial Discourse," *History and Anthropology* 5 (1990): 1–18.
2. Samuel Gill, *Sacred Words: A Study of Navajo Religion and Prayer* (Westport, Conn.: Greenwood Press, 1981).
3. Witherspoon, *Language and Art in the Navajo Universe*. See also Dell Hymes, *'In Vain I Tried To Tell You': Essays in Native American Ethnopoetics* (Philadelphia: University of Pennsylvania Press, 1982); Dennis Tedlock, *The Spoken Word and the Work of Interpretation* (Philadelphia: University of Pennsylvania Press 1983).

4. Dowie, *Losing Ground,* 56. Throughout the late 1980s and early 1990s, bloated and cash-strapped mainstream environmental organizations had offered board positions, endorsements, and other benefits to corporate America in exchange for large cash donations, a process known as "greenwashing." A 1990 survey of seven mainstream environmental organizations' boards of directors showed widespread representation of top corporations. "Twenty-four of the directors [on these environmental organizations] were associated with corporations that—like Exxon, Monsanto, and Union Carbide—are on the National Wildlife Federation's list of Toxic 500." See also Jim Donahue, "Environmental Board Games," *Multinational Monitor* (March 1990): 10.

5. For the other grassroots activists, this mantra referred to the banning of commercial cuts on all public U.S. forests.

6. Among the other legal actions taken during this period was a suit filed in late summer 1994 by Steve Sugarman and Bruce Baizel on behalf of Diné CARE and eight other groups asking the federal court "to require the BIA to consult with US Fish and Wildlife Service on the effects of timber sale activities approved under the 1982 forest management plan on the Mexican spotted owl. The lawsuit also asked the court to halt any ground disturbing activities until that consultation had taken place." (from a memo to Diné CARE board from Bruce Baizel dated December 5, 1995).

7. Reichard, *Navaho Religion,* 423.

8. Luckert, Karl, introduction to Haile, *Navajo Coyote Tales.*

9. Toelken, "Life and Death in Navajo Coyote Tales," 388.

10. Ibid., 389.

11. Some of the visual allegory is rather specific. Ed Richards, general manager of NFPI, walked with a cane after an automobile accident near the end of 1993.

12. See, for instance, William Hanks, "Discourse Genres in a Theory of Practice," *American Ethnologist* 14 (1987): 668–92. Within decades of Spanish colonization of Mesoamerica, Mayan nobility adapted their own literacy traditions into letters to the Spanish Crown.

13. E.g., Lila Abu Lughod, "The Romance of Resistance: Tracing Transformations of Power through Bedouin Women," *American Ethnologist* 17, no. 1 (1990): 41–55.

14. For example, with regard to video, see Terence Turner, "Defiant Images: The Kayapo Appropriation of Video," *Anthropology Today* 8 (1992): 5–16. Regarding the Internet, see Daniel Miller and Don Slater, *The Internet: An Ethnographic Approach* (New York: New York University Press, 2000).

15. This selection of Jimmy Smith's recorded statement is a translation courtesy of Alicia Keeswood, a former student intern with Diné CARE.

fifteen

1. Peter Schwartz and Peter Leyden, "The Long Boom: A History of the Future: 1980–2020," *Wired* 5.07, July, 1997.

2. In all fairness, some of the (several thousand) millionaires spawned by that Seattle software company have become active pioneers in what has come to be known as "The New Philanthropy" (*Time,* July 24, 2000). And, in fact, Navajo Nation just recently achieved a major milestone of wiring 110 chapter houses to the Internet, something unimaginable even five years ago. The feat was achieved in no small part through a grant from the Bill and Melinda Gates Foundation. (See "Navajo Nation All Wired Up to the Net," *Indian Country Today,* October 20, 2000). For an alternative perspective see Paulina Borsook, "Cyberselfish," *Mother Jones* (July/August, 1996).

3. GIS (Geographic Information Systems) is a computer-based mapping tool that allows the visualization of statistical data. It's based on the idea that any number of features in a landscape—rainfall, slope, soil quality, human demographic data—can be correlated and visualized in ways that would be impossible without computing power.

4. The anthropologist and the intern were married after leaving the Diné Bikéyah, prompting considerable glee among the members of Diné CARE, who not only took credit for bringing the two together, but who also enjoyed the extended kinship implications. Adella's comment on learning the news was simply: "Now I'll have to buy Lori some cows."

5. A pseudonym.

6. *Indian Country Today*, January 27–February 3, 1997. More recently, other oil companies have also been implicated in the careless polluting of Navajo lands. In late March 1998 the federal government sued Texaco for dumping more than 500,000 gallons of polluted water into the tributary system of the San Juan River on Navajo lands in southern Utah.

7. As of mid-2000 approximately 180 residents still held out against forced relocation, according to John Redhouse (personal communication).

8. Anna Frazier was a clan grandmother both to Alexander Thorne and to Lori Goodman.

9. "Former Uranium Miners Getting IOU's Instead of Cash," Boulder (Colorado) *Daily Camera*, August 16, 2000.

10. Adapted and summarized from Matthews, *Navaho Legends*, 133–34.

"Twenty Years of Growth"

Alonso, "Politics of Space, Time and Substance"

Barsh, "The Challenge of Indigenous Self-Determination"

Basso, *Wisdom Sits in Places*

Cicourel, "Integration of Distributed Knowledge"

Dowie, *Losing Ground*

Eichstaedt, *If You Poison Us*

Escobar, *Encountering Development*

Gilles, "Navajo Miners Falling Victim"

Griffin-Pierce, *Earth Is My Mother*

Howerton, "Indian Dollars Grease the Gallup Economy"

Hutchins, *Cognition in the Wild*

Iverson, *The Navajo Nation*

Lamphere, *To Run after Them*

Kelley and Francis, *Navajo Sacred Places*

Matthews, *Navaho Legends*

Mitchell, "Everyday Metaphors of Power"

Redhouse, *Holy Land*

Redhouse, "Overview of Uranium and Nuclear Development"

Redhouse, *Short History of Logging*

Reichard, *Navaho Religion*

Reno, *Mother Earth, Father Sky*

Shoumatoff, *Legends of the American Desert*

Toelken, "Life and Death in Navajo Coyote Tales"

Western, Wright, and Strum, *Natural Connections*

Young, *The Navajo Language*

Zolbrod, *Diné Bahane'*

problems with grants, 110; proposes cartoon response to industry ads, 201; in Protection Way ceremony, 197; receives recognition for Diné CARE work, 100; response to timber industry ads, 200–201; as tough and effective negotiator, 121–22; as unofficial executive director of Diné CARE, 103–6, 218; at Window Rock special council session on forests, 187; working with Lucy Charlie, 60–61

Goodwin, Charles, 232n. 16

Gorman, Nelson, 177

Grants Mineral Belt, 145

Greenpeace, 52

greenwashing, 238n. 4

hand tremblers, 156, 170

Harrison, Phil, 148, 220

Hatch, Orrin, 221

herbal medicine, 34

Hicks, Paul, 222

High Country News, 91

Hitt, Sam, 67, 69, 88–89, 92, 116, 120, 189, 199–200, 211, 213; announces hiring of private investigator, 190; and breach of trust, 90

Hobbyists, 150–51

Holy People, 5, 8, 34, 73, 161, 185, 188, 197, 198, 219, 223, 226

Holy Wind, 34, 77–78, 161

Hopis: land dispute with Navajos, 137

Huerfano, New Mexico, 58–62

Hutchins, Edwin, 106, 109

incinerator, toxic-waste, 50–52

Indian boarding schools, 40, 49

Indian Country Today, 91

Indigenous Environmental Network, 53, 90, 152

information as social process, 93

Insulation Contractors Unlimited, 58–62

Interior Board of Indian Appeals, 88

Italian film crew, 135

Jackson, Leroy, 1–8, 13, 32, 38–40, 57–58, 67–73, 212; burial of, 178; consultation with others, 93; convenes first Diné Spiritual Gathering, 92; and daughter, 115; disappearance of, 169–72; discovery of his body, 172;

hung in effigy, 91, 99; marriage to Adella, 42; meets with loggers and mill workers in Crystal, N. M., 127; migraine headaches, 154, 163; office in home described, 14; private investigator looks into death of, 189; receives poem in mail, 165; at scoping session, 83–85; the search for, 172; seeks funding to oppose Tó Ntsaa timber sale, 126; seeks help from medicine man, 155–57; and son Eli, 4–7, 13–15, 87–88; as substance-abuse counselor, 42

Joe, Ivan, 215

Joe, Robert, 46–47; home of, 48; and liver cancer, 144

Johnson, Fred, 178

Kelly, Kevin, 110

Kinaaldá (puberty ceremony), 224–25

Krahl, Lane, 67

KTNN radio, 93

land: connection to wind and words, 78

Land and Water Fund, 126

land grants, unfulfilled, 21

Lange, Dave, 176

language: and ritual, 78. *See also* Navajo language

Lighthawk, 113

Little, Keith, 128

livestock reduction program, 21

loggers and mill workers: airing of grievances by, 138

logging, commercial, 23, 24, 67, 80–81, 100; environmental effects of, 32

Long Walk, 19

Los Alamos National Laboratories, 25

MacDonald, Peter, 50, 52

MacDonald, Rocky, 50

Manuelito, 19, 178, 219

Marcus, Mark, 168, 179, 191

Martinez, Melton, 219, 220

Martinez, Paddy, 219

Maryboy, Mark, 217

May, Karl, 150

McFeeley, Patricia, 175, 190

medicine man, 210; German couple searching for, 135–36; Leroy and Adella consult, 155–57

Medicine Man's Association, 69